PETER EDWARDS

Rural Life

GUIDE TO LOCAL RECORDS

D1380296

B.T. Batsford Ltd ·

Acknowledgements

I am grateful to the following for giving me permission to reproduce the whole or part of documents in their possession or ownership:

His Grace, the Duke of Northumberland, for fig. 1 (Surrey R.O. 1322/1/5); the Trustees of the Davenport-Greenshields Estates for fig. 15 (Shrops. R.O. 2713); Mr. M. C. Lack, M.A., B.Ed., the Headmaster of Bookham Middle School, for fig. 27; Sir Lyonel Tollemache for fig 33. (Surrey R.O. 58/3/3/2); Rev. A. C. Warner, M.A., Rector of Great Bookham, for fig. 34; Mr. Yarham of Cambridge for fig. 37; Mr. J. Howarth of Bookham for fig. 39; the National Trust for fig. 41 (Surrey R.O. 34/3).

Crown copyright material in Shrops. R.O. and Surrey R.O. is reproduced by permission of the Controller of Her Majesty's Stationery Office, viz. Shrops. R.O. fig. 32 (QR 334/154), Surrey R.O. fig. 4 (QS 2/1/1), fig. 5 (QS 2/1/19), figs. 10 & 40 (QS 6/7 Great Bookham 1780), fig. 12 (P5 Wimbledon Parish Records), fig. 31 (QS 2/6/1790 Mids.).

Fig. 2 (B/V/5/1772 Mackworth); fig. 23 (B/V/5/1726 Kinver) and fig. 25 (B/A/11b Great Harborough 1713) are reproduced by permission of the Lichfield Diocesan Registrar.

I am also grateful to the archivists at the following record offices for permission to reproduce documents in their keeping: Hampshire R.O. fig. 35 (1582 B41), fig. 38 (1593 B62); Herefordshire & Worcestershire R.O. for fig. 36 (B.A. 2252/7(iv) class 705:366); Lincolnshire A.O. for fig. 42 (INV 145/141); Northumberland R.O. for fig. 16 (QSB Epiphany 1721); Surrey R.O. for fig. 11 (PSH/STK.DAB/1/1), figs. 20–22 (PSH/CRON/6/1), fig. 43 (181/11/53); Wigan Heritage Service for fig. 9.

First published 1993

Typeset by J&L Composition Ltd, Filey, North Yorkshire
and printed in Great Britain by
Butler & Tanner, Frome, Somerset
Published by B.T. Batsford Ltd
4 Fitzhardinge Street, London W1H 0AH

A CIP catalogue record for this book is available from the British Library

ISBN 0 7134 6787 8

Title page: The village street in the mid-nineteenth century

Contents

CHAPTER ONE

The governance of rural England

Over the centuries villagers have been subject to the jurisdiction of a number of administrative and judicial bodies. Some of the links have been local and personal, others more distant and formal, though the nature of a particular relationship might change over time. Thus, the church now plays a far smaller administrative (and perhaps spiritual) role in the lives of the ordinary person but the State has become a much more intrusive force. The interaction between the individual and society can be seen in the records of these institutions. These documents, which provide a rich source of information for the local historian, form the basis of this study.

Of course, there has been a qualitative as well as a quantitative change in the nature of the material over time; for centuries much business was conducted locally and by word of mouth. It was not for some time after the Norman Conquest that the oral tradition began to break down. This change is revealed by Michael Clanchy in his book *From Memory to Written Record: England 1066–1307*, in which he charts the development of a literate society in the 250 years after the Conquest and the growing importance of the written record. By 1300 laymen were using documents as a matter of course, and even serfs (at least the more prosperous ones) were familiar with them. Nowadays, there is often too much material and, apart from the problems of processing it, a major task for archivists is to keep it down to manageable proportions. At times this may result in the sampling of certain classes of record and the destruction of the rest of the documentation.

Some of the manuscripts can still be found in their original repositories – in the parish chest or in the estate muniment room, for instance – but the establishment of special archive offices, most notably the foundation of county record offices, has led to the concentration of documents in certain centres. Readers with local knowledge may be aware of material held in private hands in the locality and, using personal contacts, may gain access to it. Thereafter, the county record office is a good place to start since many records are likely to have been moved there, and (eventually) indexed and calendared, too. If not, there is often a note to indicate where the manuscripts are being held.

Local administration

The manor

In the Middle Ages the basic unit of administration was the manor, the body with which the ordinary villager came into closest contact. Manors varied in size, scope and structure, reflecting differences in local circumstances and the fact that as an organization they were laid on top of pre-existing territorial units. Some manors, especially those in central England, were conterminous with a village, while elsewhere, notably in eastern England, the village was divided up between two or more manors. In other places manors incorporated several villages or consisted of a manorial centre with outlying properties.[1]

The central institution was the manor court, and all the tenants and freeholders owed suit of court there, attending the sessions and being bound by its decisions. By the end of the Middle Ages servile tenure had almost disappeared, having been converted to copyhold. This, however, did little in itself to diminish the work of the court. Essentially the manor court was an administrative rather than a judicial body, overseeing the social and economic life of the community, but it did fine people who did not abide by its regulations.

The steward, as the lord's representative, presided over the court. To help him he had a jury of local inhabitants who presented matters to be dealt with there, giving reports or making accusations in response to specific questions asked by the steward. Much of the work was carried out at the court baron, the main adminstrative arm of the manor. There, farming practices were regulated, land conveyed and the peasantry supervised. In manors where lords had been given special judicial rights from the Crown, court leets were also held, with authority to determine misdemeanours. Often the separate jurisdictions were combined in one court, and the rolls recording its decisions contain evidence of the work of each.[2]

The day-to-day running of the manor was the responsibility of the reeve, sometimes assisted by other men such as the beadle and hayward. These officials, normally unfree tenants, were compelled to serve, though not infrequently they were chosen by their fellow villeins. The reeve, in turn, was answerable to the bailiff, who had the care of two or three manors. The administration of the whole estate was the job of the steward. The latter travelled from manor to manor, checking on the work being done by the bailiffs and reeves and holding the manor courts. Exercising financial oversight, the lord of a single manor might audit his reeve's account himself. On larger estates a receiver did the work for him. On the most substantial estates there were several receivers, all under the control of a receiver general.

The accounting system practised was the charge/discharge method; in the

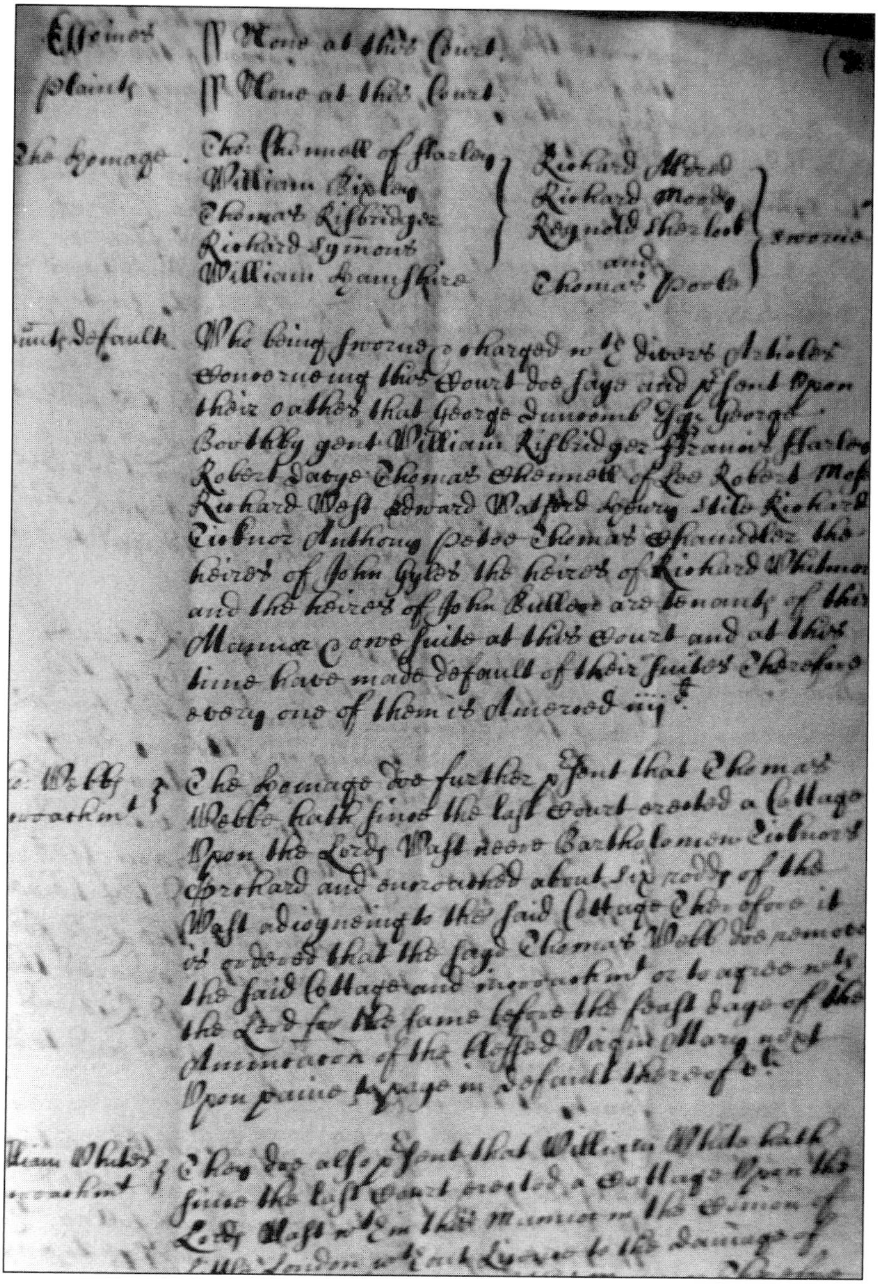

Essoines || None at this Court

plaints || None at this Court

The homage . Tho: Chennell of Farley, William Ripley, Thomas Risbridger, Richard Symons, William Hamshire } Richard More, Richard Moody, Reynold Shorlock and Thomas Poole } sworne

Suit default — Who being sworne & charged wth divers Articles concerning this Court doe saye and prsent upon their oathes that George Duncombe Esqr George Boothby gent William Risbridger Francis Farley Robert Daye Thomas Chennell of Lee Robert Mose Richard West Edward Walford Henry Stile Richard Tickner Anthony Peter Thomas Chandler the heires of John Gyles the heires of Richard Whitmore and the heires of John Butler are tenants of this Mannor & owe suite at this Court and at this time have made default of their suites Therefore every one of them is Amerced iijd.

[illegible] Webbs incroachmt { The homage doe further prsent that Thomas Webbe hath since the last Court erected a Cottage upon the Lords Wast neere Bartholomew Tickners Orchard and encroached about six rodds of the Wast adioyning to the said Cottage Therefore it is ordered that the sayd Thomas Webb doe remove the said Cottage and incroachmt or to agree wth the Lord for the same before the feast daye of the Annunciacon of the blessed Virgin Mary next Upon paine [illegible] in default thereof [illegible]

William Whites incroachmt { They doe also prsent that William White hath since the last Court erected a Cottage upon the Lords Wast wthin this Mannor in the Common of [illegible] to the damage of [illegible]

1 View of frankpledge, Manor of Albury (Surrey), 15 October 1653.

charge the accountant listed all the money and goods he had to answer for, against which he set the discharge, recording all items of expenditure. The earliest accounts were made in the early twelfth century and a few survive for that period, but as the habit of keeping written records had not yet become universal, even some large estates had not adopted this practice. The idea spread rapidly in the second half of the twelfth century, even among lords of single manors, and the number of extant accounts rises dramatically (though lay estates are still under-represented).[3]

Occasionally, surveys of the manor were drawn up which include data on the home farm and the holdings of the peasantry, together with the rights and obligations of the latter. Some were made at courts of recognition, the first to be held on the succession of a new lord. The tenants came to do fealty and to present for the steward's scrutiny their deeds and evidences, recording their right to the land they held of the manor. During the thirteenth century the number of surveys rose, and by 1400 they had become a normal part of estate administration. At the same time a particular form of survey known as an 'extent' developed. Basically it comprised a survey with valuations added and in it were included all sources of profit to the lord – demesne buildings and land, manorial dues and tenants' rents and services.[4]

In the early modern period the right to hold a manor court came to define the manor itself – if there were no court, there was no manor.[5] In consequence the number of records designated as manorial shrank, being restricted to documents dealing with the work of the courts. At the same time the rise of the vestry affected the amount of business being conducted. Over the years much customary land was enfranchised and what remained was finally abolished by an act of 1922. Because they might still be needed to prove a title to erstwhile copyhold land, the task of preserving manorial records was given to the Master of the Rolls. As a result, a register of manorial documents, recording ownership and location, was set up. The list is maintained by the Historical Manuscripts Commission (HMC), and even if its information is not always up to date, it is a useful guide. The register, arranged by county and then alphabetically by manor, can be consulted at the offices of the HMC at Quality House, Quality Court, Chancery Lane, London WC2. This list should be examined in conjunction with the National Register of Archives, also kept by the HMC.[6]

The topographical volumes of the Victoria County Histories should also be consulted. They record the manorial history of each parish and, in those counties where such volumes have been completed, references to the family and estate papers will be found. Many manuscripts are still in private hands but increasingly they have been deposited in county record offices and other repositories, where they form part of wider estate collections. As the Copyhold Commission, set up by the Copyhold Act of 1841, merged with the Board (later Ministry) of Agriculture, some material has been sent to the Public Record Office at Kew, along with other records of the ministry.[7]

The parish

The parish, as an ecclesiastical unit, dates back to the Middle Ages. From the spiritual (and social) point of view, it exerted a great influence over the villagers' lives. To help the incumbent maintain the fabric of the church, its goods and ornaments, church-wardens were appointed, the first reference to them appearing in a canon of 1127.[8] These officials made annual accounts, recording their expenditure during the course of the year. The earliest extant accounts are those of St Michael's, Bath, which begin in 1349. From the end of the fifteenth century enough examples have survived to show that church-wardens were involved in all aspects of church and community life.[9]

Parish registers, first kept in 1538, record details of baptisms, marriages and burials. Initially written on loose sheets of paper, the earliest surviving entries tend to be those copied into the new books ordered by Elizabeth I in 1598. The information for the period 1538–98 (especially pre-1558) is therefore patchy. From 1598 incumbents had to make a transcript of all the previous year's entries and send it to the diocesan registry. These documents, commonly called 'BTs' (bishops' transcripts), can be found with the rest of the diocesan records.[10] The quality of the parish registers is also affected by the growth of nonconformity. For some time nonconformists used the established church for the basic sacraments but gradually they became more independent. With the introduction of civil registration on 1 July 1837, the problem of under-registration diminished, though it did not disappear until a measure of 1874 permitted the punishment of defaulters.

In the sixteenth century the parish's importance increased with the extra administrative duties imposed on it by the government (though in large parishes with scattered settlement the township was often the administrative unit). The constable, for instance, became an important executive officer, as well as a quasi-law-enforcement agent.[11] In 1555 each parish was made responsible for its highways and a surveyor was appointed annually to oversee them.[12] Parishes, acting through overseers of the poor, were also charged with the relief of their poor and, through the constable, with the punishment of vagrants. These duties had been imposed on them by a series of measures in the second half of the sixteenth century, culminating in the codifying acts of 1597 and 1601.[13] Overseers of the poor were chosen to carry out the task. All officials, elected annually, were normally chosen at Easter at a meeting of the parish vestry. There, too, the outgoing officials accounted for their expenditure, drawn from funds raised by parish rates. Rating lists indicate each person's liability (normally assessed on land) and often the names of the properties so charged. The rate was paid by the occupier but later documents refer to owners too.

The vestry had medieval antecedents, having been established at least as early as the fourteenth century to manage church affairs, but in the early modern period it became a general administrative body. Sometimes, notably in populous industrializing parishes or in places where the leading inhabitants formed a cabal, executive committees, known as 'select vestries', were set up which excluded most of the population.[14]

The rise of the vestry did not necessarily mean the demise of the manor, and in some places the two bodies coexisted side by side, each carrying out separate functions. It is no coincidence, however, that as the vestry grew in importance, the manor declined as an institution. The right to set parish rates to finance the work of its officials and to hold them to account at the end of the period of office gave the vestry undoubted prestige. Inevitably it began to involve itself in every aspect of local administration, making by-laws and issuing instructions to the parishioners on all manner of subjects, and as a result the minutes of the meetings cover a wide range of themes. Its influence only declined after 1834 when the administration of the poor law was assumed by Boards of Guardians. In 1894 it was finally replaced by the parish councils which took over its work (and records).[15]

Of the records of individual parochial officers, those of the overseers of the poor are the fullest and the most informative for the social historian. The accounts of expenditure that were made under the system of outdoor relief that prevailed before 1834 show fluctuations in the incidence of poverty and indicate those members of rural society most at risk. They also provide evidence of the ways in which the poor were relieved.[16] After the reform of 1834 paupers were forced into workhouses, though in practice many parochial officers continued to give a certain amount of outdoor relief. The documents tell us a great deal about society's attitude towards the poor, as do ancillary records such as pauper apprenticeship indentures, bastardy bonds and settlement papers.

Many parish records can be examined in print or in transcription. In particular, the popularity of genealogy has led to the formation of specialist family history groups who have done a good deal of work in transcribing parish registers. These lists augment the ones published by record societies and are readily available in county record offices and in the local history section of reference libraries. County record offices will also have microfiche copies of parish registers photographed by representatives of the Mormon Church. Other parish records have not received the same blanket treatment, and the reader will have to take pot luck. Particularly good examples of specific types of records tend to be singled out – a set of churchwardens' accounts that span the Reformation or a comprehensive collection of settlement papers, for instance. Even if nothing has been printed for a specific parish, such volumes do have a general value. Apart from providing examples of the subject matter itself, there will normally be a detailed introduction in which the editor describes the documents, their provenance and the methodology adopted in dealing with them.

Some collections are still in the parish, and if not in the parish chest itself, then in the home of the minister or in that of the churchwarden. Mostly, however, they have been deposited in the diocesan record office which in many cases is the county record office. In 1929 the synod of the Church of England passed an ordinance enabling diocesan record offices to be set up, and allowing bishops to take steps to protect documents at risk. In 1978 the measure was strengthened. Henceforth, all parishes were required to transfer all their documents over 100 years old to diocesan record offices unless they possessed adequate storage facilities. Many later documents have been transferred there too.[17]

The records of the civil parishes established by the Local Government Act of 1894 are to be found in the county rather than in the diocesan record office (even if in practice they are often the same place). Many civil parishes, especially in the countryside, have exactly the same boundaries as the ecclesiastical parish, but the reader should be aware of the distinction and check on any changes that might have occurred. Topographical volumes of the Victoria County Histories, organized by ecclesiastical parishes, reveal the older units. The same information can be obtained from the parochial maps of counties printed by the Institute of Heraldic and Genealogical Studies, Northgate, Canterbury, Kent. Apart from noting when surviving parish registers begin, they also show detached portions of parishes, a common feature in the days before Victorian rationalization. They even include those parishes (or parts of them) physically separated from their administrative county.

The town

Although this book is concerned with rural sources, the links between town and country were numerous, and many urban records have a bearing on the subject. First and foremost, towns served as the normal marketing outlets for agricultural produce – the importance of this function is reflected in the prominent position given to the market place. The weekly markets and the annual fairs brought both communities together; if villagers disposed of their goods there, they could also buy items unobtainable at home. At the same time they met friends and acquaintances and heard news of the outside world.

Towns used the human resources of the countryside too. Much of the urban population increase was caused by immigration from outside, mostly of poor people, travelling more in the hope of finding a job than in the expectation of getting one. There were also 'betterment' migrants, with apprenticeships to take up or jobs or positions to fill, though they constituted only a small proportion of those coming in. At the top, some towns became the resort of country gentlemen, especially after the development of a distinct urban culture in the late seventeenth century. Of the movement away, some townspeople took jobs in the burgeoning industrial areas in the countryside. Members of the elite left too; the very rich bought landed estates and set themselves up as gentlemen. During the last 150 years or so the flight from the town has increased, to the extent that many villages are now mere dormitory suburbs for people working elsewhere.

The connection between town and village can be seen in the lists of freemen and apprentices. In corporate towns freemen's (or burgess) rolls give the names of people who had gained the freedom of the borough, together with their occupations and residences (and perhaps those of their fathers too). Some of the freemen lived in the countryside and earned a living from farming. Many more had a rural background, as is shown by the occupations and abodes of their fathers.

Apprenticeship records should also be consulted; serving an apprenticeship was one of the commonest ways of obtaining the freedom, and many of the lists (but by no means all) relate to corporate towns. There seems to have been a marked decline in the number of entries in freemen's and apprenticeship rolls during the course of the seventeenth century. The latter, in particular, suffered from the decay in apprenticeship regulations at this time and the growth of industry in non-corporate towns and in the countryside. The situation did vary from town to town; in Parliamentary boroughs where the freemen possessed the franchise, the records tended to be maintained more carefully.

Administratively many towns were run in the same way as villages; the manor court or vestry provided the most common form of local government but in some places other arrangements evolved. Trustees of an influential charity might assume the role, while increasingly in the eighteenth century improvement commissioners took over the management of affairs.[18] Corporate towns, on the other hand, with their mayors, aldermen and ruling councils, had a more formal structure. The details were set out in the charters that incorporated individual boroughs or confirmed (or modified) existing arrangements. From time to time they were reissued or updated. For the day-to-day administration of the borough some sort of minute book was used in which all the varied business of the council was entered. Details of financial management appear in the chamberlain's accounts. A number of towns had their own magistrates, usually with petty sessional jurisdiction but in some instances with the right to hold quarter sessions.

Town records, like those of rural estates, may still be in their original repository. As a result, there may be problems of access, though most authorities are willing to accommodate serious students. Further difficulties might be encountered if storage facilities are poor and the documents inadequately indexed. The situation is better in corporate towns; their archives are fuller and more comprehensive than those of non-corporate towns, and therefore greater attention tends to be given to their preservation. If not in the town hall, they may have been moved to the local reference library, many of which have been developing their own local history collections. Others have been transferred to the county record office. For a fuller discussion of urban records, readers should see Stephen Porter's book, *Exploring Urban History* (Batsford, London, 1990).

Regional records

Estate records

In many ways the system of estate management that had developed in the Middle Ages continued into the early modern period. Even if records designated as manorial were more restrictive in scope, the manor remained the basic unit of estate administration, and records such as accounts, surveys, rentals and deeds were normally arranged in this way (at least in the early part of the period). Ordinary villagers came into contact with local bailiffs, similar in status to the medieval reeve, and with the same duties too. On larger estates the bailiffs were answerable to under-agents, appointed to oversee each major block of property and to give an account of it to the chief agent. The under-agents also carried out such jobs as inspecting farms, seeing that leasing covenants were being carried out and making use of their local knowledge to further the landowner's interests. On smaller estates the organization was much more informal for, as in the Middle Ages, the owner often dealt directly with his bailiffs.

Over time changes did occur. Control of income and expenditure was tightened up by the gradual replacement of the medieval charge/discharge method of accounting by a system of double entry book-keeping.[19] Administratively there was a tendency to base management of the estate on blocks of territory (or even on the whole estate) rather than upon the manor, though the speed of this change varied from estate to estate. The documentation itself becomes more fragmented and specialized. The problems thus caused are discussed in Alan Simpson's book, *The Wealth of the Gentry 1540–1660*.

In the late sixteenth and seventeenth centuries the dramatic rise in agricultural prices prompted many landowners to manage their estates in a more positive way. They farmed their demesne again, were active in the administration of their property and carried out various improvement schemes. Their knowledge of their estate, moreover, was improved by regular use of surveys and enhanced by developments in mapping techniques.[20] This concern is also reflected in the material to be found in the diaries and in the commonplace and memoranda books which they kept and especially in the correspondence that passed between them and their agents.

For many tenants the Tudor and Stuart ages witnessed a change in their tenurial position. Copyhold tenure came under attack, and by the end of the period the number of customary tenants had fallen dramatically. Some had enfranchised their holdings but far more had become leaseholders. For landowners leasehold was preferable because it enabled them to exercise greater control over their tenantry, their rents and methods of farming. Instead of being bound by custom they could, through clauses inserted in leases, define the conditions on which tenants held their land from them and these could be altered as circumstances dictated.[21] Such changes gave estates a greater sense of cohesion because it made the formulation of an overall policy that much easier. While care had to be taken not to ride roughshod over local traditions, adjustments could be made more readily, since it was no longer necessary to treat the estate as a series of discrete units, bound by their own immutable customs.

Apart from leases, estate records include deeds relating to the transfer of property. For the medieval period the information may be found on separate deeds or, especially on ecclesiastic estates, enrolled in cartularies. Methods of conveyancing varied; in the Middle Ages and the early modern period an important factor was the desire to keep the transaction secret, and the ways in which this was achieved owed much to the fertility of lawyers' imaginations.[22] In the seventeenth century other deeds like mortgages and family and marriage settlements became more commonplace. The non-specialist might be put off from using title deeds because of their complexity but they do contain much of interest and the basic information can be extracted without too much trouble.

Landowners often established muniment rooms in their houses for the storage of documents or even housed them in estate offices built for the purpose. In 1737, for instance, Lord Gower had an office constructed in the grounds of Trentham Hall (Staffordshire) at a cost of £25.[23] Estate records might still be in such rooms today. Owners, in general, allow bona fide students access to their manuscripts, though they often exact a fee for permission to do so. Nonetheless many collections have been deposited in county record offices, where they join others sent from solicitors' offices.

The diocese

While it was at the parochial level that most villagers came into contact with the church, much of the administration was carried out by the diocese. Some parishes, it is true, were exempt from the bishop's jurisdiction – these 'peculiars', as they were known, were controlled by a variety of bodies, perhaps a monastery, a cathedral chapter or a manorial lord. Documentation pertaining to the latter institutions will be found in the place holding the rest of the archive.

For a record of the relationship between the diocese and the parish, local historians can turn to the bishops' registers. In England they originate in the thirteenth century and, because many of them have been printed, the information they contain is reasonably accessible. Some of the registers contain the findings of the periodic parochial visitations that bishops conducted in their sees. Held at convenient centres in the diocese, they were run by the bishop's chancellor, or in larger dioceses by commissaries sent to each archdeaconry. In particular, the enquiries sought information on the

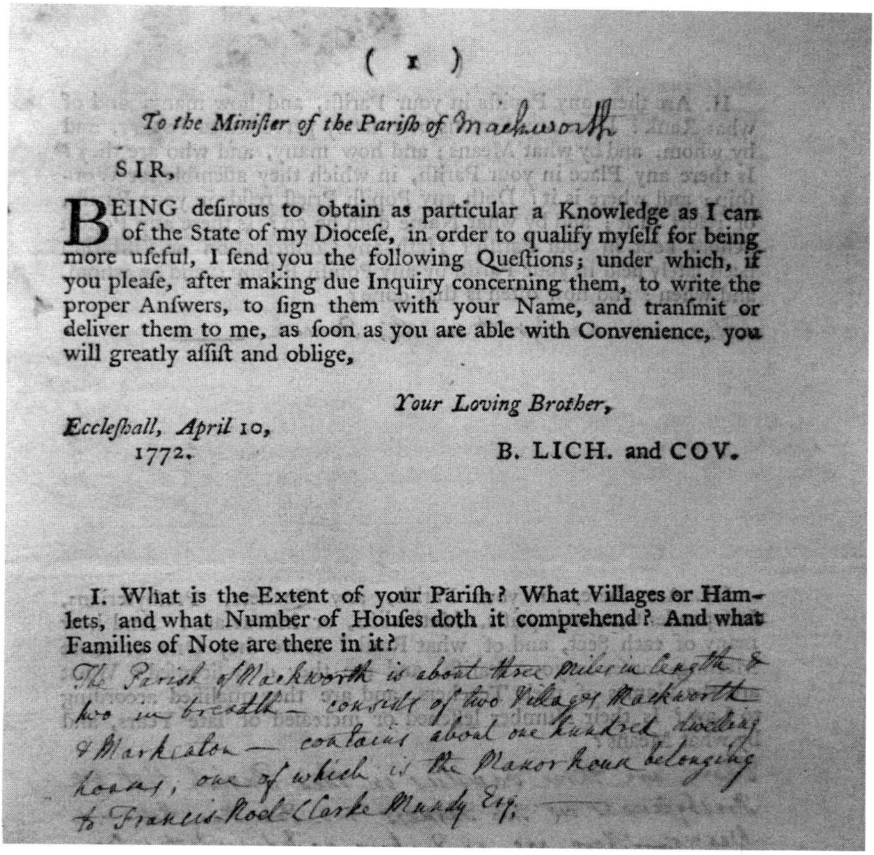

(1)

To the Miniſter of the Pariſh of Mackworth

SIR,

BEING deſirous to obtain as particular a Knowledge as I can of the State of my Dioceſe, in order to qualify myſelf for being more uſeful, I ſend you the following Queſtions; under which, if you pleaſe, after making due Inquiry concerning them, to write the proper Anſwers, to ſign them with your Name, and tranſmit or deliver them to me, as ſoon as you are able with Convenience, you will greatly aſſiſt and oblige,

Your Loving Brother,

Eccleſhall, April 10,
1772.

B. LICH. and COV.

I. What is the Extent of your Pariſh? What Villages or Hamlets, and what Number of Houſes doth it comprehend? And what Families of Note are there in it?

The Parish of Mackworth is about three miles in length & two in breadth — consists of two Villages Mackworth & Markeaton — contains about one hundred dwelling houses, one of which is the Manor house belonging to Francis Noel Clarke Mundy Esq.

2 Bishop of Lichfield's visitation of his Diocese, 1772.

fabric of the church, its books and equipment, the conduct of the clergy and the morals of the laity.[24]

Bishops normally made their first visitation as soon as they were instituted and thereafter (in theory) every three years. Archdeacons held theirs annually. As early as the fifteenth century it had become customary for the bishops to ask churchwardens to present matters of concern to them. In the following century Elizabeth's prelates issued articles of enquiry to guide the churchwardens. By this time the information was being written down in two special visitations books (largely written in English). The first, known as the *Liber Cleri*, contains the names of all the clergy, churchwardens and schoolmasters called to exhibit, while the second, the *Liber Compertorum*, includes the churchwardens' presentments. In the latter, spaces may have been left to record actions but, if not, they were noted in a separate act book.

Other information was collected at the visitation. Occasionally incumbents were asked to take a census of their parishioners, usually to find out their religious affiliations but not always so. Most of these counts were limited to the diocese, but in 1563, 1603 and 1676 they were organized provincially or nationally.[25] Moreover, as a result of a canon of 1571, regular surveys were taken of church property in each parish. These documents, known as glebe terriers, give a description of the parsonage and other buildings, together with an account of its lands. Other possessions, sources of revenue and privileges were also recorded.[26]

People presented at the visitations were tried at the archdeaconry and consistory (bishops') courts, along with others accused of offences which came within the courts' jurisdiction. Unfortunately the material contained in the act books is difficult to analyse because the entries are written in Latin and in a crabbed and heavily contracted hand.[27] The depositions of witnesses are easier to use because they were written out almost verbatim in English. Apart from information on the cases themselves, they generally give personal details of the witnesses.

Until 1858, when probate of wills was transferred to a lay court, the church had jurisdiction over testamentary matters. Apart from the inhabitants of peculiars who possessed their own exempt jurisdictions, the first court to deal with probate was that of the archdeacon. The court proved the wills of people with property solely in that archdeaconry. Larger owners or occupiers of land (if located in a single diocese) had their wills proved at the consistory court. Disputed and difficult wills, and those of persons with land in more than one diocese, were administered by the Prerogative Courts of York or Canterbury.[28] By an Act of 1529 the administrator of an estate had to make, or have made, an inventory listing the personal goods of the deceased. It did not initiate the practice, however, for many medieval inventories are known.[29] Originally the inventories were folded in with the wills, but in many record offices (though not in all) they have subsequently been separated.

Wills, as a source, span a much longer period than do inventories. They were made in the Middle Ages and continue to be drawn up today, though they are no longer administered by the church. Inventories, on the other hand, only become numerous in the mid-sixteenth century and tail off after 200 years or so. The survival rate is variable too. The best period is the one between the late seventeenth and early eighteenth centuries but by then the inventories often give less detail. Peculiar jurisdictions tend to have later inventories, as does the Prerogative Court of Canterbury. As the church continued to exercise authority over disputed probate cases until 1858, cause papers may include contemporary inventories.[30] After 1858 a new Court of Probate was set up and grant of probate could be made at the principal registry at Somerset House in London or at one of the district registries elsewhere in the country.[31]

3 A medieval priest receives tithe animals from his parishioners.

Outside the spiritual sphere (and perhaps including it, too) the payment of tithes was the issue which most concerned villagers in their dealings with the church. Tithes originated before the Norman Conquest; the essential purpose was to provide an income for the minister but a portion might be used to repair the church or relieve the poor.[32] Some tithes were personal ones but in general they comprised a charge on land. There were exemptions, the most well-known being old monastic land, but also including glebe (church) property, Crown forests, barren lands and improved wastes for the first seven years after being brought into cultivation.[33] In many parishes tithes were commuted at the time of an enclosure award.

Even in the Middle Ages tithes were appropriated by laymen, especially by lessees of monastic property, and this trend became more pronounced after the Dissolution. In all essentials, tithes had become a form of property, like any other, liable to be bought and sold at will, and often divorced from its real function. It is, therefore, hardly surprising to learn that payment became a vexatious issue. Farmers felt particularly aggrieved because it not only bore heaviest on them, but also penalized them for any improvements they had made. Evasion was rife and, as a result, tithe owners had to maintain constant vigilance and even at times have recourse to the law. All this was time-consuming, costly and socially disruptive. It did generate a large volume of

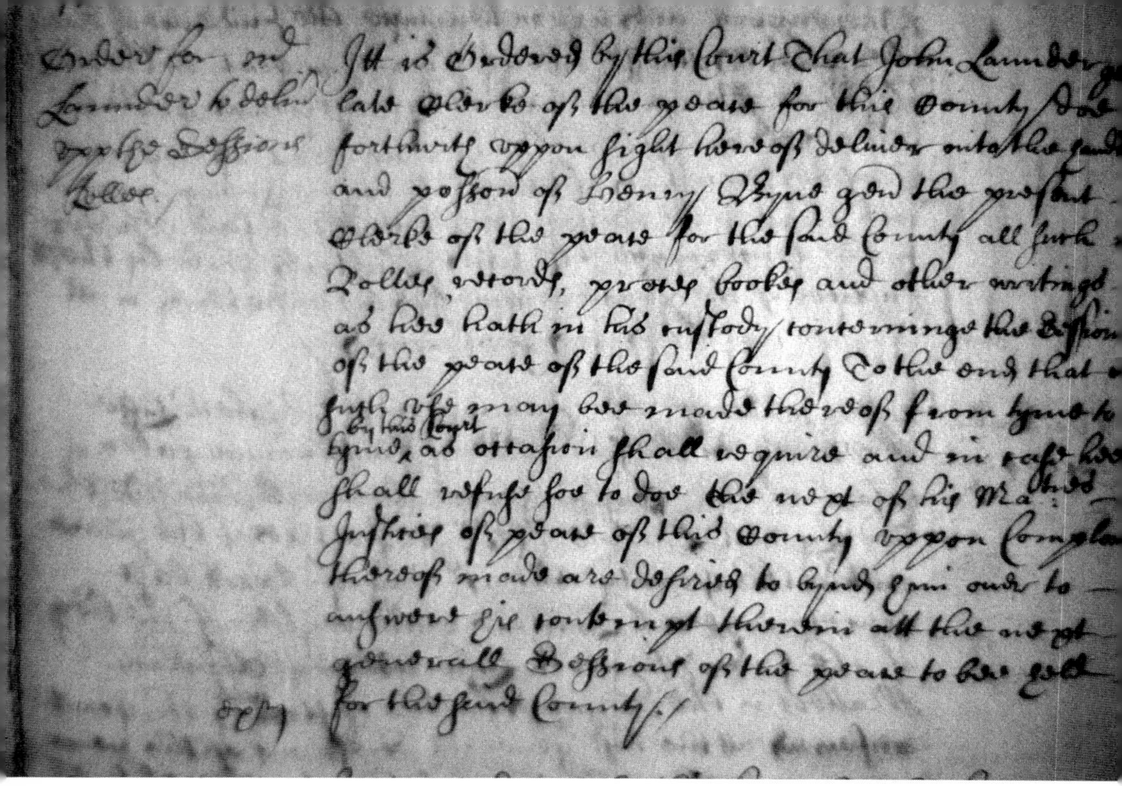

Order for mr Saunders to deliver the Sessions Rolles

It is Ordered by this Court That John Saunders gent late Clerke of the peace for this County doe forthwith uppon sight hereof deliver into the hands and possession of Henry Wyne gent the present Clerke of the peace for the said County all such Rolles, records, proces bookes and other writings as hee hath in his custody concerninge the Sessions of the peace of the said County To the end that such use may bee made thereof from tyme to tyme by this Court as occasion shall require and in case hee shall refuse soe to doe the rest of his Maties Justices of peace of this County uppon Complaint thereof made are desired to bynd him over to answere his contempt therein att the next generall Sessions of the peace to bee held for the said County./

4 A Clerk of the Peace hands over the records to his successor, Surrey, 1660.

material, however, for many cases survive in the records of the diocesan courts or in the archives of the Chancery and the Exchequer.[34]

Tithes were finally abolished by the Tithes Commutation Act of 1836 which converted the duty into a money payment. Altogether, some 11,800 parishes in England and Wales were surveyed by commissioners, although the amount of tithable land remaining varied regionally and even between neigbouring parishes. The work was speedily carried out and after ten years very little remained to be done.[35] The tithe records comprise three main elements – a large-scale map; an accompanying apportionment, on which are listed the names of owners and occupiers of property, together with the size of their holdings; and a file of material collected by the commissioners during the course of their work.

The county

In the Middle Ages the sheriff was the leading officer in the county and the one who carried out the wishes of the government, implementing policy and collecting taxes and other forms of revenue. Through the sheriff's court he also dispensed justice. By the early modern period, however, the office had become largely honorific (if costly), as much of his work had been taken over by the Justices of the Peace. Though their name is indicative of the judicial role they played, JPs over the course of centuries acquired wide-ranging administrative duties too. Even before the end of the Middle Ages they were being used in this capacity and, as government increased its regulatory control in the Tudor and early Stuart periods, their duties were enlarged. From the Crown's point of view they provided an answer to the basic medieval problem of how to control the provinces without creating over-mighty subjects.

The main administrative organ of the JPs was the quarter session, so-called because the courts met four times a year. As the pressure of work increased, some devolution of function took place. Magistrates, acting alone or in twos and threes, were given authority to deal summarily with a variety of offences. As they met more frequently than the quarter sessions, they could therefore give cheap, local and speedy justice. This trend led to the development of the petty sessions during the course of the seventeenth and eighteenth centuries, the boundaries of which often coincided with the old hundredal divisions of the county.[36]

For a period during the middle of the seventeenth century, at the time of the Civil War and the Interregnum, the administration of the county by the Justices of the Peace was dislocated. In areas controlled by Parliament, County Committees were established which over time usurped many of the administrative functions of JPs. In royalist districts similar expedients were attempted but without the same degree of success. The committees tended to come into existence primarily to supervise the collection of taxes and to administer the revenues thus brought in but gradually they acquired other powers.[37] For evidence of their work local historians should look at the records they left, which mainly consist of minutes, order books and accounts.

Public records, like those of the quarter sessions, were kept by the Clerk of the Peace. When the office was abolished in 1971 the documents were transferred to county record offices, though many had already been moved there.[38] At the end of each quarter session the records were normally bound together in a single file and rolled up in a parchment cover, though in some populous counties the sheer volume of paperwork necessitated some division of the material from the outset.[39] Certain classes of quarter sessions' records such as the land tax returns or deposited maps and plans were 'enrolled' with the Clerk of the Peace. This entailed the clerk making a copy of the document presented to him, thereby providing a permanent public record of it and acting as a safeguard against its loss.[40]

When county councils were established in 1888 they took over the administrative work of the quarter sessions. In fact, there was a great deal of continuity between the two systems. Apart from acquiring the records of the quarter sessions, they also inherited some of its personnel too. Many of the Clerks of the Peace became clerks of the county council, while many JPs were

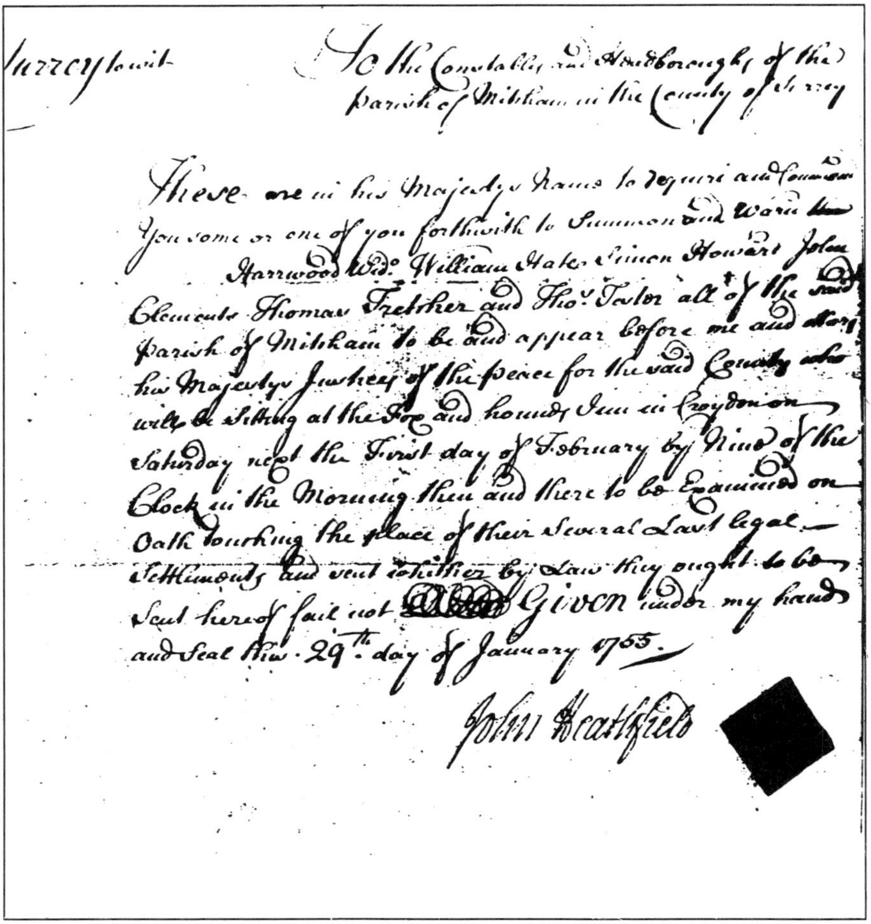
Surrey to wit

To the Constables and Headborough of the Parish of Mitcham in the County of Surrey

These are in his Majesty's Name to require and Command You some or one of you forthwith to Summon and Warn the Harwood Wid.o William Hales Simon Howard John Clements Thomas Fletcher and Tho.s Taylor all of the said Parish of Mitcham to be and appear before me and other his Majestys Justices of the peace for the said County who will be Sitting at the Fox and hounds Inn in Croydon on Saturday next the First day of February by Nine of the Clock in the Morning then and there to be Examined on Oath touching the place of their Several Last legal Settlements and sent thither by Law they ought to be. Seal hereof fail not [illegible] Given under my hand and Seal this 29th day of January 1755.

John Heathfield

5 The Surrey JPs order six people living in Mitcham to appear before them, touching their place of settlement, 29 January 1755.

elected on to it.[41] Much of the subsequent history of county administration can be followed in the records, notably in the minutes of the various committees set up by the council. This material has been under-used, not only because of the sheer bulk of the archive but also on account of its rather general nature. Nonetheless, there is useful information to be found there, even though a considerable amount of stamina is required on the part of the researcher. Of particular interest are the records of the executive committees that were established during the course of the two World Wars to mobilize the nation's resources in the counties.

Central government

At first the various organs of government formed part of the king's court and moved around with him. During the course of the Middle Ages, however, specialization of function occurred and, as separate bodies evolved, they acquired permanence and an independent existence. Over time the business of government became more complex; old departments were subdivided and new ones were developed; as a result, a vast archive of material was created. According to class, these records have been deposited in the Public Record Office (PRO) either at Chancery Lane, London, or at Kew. Much of the evidence is of a local nature but relevant material for individual communities is often hard to find. The sheer bulk of the documentation makes the examination of some classes of record a daunting prospect, while inadequate finding aids often compound the problem. For guidance on this complicated subject, Philip Riden's book *Record Sources for Local History* (Batsford, London, 1987) is recommended.

Administration

In the Middle Ages the Chancellor, as the keeper of the Great Seal, was the leading administrative officer of the Crown. From the Chancery (which went out of court in the thirteenth century) a stream of documents – orders, instructions, grants, confirmations and the like – issued forth to individuals, officials and corporate bodies all around the country. These were entered variously on to the charter, patent, fine and close rolls. Of particular interest are the various enquiries or inquisitions initiated by the Chancery, especially the inquisitions *post-mortem* (IPMs), which contain surveys of the property of deceased tenants-in-chief.[42] Enrolled copies were kept from the early thirteenth century and, as they have been calendared and indexed, are easy to use by local historians. Sadly, many of the surveys in the IPMs have not been transcribed.

As the Chancery developed as a separate institution, the monarch had to resort to more personal means of authorization. First of all the privy seal was employed, but when its keeper went out of court, use was made of the signet ring.[43] The keepers of this seal, the king's secretaries, became the fulcrum of the administration in the early modern period and the vital link between the Crown and government. Normally two secretaries were appointed and they dealt with all manner of domestic and foreign business. Their records have been calendared from the beginning of Henry VIII's reign; for local historians the important series are the Calendars of Letters and Papers for Henry VIII's reign and the run of Calendars of State Papers (Domestic) which stretch into the eighteenth century. In the Commonwealth period the material can be supplemented by information contained in the Calendars of the Proceedings of the Committee for the Advance of Money and the Calendars of the Proceedings of the Committee for Compounding.[44]

Also printed are the early modern records of the Privy Council, the inner circle of advisers close to the monarch. It dealt with a host of local issues; petitions came to it from the provinces seeking redress in matters of local concern, while it, in turn, sent out orders to the localities. It was particularly involved in preventing disturbance and disorder which might occur, for instance, at a time of harvest failure or after an enclosure scheme had been carried out.[45]

For some parts of the country, extra administrative material is available. In the Middle Ages a number of exempt palatine jurisdictions were established, basically covering the counties of Cheshire, Durham and Lancashire. Their records have now been transferred to the PRO in Chancery Lane (with the exception of the material relating to the estates of the bishop of Durham, deposited at the University of Durham). In the 1530s a number of councils were set up in the outlying parts of the country. The Council of the West was short-lived, disappearing about 1543, but the other two, the Council of the North and the Council of the Marches of Wales, lasted longer.[46]

In 1782 the work of the two Secretaries of State was rationalized, with one handling domestic concerns and the other foreign affairs. Local historians will be mainly interested in the Home Office papers, desposited at the Kew branch of the PRO. Separate files were made for incoming and outgoing letters, and within each category the documents were arranged in chronological order. Readers, therefore, have to look through a mass of material, covering the whole country, if they want to find something about their locality. If they know the date of a significant local event – an enclosure – or a food riot, for instance – this may help them discover something of interest.[47]

The Registrar General

The office of the Registrar General was created in 1836 to oversee the national system of registering births, marriages and deaths. For this task the new poor law unions of 1834 provided a handy organization and they invariably served as registration districts. In addition, many clerks to the poor law guardians acted as superintendent-registrars. The registration districts themselves were divided into subdistricts, each with its registrar of births and deaths, and perhaps of marriages. Both sets of local officials kept their own books (when full, the volumes were given to the superintendent) and every three months a copy of all entries was sent to the Registrar General. Superintendents also received duplicate books of marriages solemnized in local Anglican churches, Quaker chapels and Jewish synagogues and personally registered the marriages of Roman Catholics and nonconformists who, until 1898, were not allowed to perform the task themselves. In some subdistricts registrars were deputed to do the job. Copies were sent to the Registrar General.[48]

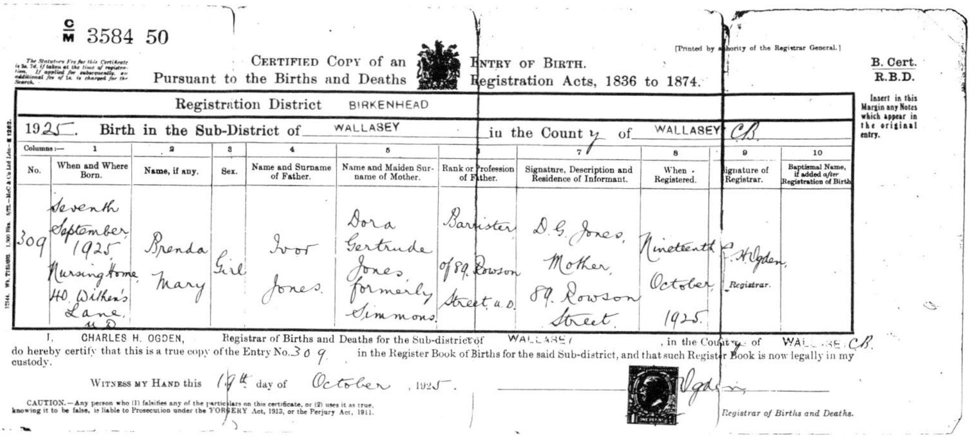

C/M 3584 50

The Statutory Fee for this Certificate is 3s. 7d. if taken at the time of registration. If applied for subsequently, an additional fee of 1s. is charged for the Search.

[Printed by authority of the Registrar General.]

B. Cert. R.B.D.

CERTIFIED COPY of an ENTRY OF BIRTH.
Pursuant to the Births and Deaths Registration Acts, 1836 to 1874.

Registration District BIRKENHEAD

1925. Birth in the Sub-District of WALLASEY in the County of WALLASEY CB.

No.	When and Where Born.	Name, if any.	Sex.	Name and Surname of Father.	Name and Maiden Surname of Mother.	Rank or Profession of Father.	Signature, Description and Residence of Informant.	When Registered.	Signature of Registrar.	Baptismal Name, if added after Registration of Birth.
309	Seventh September 1925 Nursing Home 40 Wilkin's Lane U.D.	Brenda Mary	Girl	Ivor Jones	Dora Gertrude Jones formerly Simmons	Barrister of 89 Rowson Street U.D.	D. G. Jones, Mother, 89 Rowson Street	Nineteenth October 1925	F. H. Ogden, Registrar.	

Insert in this Margin any Notes which appear in the original entry.

I, CHARLES H. OGDEN, Registrar of Births and Deaths for the Sub-district of WALLASEY, in the County of WALLASEY CB. do hereby certify that this is a true copy of the Entry No. 309 in the Register Book of Births for the said Sub-district, and that such Register Book is now legally in my custody.

WITNESS MY HAND this 19th day of October, 1925.

Registrar of Births and Deaths.

CAUTION.—Any person who (1) falsifies any of the particulars on this certificate, or (2) uses it as true, knowing it to be false, is liable to Prosecution under the Forgery Act, 1913, or the Perjury Act, 1911.

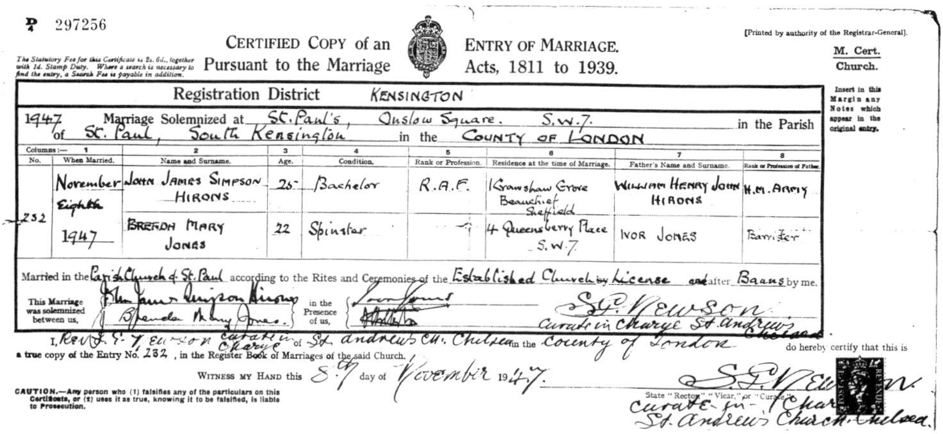

P/4 297256

The Statutory Fee for this Certificate is 2s. 6d., together with 1d. Stamp Duty. Where a search is necessary to find the entry, a Search Fee is payable in addition.

[Printed by authority of the Registrar-General].

M. Cert. Church.

CERTIFIED COPY of an ENTRY OF MARRIAGE.
Pursuant to the Marriage Acts, 1811 to 1939.

Registration District KENSINGTON

1947 Marriage Solemnized at St. Paul's, Onslow Square. S.W.7. in the Parish of St. Paul, South Kensington in the COUNTY OF LONDON

No.	When Married.	[Name] and Surname.	Age.	Condition.	Rank or Profession.	Residence at the time of Marriage.	Father's Name and Surname.	Rank or Profession of Father.
232	November Eighth 1947	John James Simpson Hirons	25	Bachelor	R.A.F.	1 Grawshaw Grove Beauchief Sheffield	William Henry John Hirons	H.M. Army
		Brenda Mary Jones	22	Spinster	—	4 Queensberry Place S.W.7.	Ivor Jones	Barrister

Insert in this Margin any Notes which appear in the original entry.

Married in the Parish Church of St. Paul according to the Rites and Ceremonies of the Established Church by License after Banns by me.

This Marriage was solemnized between us, John James Simpson Hirons / Brenda Mary Jones in the Presence of us, [signatures]

S. G. Newson. Curate in Charge St. Andrew's Chelsea

I, Rev. S. G. Newson Curate in Charge of St. Andrew's Ch. Chelsea in the County of London do hereby certify that this is a true copy of the Entry No. 232, in the Register Book of Marriages of the said Church.

WITNESS MY HAND this 8th day of November 1947.

State "Rector," "Vicar," or "Curate." Curate-in-Charge St. Andrew's Church. Chelsea.

CAUTION.—Any person who (1) falsifies any of the particulars on this Certificate, or (2) uses it as true, knowing it to be falsified, is liable to Prosecution.

6 and 7 Certificates of the birth and marriage of Brenda Mary Jones.

By law people had to register a live birth within 42 days and a death within five days but comprehensiveness was only achieved in 1874 when defaulters became liable to punishment. Researchers do not have direct access to the archive, as the information in the local registers and the national copies can only be supplied in the form of a certified copy. Nonetheless, they can look at the indexes compiled by the registrars and the Registrar General. For the national records one has to go to St Catherine's House in London, the headquarters of the Registrar General, now the Office of Population Censuses and Surveys.[49]

In 1841 the Registrar General assumed responsibility for collecting the data for the decennial national censuses, begun in 1801. Hitherto the work had been undertaken by parish overseers of the poor but they had only gathered a limited amount of information from which a few rudimentary calculations were made. Because of his network of officials, augmented for the purpose by an army of enumerators, the Registrar General was able to conduct a much more thorough enquiry. The enumerators gave a printed census form to a person in each household and collected it, duly completed, the following day. The forms were then sent to the registrars who checked them before giving them to the superintendents of each district. They, in turn, dispatched them to the Registrar General.[50]

Inevitably there were problems. Many people were suspicious of the census and may have made false or vague returns. Others simply did not know the requisite information or were confused as to what was being asked of them. Often the enumerators themselves were unsure of what instructions to give. Errors occurred in transcription too: data was put into the wrong column and occupations and place-names were misspelled. Because they deal with information of a personal nature, censuses can only be examined after 100 years have elapsed, though later abstracts are in print. A complete microfilm set is available for examination in the PRO, Chancery Lane, but in practice researchers can normally find copies more locally in reference libraries and record offices.

Financial administration

In the Middle Ages financial matters were controlled by the Exchequer. It was the first branch of the *Curia Regis* to go out of court, establishing an independent existence at Westminster before the end of the twelfth century.[51] From there it grew into a great department of state with an influence not merely in financial affairs but also in many other branches of the administration. In spite of the return to chamber government in the late fifteenth and early sixteenth centuries, it was not until the rise of the Treasury in the late seventeenth century that its supremacy was permanently challenged.[52]

The Domesday Book occupies pride of place among the Exchequer records. In effect, the survey is made up of several parts, not all of which give the same amount of detail, a reflection of the variable survival rates of successive drafts for different parts of the country.[53] In 1279 an even more ambitious survey was undertaken by Edward I. Known as the Hundred Rolls because the information was supplied by juries meeting at hundred or wapentake courts, the survey formed part of a more general enquiry into forms of landholding and resources in the country. The enquiry was never completed; it seems that some eight counties, mainly in the south and east Midlands, were surveyed but even there the survival rate of the material is variable.[54]

The Exchequer records naturally contain taxation returns and information on other sources of revenue. Between the thirteenth and seventeenth centuries, whenever taxes were granted by Parliament, they most commonly took the form of a subsidy. In the Middle Ages this involved an assessment of some fraction of the taxpayers' moveable wealth, extended in the sixteenth century to include wages and land. (In 1342, however, Parliament granted Edward III a tax known as the *Nonarum Inquisitiones* because it was assessed on one-ninth of the value of corn, wool and lambs produced in the year ending 1341.[55]) Between 1290 and 1332, and after 1523, the returns list individual taxpayers. Unfortunately, the tax tended quickly to get out of date and thus ceased to reflect the taxpaying capacity of the population. In the 1520s a new listing was made but this, too, became fossilized in Elizabeth's reign.[56] During the Commonwealth period the lay subsidy was replaced by the monthly assessment, at a rate far higher than the taxpayers had known before.[57] For the latter, extant material has to be sought in private collections and at county record offices, for no lists were sent to the Exchequer.

The clergy were taxed separately. Clerical incomes, for instance, were assessed in 1291 (the so-called Tax of Pope Nicholas IV), and these have been printed in full by the Record Commission in the *Taxatio Ecclesiastica* (1802).[58] In 1535 the *Valor Ecclesiasticus*, a survey of church income, was made in conjunction with a new tax of one-tenth on clerical wealth. The commissioners sent out to obtain the information had to work quickly (the returns were called for within four months) and there are signs of haste. Nonetheless, the enquiry was a major achievement and (with some gaps) provides a countrywide survey of ecclesiastical property at the time.[59] The material is readily available in print, having been published by the Royal Commissioners in six volumes between 1810 and 1834.

In 1692 a new property tax was introduced. Initially intended as a tax on offices and personal estates as well as on land, it soon became a charge solely on land. Indeed, by 1702 it was being called a 'land tax'. By 1698 the tax had become stereotyped, the rate being fixed at the county quotas of 1692. Within the county the commissioners could apportion the rate as they saw fit. Between 1780 and 1832 copies had to be deposited with the Clerk of the Peace since the tax was used as a means of identifying those who could vote for county MPs and they are the ones most likely to be found in county record offices.[60]

More recently valuable information can be gained from the documentation generated by the reform of the land tax that resulted from Lloyd George's Finance (1909–1910) Act 1910. Surveys of landed properties were made and from them one can obtain material on landownership and rural society. The tax caused an uproar among the landed classes and only became law after its rejection by the House of Lords had provoked a constitutional crisis; it continued to meet opposition and the land clauses were replaced in 1920.[61]

From time to time other schemes were adopted. In 1377, 1379 and 1381 a poll tax was levied, assessed in 1377 at a flat rate of 4d a head for all lay tax-payers and unbeneficed clergy and 6d for beneficed clergy, but graded according to wealth in 1379 and 1381. It was as unpopular then as it recently has been.[62] Similarly the imposition of ship money in the 1630s met with opposition. Sadly, extant material does not include lists of individual tax-payers, though county totals exist.[63] Other items were occasionally subject to tax. Eighteenth-century legislators were particularly fertile in their choice of commodities, and included windows, bricks and wigs in the list. For the local historian only the records of the first named tax have any value.[64] Income tax was introduced at the end of the century. First used by Pitt in 1799 as a temporary wartime expedient, it was never withdrawn, although the rate has fluctuated periodically.

Best known of the 'commodity' taxes is the hearth tax, first levied in 1662 and reimposed at intervals until 1689.[65] Extant material is confined to the years 1662–5 and 1670–3, for on other occasions the tax was either farmed out or managed by a commission. All householders were rated at 2 shillings a hearth, except for those exempted on grounds of poverty or other reasons. Many of the returns include the exempt at the end of each township or parish and this makes them more comprehensive. The Lady Day 1664 returns are usually good but researchers should certainly look at more than one list, not only to discern the one that gives the most information for their community but also to fill in the gaps.

The government (before modern times), in the person of the monarch, also drew an income from land, some of it belonging to the Crown and some of it owned by others but temporarily in its hands. Evidence for this can be found in the class of Exchequer documents known as the Pipe Rolls, which run in an almost unbroken sequence from the middle of the twelfth century to 1832. The rolls record the accounts presented to the Upper Exchequer by sheriffs and other accountants for auditing, and as such will refer to the various sources of income at their disposal and the ways in which they disbursed it. The rolls have been calendared up to the early thirteenth century and the work is continuing under the auspices of the Pipe Roll Society.[66]

In the sixteenth century the dissolution of the monasteries led to the creation of a special body, the Court of Augmentations, to administer the newly acquired lands and their revenues. The records of the court are voluminous and diverse, providing information on the properties themselves, their administration and subsequent disposal (if it occurred). Local historians will find much of interest in these documents and there are various finding aids in the Round Room of the PRO. In 1554 the court became part of the Exchequer but retained its identity as a subdepartment there, the Office of the Auditors of Land Revenue.[67]

Justice

Of the three branches of the judiciary that emerged out of the *Curia Regis*, the ones with which the population at large had the closest contact were the courts held in the counties by itinerant justices. The earliest courts were those of general eyre; every few years royal justices came to each county to hear cases that had arisen since their last visit and pass judgment on them. These courts only operated for 100 years or so, ending abruptly in 1294 at a time when war with France was imminent, but there are extant rolls for all counties except Cheshire.[68] Non-specialists may balk at reading the originals, though a finding aid is available at Chancery Lane and sections dealing with individual counties are identified by a note in the margin.

One of the reasons for the demise of the general eyre was its intermittent nature, which enabled other bodies, notably the courts of assize, to take its place. Judges of assize, holding several sessions a year in each county, were operating well before the end of the thirteenth century and by 1300 had gained formal recognition. By 1337 the six circuits had crystallized, though minor adjustments were made in the sixteenth century. In Wales assize judges were appointed for the six counties created by Edward I in 1284. In 1543, shortly after the rest of the country had been divided into shires, a Court of Great Sessions was introduced and four Welsh circuits established.[69] Until their abolition in 1971 the assizes, for all practical purposes, formed the apex of the legal system for the ordinary citizen.

Cases could be taken out of the assizes by a writ of *certiorari* issued out of King's Bench or Chancery and transferred to the Court of King's Bench, the highest common law court in the land. In origin, it comprised those judges who continued to attend the king after the other two branches had left the *Curia Regis*.[70] Local historians may find information on their community in the court's records but only the truly committed will attempt the task. There is certainly a mass of material to look at, but it is not organized by county and is inadequately indexed. The handwriting is difficult to read too. Some medieval material has been printed, most notably in the volumes of the Selden Society. The third branch of the *Curia Regis* consisted of those judges who remained at Westminster to hear pleas brought to them, and which evolved into the Court of Common Pleas. For researchers, there are the same problems as those encountered when examining the records of King's Bench.

The courts of Chancery and Exchequer also possessed some common law jurisdiction; aspects of their work, especially in the context of economic regulation, are of interest to local historians. Far more wide-ranging was their equity jurisdiction, which they shared with the Courts of Requests and Star Chamber.[71] The work of these courts expanded during the course of the sixteenth century to fill in the gaps left by the common law and to complement the business being conducted there. With regard to the Exchequer, provision was also made for special commissioners to hear cases locally.

Regional administrative bodies such as the Councils of the North and of the Marches of Wales, and the county palatines of Cheshire, Durham and Lancashire had their equity jurisdictions too. In spite of their undoubted popularity, not all of the equity courts survived the seventeenth century. The Courts of Requests and Star Chamber were forced to close, though the equity jurisdiction of the courts of Chancery and Exchequer did continue.

Summary

From the records of local administration, one can gain an impression of the daily routine of life in the countryside, as well as an indication of matters of concern to rural society. Apart from providing us with important evidence of the running of affairs in general, they also enable us to examine specific issues or particular sectors of the population. The records of outside bodies also contain valuable information, especially as they often deal with events that were central to rural life. All villagers were subject to the jurisdiction of the Justices of the Peace and, as the business they conducted was so varied and wide-ranging, their impact on the local community was considerable. Similarly, bishops, within their dioceses, possessed an authority which transcended the spiritual sphere. Even the records of an estate list more people than those who lived on it.

Local historians should also make a positive effort to study the records of central government. Some will have looked through the calendars of documents shelved in local reference libraries or published in county record society volumes but fewer will have gone to examine original material in the PRO. Apart from the inconvenience, there are other practical problems to be faced. Because many of the records are inadequately indexed, especially those at Chancery Lane, the task of finding relevant information is something of a lottery. Medieval documents such as those produced by the courts of assize and King's Bench are also very difficult to read so that they tend to be ignored, even though they may contain useful local references.

While the difficulties to be encountered when using these records must not be minimized, readers should not overlook an archive which is not only rich in local material but which also contains information that could give them insights into the history of their community. Many a study has been enlivened by the discovery there of a vital piece of evidence. Furthermore, serendipity is not the sole guiding principle to be followed when examining the records. Some sources are relatively easy to use and, if they have a nationwide coverage, can be confidently scanned for interesting and relevant information.

CHAPTER TWO

Village society

Medieval developments before the mid-fourteenth century

Medieval society was not static. The number of people in each social group, and their relationship with one another, varied over time and with it the fortunes of individuals. In particular, the distribution of land among small, medium and large owners (and occupiers) altered. Many people stayed in the same class but some improved their position, while others fared less well. A major factor influencing change in the centuries after the Norman Conquest was the fluctuating level of the population. Clearly the situation in the first half of the period, characterized by growing pressure on land, was a far more difficult one for the mass of the population than that which faced them in the aftermath of the plague of 1348–9.

To begin with, the Domesday Book can be used to give some indication of the division of land between the constituent groups on the manor. According to the survey, manorial lords only directly exploited one-third to two-fifths of the land, the rest being held by freemen, leaseholders and serfs.[1] To find out the ratio between the two on a specific manor, the number of ploughs on the demesne can be compared with those in the hands of the villagers. The ploughs of the villagers were usually totalled together and, where this happened, it is difficult to make an assessment of each group's holdings, let alone calculate the area farmed by one person. Fortunately some entries are more precise. Important freeholders were often treated individually, while the ploughs belonging to freemen as a group were frequently listed separately from those of the bondmen. At Wigston Magna (Leicestershire) 31 sokemen, one clerk, two knights and four Frenchmen possessed eight ploughs; 32 villeins, twelve bordars and a priest had five.[2] It is not clear how the land was distributed within the former group, though we might expect the knights to have held more land than did the sokemen.

We do know that in those parts of the country where the Domesday Book provides more detailed information disparities did exist. In Middlesex villeins, on average, held between one-half and a whole virgate of land, but nearly one-third of them had one to two virgates. At the extremities a few occupied larger or smaller holdings.[3] In Leicestershire, Lincolnshire, Northamptonshire and Nottinghamshire the commissioners presented the material in a more indirect way, noting down the number of oxen separately kept by sokemen and villeins. The pattern – a large group in the middle and smaller clusters at either end – remains the same. Nearly half of the peasants owned two to four beasts, while 20 per cent had four to eight oxen and 28 per cent had less than two.[4] In these counties, at least, the average sokeman possessed more plough animals than did the villein, though he was also more likely to have kept fewer of them. Both classes seem to have been worse off than villeins in some other parts of the country, illustrating the point that in general the size of holdings in an area was related to the availability of land.[5]

With the Domesday Book as a base, later surveys should be examined for comparative purposes. The Hundred Rolls of 1279, for instance, can act as a convenient benchmark for assessing the changes that had occurred in the intervening centuries, at least in those parts of the country for which the documentation survives. More detail is in the Rolls, too. Not only do they record the status of individuals, listed in different socio-economic groups, but they also indicate the amount of land they farmed and the rents and services owed. In Warwickshire the percentage of freemen was higher in the wooded half of the county, the Forest of Arden, than in the felden half.[6] This seems to have been due to the greater opportunities for individual initiative provided by the availability of waste land and other economic resources in the Forest. The rolls also show that freeholdings continued to be less uniform in size than those of the unfree tenants.[7]

For communities not covered by the Hundred Rolls, manorial surveys, extents and custumals provide similar information. An extent of Hodstock (Nottinghamshire), taken in 1324, reveals that the pattern of landholding there was like the one just outlined.[8] The manor's 20 freeholders formed a very disparate group, with wide variations in the size of their holdings. Among the unfree tenants there, those occupying standard holdings remained numerous: over half of them had holdings of between one and two bovates (mostly one). A handful of peasants had thriven, increasing their acreage as they had done so, but most of the rest were cottagers. As with most documents of this type, no mention is made of subtenants, and thus they do not provide us with a completely accurate picture of the social structure of the manor. Surveys in which this information is given, coupled with the evidence of manor court rolls, indicate that subletting was a widespread practice and greatly affected the amount of land actually occupied by individuals.[9]

Local historians can also use the manor court rolls to build up a picture of landholding in a community by looking at entries which record the surrender of properties into the hands of the steward and their subsequent regrant to tenants. Freehold land was dealt with at the court too. In this period population pressure did have an impact upon the size of the holdings but the rolls reveal that the amount of land held by an individual was also influenced by his life cycle. As a person's family increased, for instance, extra land might be acquired, only for it to be surrendered later on in life when it was no longer needed.

In addition, rentals may list the details of each person's property, though many merely give the name and a generalized description. At least they refer to individual tenants, both free and unfree, and provide evidence of rents and services. As they were made annually (or annotated regularly), they should be more sensitive to change than were surveys or extents. On the other hand, like the latter sources, they do not often include subtenants in the list.

Tax returns provide another source of information on social structure and one that covers more places than do manorial surveys. Because the lay subsidies of the years up to 1332 record individuals and their assessments, the people concerned can be put into wealth bands. The lord of the manor (if a lay person) often stands out from the other taxpayers by the size of his assessment, though this depends upon the extent of the demesne and the presence or not of other substantial landowners. Researchers should be careful when drawing conclusions from the figures. When the returns have been related to entries in surveys and extents a large number of omissions have generally been found. Many people evaded the tax or paid less than they should have done, while others were deemed too poor to contribute anything. These shortcomings obviously affect the accuracy of the picture of local society that can be drawn from the data, especially if the omissions are not evenly spread among the social classes.

The absence of the exempt from tax lists highlights the difficulty of finding out information on the rural poor of medieval England. Their number certainly grew in the period before the mid-fourteenth century, as population pressure reduced the real income of many villagers by raising prices without a compensatory increase in wages. To a certain extent the problem was eased by assarting, and thousands of acres of waste were brought into cultivation. Evidence for the practice, which appears in manorial surveys and extents, as well as in manor court rolls, had an impact upon the size of holdings. A considerable number of encroachments were made by peasants and, as these were often only a fraction of an acre, they had the effect of increasing the number of smallholdings in the country. At Great Shelford (Cambridgeshire), where the tenant population more than doubled between 1086 and the early fourteenth century, the average holding of the middling peasant had halved, while the number of very small holdings rose by more than 300 per cent.[10]

One section of the poor comprised those with little or no land (or a trade or craft). Such people had to rely upon their labour to earn a living and many of them suffered as the struggle for land and jobs intensified. They may appear in surveys, rentals and manor court rolls, occupying cottages and perhaps a small plot of land but, if subtenants, they were often omitted. As the court rolls record licences for subletting, as well as fines exacted for infringements of the rule, these people may turn up there. Incidental references to them can be unearthed in the rolls but the problem remains one of identification. More commonly the poor are mentioned as a group, often when something was being done for them (in the records of charitable foundations, for instance) or if they were creating difficulties for the authorities.

Others classed as poor were those who do appear in the records as landholders but who had become destitute through injury, illness or old age. Because they could no longer farm, their economic standing deteriorated. Manor court rolls are full of references to the arrangements that were made whenever such a situation arose; specific mention is often made of the fact that the tenant was incapable of working the land.[11] Another member of the family, if there were one, normally took over the holding and provision may have been made for the outgoing person's maintenance. Those described as poor, therefore, may have been peasant farmers who could not count on the support of a family and who had no means of gaining an income from the land either directly or indirectly.

Developments in the late Middle Ages

After the demographic crisis of the mid-fourteenth century the situation became more favourable to the peasantry and offered them the opportunity to improve their position. Conditions did not change overnight, however. In spite of the large number of vacant holdings, the records show that in many places deficiencies were soon made good. The process can best be seen in the manor court rolls, wherever the proceedings of the court baron were recorded. Vacancies were reported and thus the scale of the problem can be assessed. Moreover, as new tenants were admitted to their holdings at the court, the speed with which the gaps were filled up can be gauged. At Kibworth Harcourt (Leicestershire), when the court convened in April 1350, tenants for 44 holdings had to be found. By the end of August 1350 only four remained untenanted.[12] The documents should also tell us about the people who succeeded the former tenants. Some were heirs or relatives but others were fellow-parishioners or even outsiders. Undoubtedly one of the reasons why the land was retenanted so quickly was the existence of so many landless people in the country. It was also due to the tightening up of control by the landlords.

The tide started to turn in the 1370s when the effects of a continuing fall in the population of the country began to be felt.[13] Peasants, with plenty of land available and labour in short supply, were no longer willing to accept the old restrictions. Thousands left their homes, looking for a better place to settle, and this led to competition among landowners. All sources linking individual tenants with holdings – surveys, extents, rentals and manor court rolls – reveal that the turnover rate increased in the late Middle Ages. Manor court rolls show the difficulties facing landowners as they tried to retain their tenantry and find replacements for those who had fled. On the bishop of Worcester's estate, court rolls occasionally list holdings in the lord's hands because of vacancies. From these we can see that a peak was reached in the last two decades of the fourteenth century.[14]

Because of the difficulties experienced by landlords in securing tenants, much land went out of cultivation. Some villages, especially those on the margins, were deserted, while others shrank. In tax lists the former vanish from the record and the latter appear as dwarf settlements. In many places land became derelict as people could not be found to work it. Apart from holdings with poor soil, the ones most likely to remain unfilled were those heavily burdened with labour services.[15] In order to attract tenants landowners reduced rents and commuted surviving labour services. This information can be found in custumals, extents and surveys and in individual entries in the manor court rolls.

As vacant holdings meant less rent, the problems should be reflected in rentals and manorial accounts. The desertion of Hatton (Worcestershire) between 1371 and 1385, for instance, is recorded in the manorial account. Ten yardlands had been abandoned and, although for a time they were let to tenants from nearby Hampton, the lands had become demesne sheep pasture by 1385.[16] Surveys and extents show that other landowners adopted this solution, but it only became widespread in the late fifteenth century, at a time when wool prices rose above those of grain.

Holdings were amalgamated too, enabling the wealthier peasants further to increase the amount of land they held. This process can be charted in the manor court rolls in the increase in presentments for decayed farm houses and buildings made redundant by consolidation. Peasants were involved in leasing demesne land too. While few could afford to take on entire demesnes, more could acquire leases of parcels of the demesne whenever it was divided up. As a result, a peasant aristocracy emerged – the ancestors of the Tudor and Stuart yeomen. They held 60 acres or more of land, often by a variety of tenures, and through intermarriage increasingly formed a village elite.

These people filled most of the posts in the village, and played an important role in the community, especially if there was no resident lord. Office holding, therefore, is a good indicator of a person's standing in the community. Serving in a post not only conferred status but it gave the individual tangible benefits to offset against the burden of office. Because they were prominent in local affairs – acting as essoiners, attorneys and pledges, as well as occupying positions such as bailiff, affeeror or aletaster – these men's names (women were rarely involved) appear regularly in the manor court rolls.[17]

Others, below the elite, were also able to thrive. Vacancies caused by death or migration, for instance, allowed smallholders to acquire larger farms. In spite of such advances, a study of surveys and extents demonstrates the survival of the middling peasant with his traditional half or whole virgate of land.[18] These sources often indicate a high proportion of smallholders too. Moreover, entries in manor court rolls continue to provide evidence of the existence of a large number of poor people in the countryside. Apart from the landless, there were still those like John Baty of Kempsey (Worcestershire), described as old and decrepit (*senex et decrepitus*) in 1452, who had become impoverished through age.[19] Probate wills, a relatively new source in the late Middle Ages, reveal that many individuals made charitable bequests at the end of their own lives, often stipulating that the benefits should be restricted to the 'deserving' poor.

Some general indications of the changes that occurred in local society in the later Middle Ages can be obtained by comparing the pre-1332 lay subsidy returns with the revised assessments made in the 1520s, although as the later returns are far more comprehensive, the early sixteenth-century picture is the more accurate one. Allowing for the inevitable weaknesses – some under-recording (notably in Yorkshire) and omissions (the clergy, defaulters and the exempt and only single entries for people with scattered property) – the lists are generally thought to be fairly accurate.[20] As a new survey was made of each person's wealth parish by parish, set low enough to include all but the paupers, most wage earners should be included in it. Payment of tax was spread out over four years; all taxpayers contributed to the first two instalments and only the wealthier to the third and fourth, so the returns of 1524 and 1525 are the most complete.

The sixteenth and early seventeenth centuries

The dramatic increase in the price of agricultural products in the late sixteenth and early seventeenth centuries made it a prosperous time for many farmers. Freeholders and tenants with fixed outgoings (mostly copyholders of inheritance and leaseholders with long leases) were in a particularly good position as they had little to pay in the way of rent. Tenants who held their land on less favourable terms – mainly on short leases or at will – did not benefit to the same extent, as their landlords could regularly raise their rents. Entry fines, in particular, were high. If the sums are compared with other leases or manor court entries of the same property, the rate at which rents were moving up or down over time can be gauged. In areas where entry fines prevailed it can be difficult to obtain a base figure because many sixteenth-century leases refer to them in such vague terms as 'for divers good cause and consideration him moving' and 'for a certain sum of money'. On the other hand, the amounts paid are often noted in accounts, or even in diaries and commonplace books. Details of negotiations between landlord and tenant also appear in bundles of estate correspondence.

Less laborious to use are sets of accounts and surveys because all the information is concentrated in a single document. When comparing figures, only that part of the estate which appears in both documents should be examined to ensure the accuracy of the calculation. Where such an analysis is possible, dramatic increases in rent are invariably revealed. On the Herbert estate in the Wiltshire chalk country, data obtained from two detailed sets of surveys (1567–8 and 1631–2) indicate a fourfold increase in rents, mainly in the form of entry fines, between the mid-sixteenth and mid-seventeenth centuries.[21] In spite of rises of this order (and it was not an unusual one), evidence from estates such as Lord Bridgewater's in north Shropshire reveals that many farmers paid up readily enough.[22]

The growing wealth of the farming community was not equally distributed, however, for some gained more than others. The more substantial farmers, those with a considerable surplus to sell and who could wait for the most opportune moment to do so, did best. These were the men whose homes, improved and extended during the course of the sixteenth and seventeenth centuries, still line our village streets and country lanes. Probate inventories, listing the contents of these houses, confirm the impression that they were enjoying a rising standard of living. Apart from making their homes more comfortable, they invested their extra income in land, often in a variety of tenures. When Thomas Nash of Rushock (Worcestershire) made his will in July 1620, it is clear from the document that he had been acquiring leaseholds, as well as freehold properties, in a number of parishes. From a survey of the estate taken four years later, showing his widow holding a copyhold farm of three yardlands, we can deduce that he had probably obtained customary land too.[23]

As in the Middle Ages, these were the people who ran community affairs. Apart from holding manorial office, they monopolized the most prestigious posts in the developing parochial administration. The parish records of Terling (Essex) reveal that the churchwardens, vestrymen, overseers of the poor, as well as quarter sessions' jurymen, tended to come from the ranks of the yeomen and the wealthier tradesmen.[24] The humbler posts of sidesmen and constable, controlled by the superior officers, were filled by husbandmen and craftsmen. This pattern, in which the hierarchy of offices mirrored social gradation, was repeated in other parishes, though there were variations in the social groups involved.

The leading members of the community participated in communal life in other ways. At Terling (and elsewhere) the elite were prominent among those who witnessed wills or who stood as sureties in recognizances, activities in which the standing and probity of the person was of utmost importance.[25] Weekly, at the Sunday service, the eminence of this group was publicly displayed to the whole congregation. Apart from the lord of the manor, who often had his own special pew, they occupied the positions of honour, in the first few rows, while behind them in descending social order were seated the rest of the inhabitants. Plans and descriptions of the seating arrangements survive in some number among parochial records or in diocesan faculty papers.

For small farmers the situation was not so good. Although they obtained more from the sale of their produce and stock, the little they had to sell may have provided them with insufficient income to counterbalance the increase in their outgoings. The availability of credit facilities in the countryside, so evident in lists of credits and debts in probate wills and inventories, gave them some relief, as did the development of mortgages. A run of bad harvests, however, might prove too much for them. At Chippenham (Cambridgeshire) copyholds of inheritance were the norm. An analysis of the transactions conducted at the court baron there points to a correlation between the number of 'sales' recorded and periods of hardship.[26] When a rental of 1560 is compared with a survey of 1544 (annotated in 1636) evidence for the decline of the manor's small farmers is clear to see.[27]

This polarization of society was particularly noticeable in mixed farming areas, continuing the trend discernible in the late Middle Ages. In many communities the development of a farming elite was mirrored by a thickening of the lower strata of society, as modest farmers, forced off the land, swelled even further the already growing ranks of cottagers and landless labourers. In pastoral areas, on the other hand, surveys indicate that small farms, often organized on a family basis and with ample commons to augment the resources of their holdings, remained more viable. There, too, a greater cross-section of society tended to be involved in local administration. In the Forest of Arden in the seventeenth century even smallholders filled lesser posts such as the surveyor of the highways.[28]

Cutting across this classification of local communities according to the type of agriculture practised there was one based upon the pattern of landownership. Estate villages, with their dominant landowner, for instance, had a different social structure to those where the land was in divided ownership. Because access to the land could be more readily controlled, they tended to have smaller populations and fewer cottagers and labourers. This distinction grew over time as population pressure forced more and more people to migrate from their homes to look for a job or a place in which to settle.

The former type, the later 'closed' parishes, are well documented: details of ownership and occupancy, as well as the terms on which property was held, can be found in estate and manorial records. Less is known of the social structure of 'open' villages, though some estate material might survive and there are other sources which can be used. For the social groups covered by probate material, inventories provide evidence of the differences in personal wealth between classes, while wills often give information on a person's real estate, together with any leases or copies that he or she held.

8 Extremes of wealth in Tudor England: a beggar asks for alms from a gentleman.

Tax returns should also be examined, especially as they transcend the distinction between open and closed parishes. In this respect, the lay subsidy of 1524–5 could serve as a foundation for local historians to examine subsequent changes. Later subsidy rolls, because they record fewer tax-payers, do not give the same coverage but at least they enable us to pin-point the village elite. For comparative purposes, the hearth tax returns can be analysed; this source, because it often includes the poor, provides a comprehensive survey of local society. Even though the unit of assessment, the hearth, is completely different from that upon which the lay subsidies were based, the progressive nature of the taxes remained the same.

Apart from the hearth tax returns, other sources allow us to gain some knowledge of the lower echelons of society. References to them, both as individuals and as members of the group, continue to appear in records such as probate wills, the accounts of charitable endowments and estate and manorial documents. To them can be added the archive of material generated by the poor law legislation of the sixteenth and seventeenth centuries. In particular, overseers' accounts should be examined. These documents, which owe their origin to acts of 1563 and 1573 obliging parishioners to maintain the poor, provide a good deal of evidence on inhabitants in need of relief. From them the numbers involved can be found out, together with information on the type of people concerned, their background and the causes of their poverty. The number of extant accounts rises in the aftermath of the codifying acts of 1597–1601 but earlier examples do exist.[29] The parish rating lists, upon which individual contributions were assessed, can be used to ascertain the social structure of a community. Normally based upon the ownership or occupancy of land, they give some indication of a person's holding in the parish, though if acreages are not recorded this is more difficult to gauge. Researchers should also bear in mind the fact that some 'smallholders' might in fact be major landowners or large farmers but who only had a few acres in the parish under consideration.

The mid-seventeenth century to the mid-eighteenth century

If agriculture had been buoyant in the hundred years before the mid-seventeenth century, conditions thereafter were far less favourable. As the rate of population growth slowed down, and even stopped, demand slackened off and with it the value of farm products. At the same time farmers' expenses went up. Financial demands upon them had risen during the course of the Civil War and Interregnum and, although they did not remain at the same levels after the Restoration, they were higher than they had been in the early seventeenth century.

Locally they faced heavier and more regular rate demands, due largely to increased expenditure on the poor. Freeholders paid more in national taxation, especially after the introduction of the land tax in 1692, a measure brought in to help finance the war against Louis XIV. During the war years the rate was set at 4 shillings in the pound, although in practice the actual percentage of landed wealth tapped varied regionally. Studies based upon surviving tax lists suggest that the amount paid declined with distance from the capital.[30]

Many landowners passed on the costs to their tenantry, notably life leaseholders – those who held property for the lives of named people rather than for a term of years. Rents were adjusted accordingly but it is not easy to discern this process from the figures given in rentals and surveys. For matters of policy like this, estate correspondence is the best source. Thus, in a letter sent by the chief agent of the Duke of Newcastle to his master in 1710, he explained why he had let out for lives farms which had hitherto been leased at rack rents.[31] 'This method', he wrote, 'will excuse your Grace from what you abhor, I mean Taxes and repaires, and will ensure the succeeding rent beyond all adventure.' Rack-rented tenants, on the other hand, could not be expected to make similar payments. In the early eighteenth century the agent of Richard Hill esquire of Attingham Park (Shropshire) told him that 'tenants at rack in this country will not be tied to any repairs'.[32]

The position of the small owner-occupier deteriorated during the late seventeenth and early eighteenth centuries, making this period a significant one in the history of the declining fortunes of the small farmer, an issue which has been the subject of a vigorous debate among historians for the best part of the present century. In times of depression like this one such people always fared worse than large landowners because they had fewer resources to tide them over until conditions improved. Many did struggle on, waiting for better times, but others succumbed and sold up, often to a large landowner, seeking to enlarge and consolidate a nearby estate. As land agents were active in drawing their masters' attention to possible purchases, the correspondence between them furnishes numerous examples of this process. When a farm at Eaton (Shropshire) came on to the market in 1721, John Dickin, the agent of Richard Hill of Attingham Park, recommended its purchase because 'it lies very convenient and contiguous together with a very good common'.[33] Many deeds refer to acquisitions like this, which should subsequently appear in rentals, leases and surveys if leased out, but only in surveys if added to the demesne. The farm may have remained as a separate entity and be described by its name in the records, though if kept in hand or engrossed with other holdings, this was less likely to happen.

Small tenant farmers were also adversely affected and fell into arrears with their rent or had to give up their holding before the end of the term. Debts for rents appear in probate wills and inventories, even if they are not always distinguished as such. Instances of debt increased at times of distress. At such times rentals, especially on estates where land was rack-rented, reveal the extent of the problem as arrears mounted up and abatements were made. If entry fines prevailed, the pattern was a different one. Tenants on such estates normally could still pay their small reserved rents but sought to negotiate reduced fines when taking a new lease or copy.

Some of the farms that came back into hand were amalgamated into larger units before being relet. This practice was most noticeable in mixed farming areas, but by the middle of the eighteenth century it was also discernible in pastoral regions. As a result, farms grew in size, a trend which can be studied by looking at estate records such as rentals, leases and surveys. It also shows up in land tax lists and in local rating assessments (though these sources can only be found in any number from the mid-eighteenth century). This development, although it did not extinguish the class of small farmer (even in mixed farming areas), certainly reduced them in number and in some communities further polarized society. To emphasize this growing divide, select vestries were established in a number of places, in which attendance at meetings, as well as control of affairs, was restricted to the elite.

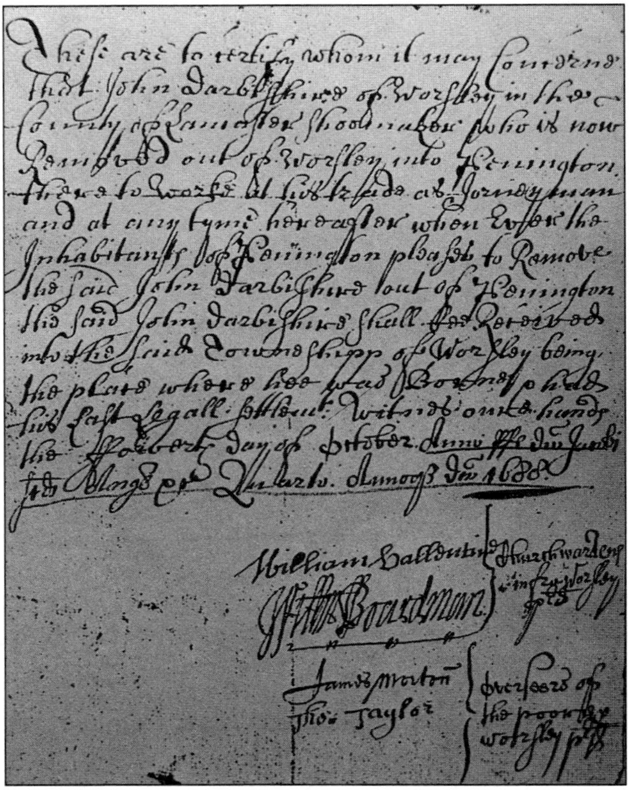
These are to certify whom it may concerne That John Darbishire of Worsley in the County of Lancaster shoomaker who is now Removed out of Worsley into Pennington there to worke at his trade as Journeyman and at any tyme hereafter when ever the Inhabitants of Pennington please to Remove the said John Darbishire out of Pennington the said John Darbishire shall be Received into the said Townshipp of Worsley being the place where hee was borne & had his last legall settlement. Witnes our hands the [illegible] day of October Anno [illegible] Anno Dom 1688

William Baldwin, [illegible] Boardman — Churchwardens in Worsley
James Morton, Tho: Taylor — Overseers of the poore Worsley

9 A removal order from Worsley, Lancashire. Dated 4 October 1688.

In general the real wages of labourers rose in the hundred years from the mid-seventeenth century, and with it their standard of living, though much depended upon local circumstances. Where large-scale enclosure schemes converted open field strips into grazing land, for instance, job opportunities fell and a surplus pool of labour was created. On the other hand, in the vicinity of towns, and in areas where rural industry was developing, incomes were higher. In spite of the more favourable economic climate, the burden of the poor relief grew, a development reflected in the greater sums noted in parish rating lists and in the accounts of the overseers of the poor. As Richard Gough of Myddle wrote, *c.* 1700, 'I have heard my father say that the first yeare that hee was marryed (which was about the yeare 1633) he payd onely four pence to the poor, and now I pay almost twenty shillings per annum.'[34]

Hearth tax returns which include the exempt provide some indication of the scale of the problem of poverty at the beginning of the period. Where sets of rating lists and overseers' accounts exist, especially if they begin as early as the tax years of the 1660s and 1670s, local circumstances can be analysed and changes over time assessed. Costs rose, not necessarily because the incidence of poverty was any greater (though it did grow in many communities), but rather because the poor had become institutionalized. By making a heavier and more regular contribution to poor relief, society hoped to contain the problem and in particular to eliminate the perceived menace of the sturdy vagabond, the fear of whom had so troubled preceding generations. At the same time, the Act of Settlement of 1662 (with its subsequent modifications) further clarified the situation by defining the rules whereby a pauper could claim relief in one parish rather than another.

Many parishes interpreted their obligations narrowly. The distinction between the deserving and the undeserving poor persisted, while numerous disputes between parishes over the settlement of individual paupers highlight their concern to provide for as few people as possible. Details appear among overseers' papers and (because the cases had to be decided by the Justices of the Peace) in the records of the quarter sessions. It was to this period that the concept of 'open' and 'closed' parishes was first attached. Parishes in divided or single ownership were not a new phenomenon but the terms came to represent (at least partially) an attitude towards the treatment of the poor. In closed parishes tight control of the population could be maintained, access to houses, lands and jobs restricted and immigration discouraged. In open parishes, on the other hand, concerted action was far less likely.

Developments since the mid-eighteenth century

From the above, it should be clear that parliamentary enclosure of the late eighteenth and early nineteenth centuries, once popularly assumed to be the cause of the decline of the small farmer, did not precipitate it. Indeed, research based upon enclosure awards and the land tax returns of the period suggest that in parishes inhabited by large numbers of owner-occupiers, enclosure was delayed for some considerable time.[35] The process was a much more drawn-out affair than has hitherto been thought, though the timing and pace varied from community to community.

The land tax returns have been extensively used by historians to examine patterns of landownership and occupancy during the critical years of the late eighteenth and early nineteenth centuries, especially as they were affected by such contemporary issues as the local impact of enclosure and the problems caused by the Napoleonic Wars and their aftermath. Although the returns were first made in 1692, most parish collections only cover those years when they were employed to determine a person's right to the parliamentary franchise (1780–1832). In any case, only the post-1772 returns can be

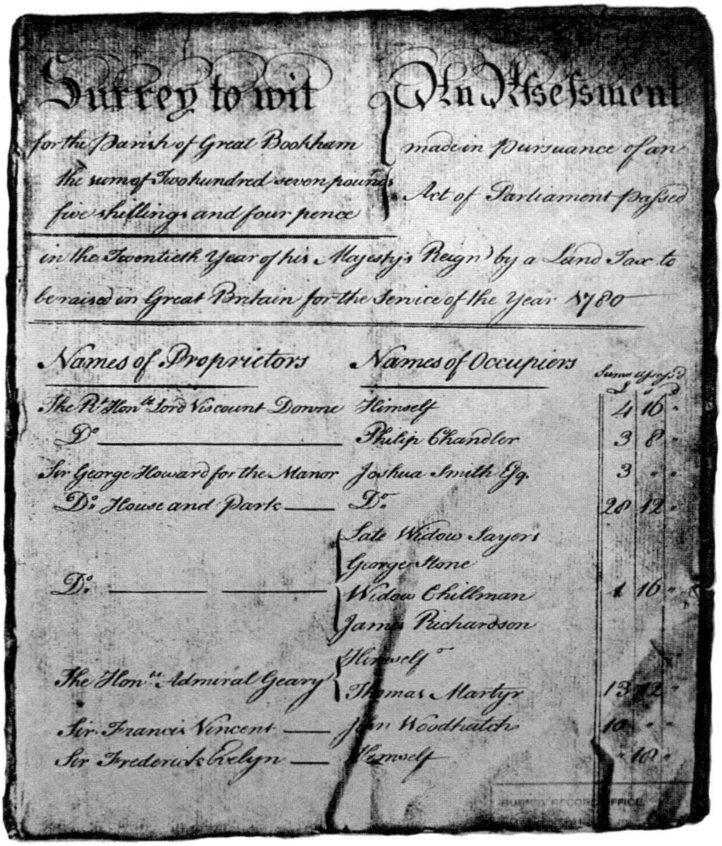

Surrey to wit } An Assessment made in Pursuance of an Act of Parliament passed
for the Parish of Great Bookham
the sum of Two hundred seven pounds
five shillings and four pence
in the Twentieth Year of his Majesty's Reign by a Land Tax to
be raised in Great Britain for the Service of the Year 1780

Names of Proprietors	Names of Occupiers	Sums assessed		
The Rt Honble Lord Viscount Downe	Himself	4	16	-
Do	Philip Chandler	3	8	-
Sir George Howard for the Manor	Joshua Smith Esq	3	-	-
Do House and Park	Do	20	12	-
Do	Late Widow Sayers George Stone Widow Chillman James Richardson	1	16	-
The Honble Admiral Geary	Himself Thomas Martyr	13	12	-
Sir Francis Vincent	John Woodhatch	10	-	-
Sir Frederick Evelyn	Himself	-	10	-

10 Land Tax assessment for Great Bookham (Surrey), 1780.

analysed as before that date no distinction was made between proprietors and occupants.[36] Some researchers have calculated acreage equivalents from the assessments, arguing that they were directly related to the amount of land held. This seems a logical assumption to make but, while it is correct in general terms, it is not necessarily accurate for individual parishes. If the returns are compared with the acreages given in the relevant tithe award, for instance, the degree of correlation varies from place to place. Research done on west Norfolk shows that there, at least, the closest fit occurred in parishes where the land was equally divided among a number of owners. In villages with few landowners the opposite was true.[37]

When analysing the returns the reader should be aware that the term 'proprietor' can be a little imprecise, for it encompasses many copy- and leaseholders. Similarly the status of the occupier, whether a main tenant or a subtenant, is not always clear.[38] From 1798, moreover, owners could redeem their contributions by making a lump sum payment. This did lead to gaps appearing in the record, but fortunately, the column for redeemed payments was often filled in. These are real problems but they are ones which local historians with their knowledge of local people and tenurial practices are well-placed to resolve. In many parishes local rating lists enable us to carry on from where the land tax returns end. Even if one list is missing or incomplete for a particular year, one of the others may survive to cover the gap.

Although there was an undoubted trend towards larger agricultural units during the course of the eighteenth and nineteenth centuries, the speed with which the small farmer disappeared from the scene can be overestimated. Owner-occupiers still formed a significant proportion of the farming population in mixed farming counties like Buckinghamshire and Leicestershire in the mid-nineteenth century.[39] For an appraisal of the local situation the tithe award should be examined. From the information given, maps and tables on the distribution of ownership and occupancy can be made. When occupancy units are reconstructed on to a map the results are often interesting. In open field communities tenants may have been renting adjoining strips from a number of owners. Differences between parishes can be mapped too. This can be done by dividing the number of owners or occupiers in a parish into its total acreage and then setting out the results on a map, linking up places of equal distribution.

In 1873 a nation-wide survey of landownership was undertaken. The Return of Owners of Land, the so-called New Domesday Survey, was compiled by Parliament to disprove the allegation that landed property was concentrated in very few hands.[40] Instead, it merely confirmed it. While it showed that over one million people in the British Isles owned some land (often only a minute amount), four-fifths of it was held by fewer than 7000 persons. The material, filed with the other parliamentary papers in the House of Lords Record Office[41] but also available in print, is arranged on a county basis and so local historians should easily find the people and places which interest them. For the large landowners, the ones with property in more than one county, they should consult a work like J. Bateman's *The Great Landowners of Great Britain and Ireland* (1883 edn.).

A more detailed account of landownership (and occupancy) can be obtained from the records produced in connection with Lloyd George's reform of the land tax in 1910. Taken together, the various documents (valuation and field books, forms 37-land and the specially marked up large-scale Ordnance Survey maps) give details of the owners and occupiers of each hereditament and the extent of their properties. The measure owed much of its inspiration to a reaction against the sort of society portrayed in documents like the New Domesday Book but it was also undertaken at a time when the landed classes were under some strain. The last quarter of the nineteenth century had been a period of distress in the countryside and many landowners had to reduce rents again and take land back in hand. Consequently, more and more large landowners, as well as small owner-occupiers, had to put land on the market. This trend continued in the years 1910–14 as prices picked up, and peaked in the welter of sales that characterized the period immediately following the end of the First World War.[42] Incidentally, the crisis which saw the collapse of the old order in the countryside enabled the small owner-occupier to make a come-back. While some had to sell, many others joined their ranks. In the main, these newcomers were tenants who bought the farms they were occupying and this development appreciably widened the landowning class.

To chart the progress of the recession in a community, estate records – accounts, rentals, leases, surveys and estate correspondence – continue to provide the best source of information but this means that once more some local historians are better served than others. Parish rating lists are one source which can be used for all sorts of communities and should be examined for evidence of changes in the distribution of land. From 1851 the national censuses often indicate the acreage cultivated by the various farmers in the parish. Newspapers become a more valuable source too. In addition, a considerable number of conveyances survive for this period. Such documents can be found in estate collections but many others, including transactions involving small freeholds, turn up among auctioneers' and solicitors' papers. Local historians should also look at sales catalogues which give details of all types of property.

At the base of society the problem of the poor continued to be a matter of concern, especially at critical times such as during the French Wars and the late nineteenth-century depression. In the first half of the period many parishes had witnessed a growth both in the number of people in need of casual relief and in those who were permanently impoverished. This trend is reflected in the pattern of rising costs in the second half of the eighteenth century which emerges from a study of most overseers' accounts. Expenditure peaked during the war years as rising prices took their toll. The experience prompted the authorities to review the provision of poor relief, many of them believing that existing measures had exacerbated the problem. As a result, outdoor relief was abolished in 1834. All paupers henceforward were to be forced to go to the workhouse, the focal point of the newly created poor law unions, which in the countryside normally served a handful of parishes. The change was not as clear cut as this account suggests for in places workhouses had already been established, while conversely many paupers continued to live outside them. The gathering together of many of the poor under one roof, however, does better enable local historians to deal with them as a group, to estimate their number and to make an appraisal on the sort of people at greatest risk.

The reform of the poor law in 1834 was based upon the report of a Royal Commission, which even if it seemed to highlight those issues which supported its authors' points of view, contains much of interest. In it are included detailed reports of the situation in many parishes and it therefore can be examined with profit by local historians in various parts of the country.[43] During the course of the nineteenth and early twentieth centuries other official investigations were carried out and these too can be found among the printed parliamentary papers. As a source, they are obviously something of a lucky dip. Not all of them have a national coverage and those that do, may not include information on a specific parish. Nonetheless, they can still be used in a general way to build up a picture of what conditions were like at the time.

Summary

Although fluctuations in the farming economy had an impact upon all sections of rural society, some people were affected more thoroughly than others. There were regional differences too. Local historians, therefore, should not only look at the general state of agriculture in their communities but also assess the extent to which events impinged upon the fortunes of specific classes. In particular, they should look at the profitability of farming for each group at certain periods and see how it affected their standards of living. They should also examine the data for variations in the size of these groups over time, as they often reflect changes in economic conditions. In general, circumstances favoured the larger farmers and this helped to promote the trend towards bigger farming units. There was little uniformity in the timing and pace of this development, however, and considerable numbers of small farmers continued to exist into modern times. This was especially the case in pastoral areas where small family farms remained much more viable than they did in mixed farming districts. Moreover, in times of population pressure the number of smallholdings increased as new land was brought into cultivation or farms were divided up. The process of consolidation also had an effect; in many places it was the class of middling farmers who suffered, leaving a society that was polarized between the two extremes. Such issues can be examined by looking at a range of documentation, much of it seeming to offer straightforward answers to a number of questions. Sources which provide acreages of individual farms suggest an easy way of assessing changes in the composition of local society over time. They can be used in this way but because of hidden variables, notably the lack of information on subtenancies, great care must be taken when analysing them.

CHAPTER THREE

Population trends

When examining social and economic life in the countryside, considerable attention has to be paid to demographic trends. Very few aspects of agriculture were unaffected by fluctuations in the size of the population and even if it were not the sole determinant of change, it was a major one. A rise in numbers, for instance, had an adverse effect on the mass of people, putting pressure on land and jobs, and causing great hardship. If demand continued to outstrip supply, the outcome was a subsistence crisis. After such a catastrophe, conditions improved. Land became plentiful and labour in short supply. In time, the population reached a critical point once more, though this might be on a different time-scale and at a higher level than before because of the farming improvements made and the various preventive measures taken.

According to Thomas Malthus, the eighteenth-century political economist, this pattern was inevitable; population growth always ended in disaster because resources could not increase at the same rate. Certainly there have been several cycles throughout history, reflecting the ebb and flow of the population even if they varied in their intensity and in their effect upon society. Bouts of expansion in Roman times and in the centuries after the Norman Conquest seem to have been checked by a subsistence crisis and on both occasions population fell sharply. However, there was little adverse reaction to the rise of the sixteenth and seventeenth centuries (except on the periphery of the country and in the Celtic regions) and none at all to the rise associated with the Industrial Revolution two centuries later.[1]

The Middle Ages

Population counts

Although the population of England was rising before the Norman Conquest, the information contained in the Domesday Book provides a good starting point for a study of local trends. Between 1086 and the early fourteenth century the population grew dramatically – even spectacularly in some places.

There then followed a period of stagnation before numbers plummeted during the well-known attack of the Black Death in 1348–9, when up to one-half of the people in the country died.[2] Recovery was slow and hampered by recurring bouts of epidemic disease but by the end of the Middle Ages the upward movement seems to have begun again.

Many have seen these events as a Malthusian reaction to over-population, with a particularly severe attack of plague delivering the *coup de grâce* to an impoverished population already weakened by under-nourishment. However, by the 1330s and 1340s there were signs that conditions were improving, even if there was still considerable poverty. More land was available, wage rates had gone up and the price of grain was falling. To a certain extent this can be attributed to the disasters of 1315–22, a time of severe harvest failures and livestock epidemics, which put a brake on population growth. Here was a real subsistence crisis and with so many people living so close to the margin, it is not surprising to note that the run of bad harvests caused many deaths.[3]

The Domesday Book provides us with our first general source of information on the population of individual communities since it lists groups of people (and a few individuals) manor by manor. Most of those included were tenants or freeholders, normally heads of households, and as such represent only a small proportion of the local population. The first task, therefore, is to use a multiplier to convert the one into the other: figures of between 4.5 and 5.0 are the ones now commonly employed. Individuals who were not married – priests, servants and slaves – must be added to the total with an allowance made for subtenants, landless labourers and others not recorded in the survey. As their number is not known with certainty, and the proportion varied between manors, many readers will think it sufficient merely to obtain a rough estimate of the population by processing the figures given. In this way, some rank order of manors can be drawn up.

When related to acreage, some places emerge as more populous than others. The reason for this is one of the questions local historians should seek to answer. Determinants include the pattern of landownership, the fertility of the soil and farming practices. Prof. H. C. Darby has plotted out the data in his *Domesday Geography of England* series and from the resultant maps, it is apparent that there was a high degree of correlation between soil fertility and population density.

For comparative material the Hundred Rolls of 1279 should be looked at. Although similar in purpose, only the figures for freeholders and tenants should be used since landless servants (normally resident on the demesne) are not listed. The comparison, nonetheless, emphasizes the point that in the intervening two centuries a dramatic rise in the population had taken place. In fact, numbers had probably risen even higher, for unrecorded groups like subtenants and landless labourers formed a larger proportion of the population in 1279. Cottagers were not always included either. Some of the most dramatic increases occurred in areas that had been under-developed in 1086, in places where reserves of waste land existed which could be brought into cultivation.[4]

Similar information can be obtained from manorial sources such as surveys and rentals. Occasionally, as in the 1299 survey of Cleeve (Worcestershire), subtenants were recorded, though this was uncommon.[5] These documents are the only sources to give lists of inhabitants of a manor (at least the tenants and freeholders) up to and through the demographic crisis of the mid-fourteenth century. They therefore provide additional evidence at a local level of the fluctuations in the size of the medieval population. In particular, they confirm the rise indicated by the Hundred Rolls. Where conditions were favourable, surveys and extents at times reveal phenomenal rates of growth. Some of the most spectacular examples can be found in manors in the Lincolnshire fens: at Pinchbeck between 1086 and 1287 the rise was more than elevenfold, while at Fleet in the years 1086 to 1315 the population increased 61 times.[6]

The effect of the plague of 1348–9 can be seen in the records of many communities. On the Bishop of Worcester's estate a survey taken in 1349, following the death of the bishop, indicates a reduction of 42 per cent in the number of tenants from 1299, most of the decline occurring in the plague years.[7] On estates where later surveys can be used it may be possible to assess the speed with which local deficiencies were made up, bearing in mind the fact that outbreaks of plague and other diseases continued to attack the population. The figures only refer to landholders; the fate of the poorer people, unrecorded in the documents, is likely to have been worse. For the impact of plague on clergymen, who may be used as surrogates for the population at large, bishops' registers should be examined. In them are recorded the names of those presented to a benefice and from the numbers involved and the places concerned, some indication of the extent of the disaster can be gained. Similarly, presentments in manor court rolls of tenants (and perhaps freeholders) who had died since the last meeting can be used to calculate death rates among these classes.

Tax lists provide names of taxpayers (who can be counted) and cover more places than do manorial surveys. Unfortunately, there are fewer numbers recorded; apart from the exempt, there were those who managed by one means or another to avoid paying their dues. At Evington (Leicestershire) an extent of 1308 notes 65 landholders, whereas the 1327 lay subsidy only lists 15 people (excluding the lord of the manor).[8] No doubt there is a correlation between the number of taxpayers and the total population but as the relationship is an unknown and fluctuating one, the figures can only give a rough estimate of the comparative size of individual communities.

The poll tax returns of 1377 offer a better base from which to work out population figures, as only those who regularly begged for a living were exempted. The main problem with the data is to estimate the proportion of people under 14 years old, the age at which one had to pay (this was increased to the age of 16 in 1379 and 1381): assessments of the number vary from one-third to one-half of the population.[9] Some allowance should be made for under-recording too, though evasion was more of a problem in 1379 and 1381. Apart from defaulters, some returns, like the one for Kibworth Harcourt (Leicestershire), only record women if they were wives or heads of households.[10] Nonetheless, the poll tax is a valuable source of information; not only does it enable demographers to obtain a reasonably clear picture of population levels but it also allows them to view it a generation or so after the Black Death of 1348–9.

Recovery cannot always be assumed; there may have been too few people to fill all the vacant holdings and some of the survivors succumbed to disease in the intervening period. Many villages, recorded in previous tax lists, were totally depopulated and do not appear in the poll tax returns (though this is not a completely infallible guide – communities missing from one tax list do occasionally appear in subsequent ones). Often their demise was foreshadowed in the earlier records, where they appear as places with low assessments and few taxpayers. For them, the plague of 1348–9 was merely the last straw. With population severely reduced and many settlements abandoned, much land went out of cultivation, especially poor quality ground put under the plough at the height of the population boom.

In spite of the impact it made, this bout of disease was not the sole cause of desertion. A large number of lost villages survived the crisis, as can be proved by references to them in later tax returns and in estate and manorial records. Undoubtedly some were weakened by the events, and in the poll tax returns of 1377 villages later to be deserted were typically smaller than the average.

Migration

To find tenants for their vacant holdings in the aftermath of a mortality crisis, landowners had to draw upon surviving members of the community and to attract others from outside. From the peasants' point of view conditions in the late Middle Ages were far more favourable to them than they had been at the beginning of the fourteenth century. Lords tried hard to maintain their hold over them in order to keep both a work-force and a tenantry on their land but they were not always successful. The records show that peasants moved between manors with considerable ease, looking for better opportunities elsewhere – to take up a holding upon more beneficial terms or to settle in a place where less irksome restrictions were imposed upon them. This could lead to the shrinkage or even desertion of individual villages.

In fact, the peasantry had never been totally immobile. In manor court rolls *merchet* fines, payments made to the lord for his consent to a bondwoman's marriage, suggest that many people found their partners from outside.[11] The general trends can also be examined by looking at the entries recording *chevage* payments, an annual due given by peasants for licence to leave the manor and to remain outside it. They reveal that even before the plague of 1348–9 some manors had experienced high rates of emigration. In the last quarter of the thirteenth century, for instance, on average 100 unfree peasants had paid to live out of the manor of Forncett (Norfolk).[12] As destinations are normally included, the distances travelled can be calculated. When they are plotted on a map it can be seen that most emigrants had only moved a few miles, settling in neighbouring villages or a nearby town. Occasionally, instances of longer distance migration appear.

Evidence can also be gained from surnames which refer to a particular place. As surnames only became fixed in the late thirteenth and early fourteenth centuries (and in some areas much later), they indicate the village or town from which many migrants had moved.[13] Local historians, therefore, should examine all contemporary records which contain names of individuals (manor court rolls, surveys, rentals, deeds and tax assessments) and make a note of all the locative names contained in them. At Kibworth Harcourt names in the manor court rolls reveal that some immigrants were coming into the village to counter-balance those who had moved away. Like the emigrants making *chevage* payments, most had not travelled far.[14]

Surnames, once fixed, provide evidence of turnover rates in a village. This could be considerable. If names in a set of court rolls are compared with those in another set 50 or 100 years later, the contrast is often a dramatic one. At Kempsey (Worcestershire) of the 103 names appearing in documents from 1432–41, only 25 turn up in similar sets of court rolls between 1499–1507. Inevitably there will be some omissions but in a good run the few who did escape detection should not seriously distort the findings.

The early modern period

By the opening of the sixteenth century the population of the country was probably rising again. The movement was sluggish and slow, however, and so hindered by setbacks that expansion had probably not progressed very far. By the mid-sixteenth century growth is more clearly discernible, as is the more rapid expansion of the following hundred years. The subsequent period, covered by the Civil War and the Commonwealth, marked a turning point: not only did the pace slow down, it also went into reverse. The late seventeenth century was a time of stagnation. By 1700 the population was on the increase once more, though it had scarcely passed the mid-seventeenth-century peak in the 1720s when a severe outbreak of disease at the end of the decade caused a marked reduction. Thereafter, growth was resumed with renewed vigour.

There were local and regional variations to this overall pattern. Growth in the late sixteenth and early seventeenth centuries, for instance, was not uniform. The expansion was particularly noticeable in towns, in industrial and open villages, and in places where reserves of waste land remained to be exploited. The availability of jobs and land not only encouraged modes of conduct amongst the native population which stimulated growth – practices such as early marriage and partible inheritance – but also attracted migrants from outside. Because the latter often comprised young adults, they further swelled the numbers by enhancing the fertility rate.

National records

Population trends in the early modern period are much easier to discern than those in the Middle Ages because the documentation is better. In particular, there are more nation-wide sources which, spaced at intervals during the course of the sixteenth and seventeenth centuries, act as benchmarks and help to highlight many of the changes that occurred both nationally and locally. They often deal with a wider section of the population too, and thus provide the basis for a more comprehensive account than is possible for previous centuries.

As before, the records only offer indirect evidence of population levels and adjustments still have to be made to convert the figures into totals. Similarly, different multipliers have to be employed for the various classes of material. When comparing data from different sources it is obviously preferable to use documents which have the same base. Unhappily, this is not always possible, especially if one wants to cover a gap in the record or to obtain a complete set of statistics in order to pin-point certain developments. Some documents, moreover, are more accurate than others and it is therefore useful to have additional sources to confirm or disprove a trend.

The most reliable records are the ones which list heads of households. They comprise the revised assessments for the lay subsidy in the 1520s, the diocesan visitation of 1563 and the hearth tax returns of 1662–89. Strictly speaking, the first source, the lay subsidies, should not be included in this group for there were households with more than one taxpayer. The entries, therefore, cannot be exactly equated with the number of taxable households, though this assumption has often been made. In practice, as extra names will help to compensate for any evasion, the figure can serve as an approximation of the total number. Because of the timing of these records, demographers are able to assess the relative importance of the two intervening periods as times of population growth. Research on parish registers has shown that the average family size fluctuated during the course of the early modern period, though if a multiplier of 5.0 is used, this will give a reasonable estimate of total population

The lay subsidies of the 1520s give us our first view of the population of early modern England. Although it was based on a new survey and therefore quite comprehensive, an estimate still has to be given for those omitted, especially the exempt.[16] In general, the rural poor constituted one-third of the village population (though there were considerable variations between communities) and an allowance of this order should suffice if a better figure cannot be worked out. Later assessments cannot be used with the same degree of confidence as fewer and fewer people were caught in the tax net.[17]

If the figures of 1524–5 are compared with the admittedly disparate material derived from the poll tax returns of 1377, an indication of the extent to which population levels had recovered from the fourteenth century crisis can be gained. More straightforward is the comparison with the diocesan returns of 1563. The material, which does not cover all sees, is to be found in the manuscripts room of the British Museum.[18] In those dioceses with surviving returns, figures for the number of households in each parish – and dependent chapelries – can be obtained. Because all households are included, these figures are reasonably accurate.

By the time that the hearth tax was introduced in Charles II's reign the population nationally had just started to decline. The returns are generally reputed to be reliable (though doubts have recently been expressed), especially if they include the exempt. Unfortunately, these people are not always noted. For Shropshire three lists exist but only one of them records the exempt and then only at the end of each hundred. Some of their names will be familiar to local historians but because branches of families tended to be found in a number of adjoining parishes, it could be misleading if they were assigned to a particular place. There may be other deficiencies in the returns. When looking at some sets of assessments many of the names which appear are different, even though the lists were drawn up in a relatively short space of time.

A second group of records consists of lists of communicants, i.e. all those people in the parish aged 14 or over. An estimate of the total population can be made by increasing the number by 30 per cent – the proportion now reckoned to represent the size of the under-14-years-old group.[19] To convert the figures into households, so that a direct comparison can be made with the first category of documents, evidence from Leicestershire suggests that a divisor of 2.8 be used.[20] The first source to provide this information is the set of chantry certificates of 1547, now deposited in the PRO, Chancery Lane. The figures can then be directly related to the *Liber Cleri* returns of 1603, which list the number of communicants, recusants and nonconformists in each parish. Most of the surviving records can be found in the same manuscript volumes as the diocesan returns of 1563, though Lincoln's (and perhaps others too) are still in the diocese.[21] The Compton Census of 1676 provides similar information to that of 1603 but only for the archbishopric of Canterbury. The original returns can be consulted at the William Salt Library, Stafford.

Less weight can be given to these documents, mainly because of the problem of under-recording. The chantry certificates are particularly suspect. Editors of collections in print disagree on their accuracy and only local historians with detailed knowledge of the places concerned can make an informed judgement.[22] There are also omissions in the first two sources. In many places the number of nonconformists is obviously too low, perhaps because the incumbent did not know the true figure or because he deliberately underestimated them to give an impression of uniformity and order. If the latter, the accuracy of the figures depends on whether he omitted them altogether or added them to the number of communicants.

Even more unreliable are the lists of adult males which were made for various purposes. The muster rolls of the sixteenth century only note able-bodied men and this means that a double set of multipliers has to be used to calculate total population. Their value lies in the fact that as a number of returns for individual counties survive, a direct comparison can be made.[23] An analysis of the Protestation Returns of 1641–2 raises the same problem of accuracy. In 1641 the king asked all males over the age of 18 to swear an oath of allegiance and the parish returns, now in the House of Lords Record Office, include the names of all those who subscribed, as well as those who did not. This makes them more comprehensive in their coverage, but not comparable to the muster rolls. In practice, they have to be used with extreme caution; many lists are missing and those that do survive are often fragmentary or obviously incomplete. In both sets of documents so much doubtful arithmetic has to be employed to convert the figures into total numbers that many local historians will not think it worth the effort.

Local sources

Details for individual communities can be supplied from traditional sources such as manorial and estate records. The lack of information on subtenants in surveys and rentals is still a shortcoming, however. Whenever such people are recorded, as in a 1554 fieldbook of the manor of Cannock (Staffordshire), they appear in some number.[24] In addition, the growing emphasis on the estate rather than the manor had the effect of creating extra gaps in the record. The names of freeholders and their tenants, in particular, are more difficult to find.

Nonetheless, these documents do provide an indication of the developments that were taking place. Where the population expanded as a result of enclosure of the wastes, for instance, surveys and rentals tend to list a greater number of tenants, either holding newly-created farms or, more likely, living in cottage encroachments on the common. There may even be a map to emphasize the point. Cottage development also shows up clearly in manor court rolls because illegal encroachments were presented there. Even if licensed by the lord, entries may still have been made in the rolls as the fines, in effect, constituted a rent rather than a penalty.

For details of the basic issues of life and death, the manor court records can be supplemented and improved upon by material obtained from the parish registers. While they are by no means perfect, a good run of documentation is an extremely valuable source of demographic information.[25] Even short and broken series of registers can help to pin-point events such as an outbreak of disease or a 'baby boom'.

For an investigation of overall population movements in the locality, an aggregative analysis of the registers should be undertaken. In particular, it will help to explain, and often correct, the impression of trends gained from looking at figures derived from national records. One of the first tasks that can be undertaken (after the reliability of the registers has been assessed) is to plot the annual totals of baptisms and burials on to a graph, an exercise which will reveal years of high mortality or increased fertility. Of course, one has to consider the relationship between births and baptisms on the one hand and between deaths and burials on the other. There was a certain amount of under-recording, and the link between births and registered baptisms, in general, was the weaker of the two. When working out annual totals it is useful to base the calculations on the harvest year rather than the chronological year because of the crucial importance of the harvest in early modern society. Having drawn the graph, it might be possible to tell at a glance if the population was expanding or contracting in spite of annual

11 Extract from the parish register of Stoke d'Abernon (Surrey).

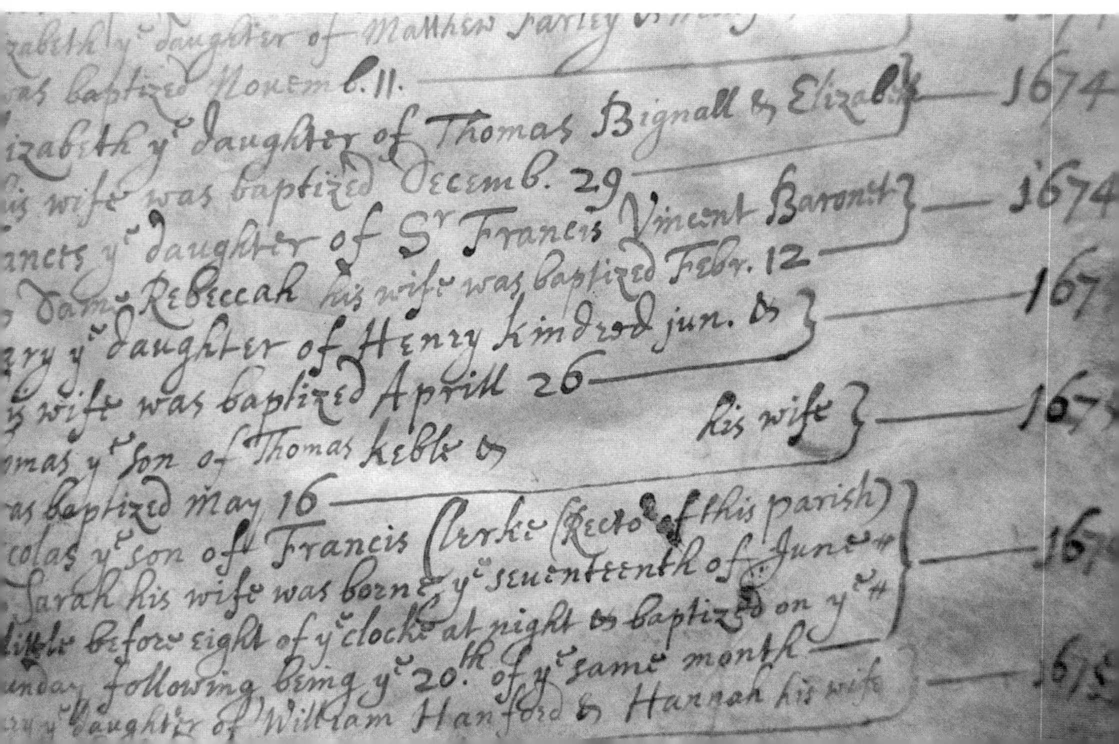

fluctuations in the figures. The underlying trend can be better displayed if a moving average of baptisms and burials is superimposed on the graph.

Greater precision can be given if the totals of baptisms, marriages and burials are recorded on a monthly basis. In this way seasonal, and even shorter term variations, show up. Monthly totals should also be gathered for a number of years as this may reveal a distinction between healthy and unhealthy months. The timing of peaks of mortality often indicates the cause of the trouble, even if the registers do not state it. They often do: at Ellastone (Staffordshire) 14 people were buried in July 1551, equal to the normal yearly total, and the register notes that this was due to 'the greate sweate'.[26] When related to individual harvest years baptism and burial rates can be linked to years of good and bad harvests. From the evidence, demographers have concluded that disease acted as an exogenous force, operating at its own pace, though clearly, people weakened by malnutrition were more likely to have been affected by it.

Migration

Parish registers also provide evidence of turnover rates in villages in much the same way as manor court records did in the Middle Ages. Studies already carried out show that there was still considerable migration in and out of individual communities.[27] Farm servants, the successors of the medieval *famuli*, remained a highly mobile group and their annual movement from farm to farm added greatly to the fluidity of the local population. At Albrighton (Shropshire) in the years 1592–1611, 133 names are recorded in the registers, only one-quarter of which are mentioned a century later (1692–1711). Such a turnover rate is not unusual, even if a few names escape the net, and it is one that can be corroborated from other sources. At Clayworth (Nottinghamshire) two out of every five villagers had moved between 1676 and 1688, the dates of two censuses taken of the inhabitants of the parish.[28]

Within a rural community any study of migration should include an examination of the documentation from neighbouring parishes. A survey of names in registers and other documents will reveal the origin of many of the immigrants into a village and the destination of people moving out of it. Marriage registers illustrate one particular facet of migration. Most people married by banns in the parish church of one or other of the partners, normally in that of the bride. The residence of non-parishioners is often given and if no place is mentioned, it often means that the person was a native. To a certain extent the pattern is complicated by the marriages carried out by licence as the couples had greater freedom in their choice of parish.

Depositions of witnesses heard at the church courts offer a particularly valuable source of information. Those of the province of Canterbury from the late sixteenth century onwards give such biographical details as residence, length of stay and occasionally previous homes, as well as the name, age and occupation of each deponent.[29] Depositions from the province of York are less informative. Like wills (which occasionally include references to the places where the beneficiaries lived), the witnesses tend to be of a reasonable social standing, although in the pre-Civil War records, at least, many poor people appear. Because the work of the courts declined after 1660, fewer cases were heard there. However, in a wide-ranging study of much of southern England and the Midlands, Prof. P. Clark was able to illustrate the continuing prevalence of short distance migration. About one-half of the migrants had travelled no further than ten miles, while only one person in ten had moved over 40 miles.[30]

Estate and farm records contain additional material. For labourers hired as servants in husbandry there may be indentures of agreement which note down places of origin. An indication of previous residence can similarly be found in leases made between landowners and tenants. Incidentally, this information could shed light on the means whereby agricultural improvements were introduced and developed. In north Shropshire in the seventeenth century the evidence suggests that Cheshire farmers were being brought in to help with the development of dairy farming.[31] When holdings were engrossed, it is interesting to see where landowners found the substantial tenants needed to stock and run the large farms.

For paupers, and for some of the respectable poor, the potted autobiographies given in settlement examinations before magistrates should be consulted. Not only do they record the subjects' place of birth but also their subsequent movements around the country. Settlement papers do not exist as such before the Act of 1662 but as earlier officials had to deal with the same problem their records contain much of relevance. Parish apprenticeship papers are another source which can be used since they reveal the destination of young paupers left in the care of the parish. Many of the children were employed in the village; boys were 'apprenticed' to local farmers as farm labourers and girls were sent to the homes of leading parishioners to work as domestic servants. Others did similar jobs outside the parish or were apprenticed to a trade or a craft. Often, but not always, this was done merely to get rid of the youths and to make them someone else's problem.

Genuine apprenticeship indentures deal with other sections of the community. Many of the youths went to a town to learn a trade but some stayed at home or were indentured to a rural master in another village. With the growth of rural industry their numbers increased, though admittedly these workers were less likely to serve an apprenticeship. The decline of guild control also had an effect upon registration.

Freemen's rolls, even more than apprenticeship papers, were an urban feature. Nonetheless, they do show the catchment areas from which urban centres drew in migrants. Even if a freeman (or an apprentice) was said to be a resident of the town in question, his place of origin, if different, can be obtained from the recorded residence of his father. It should be remembered

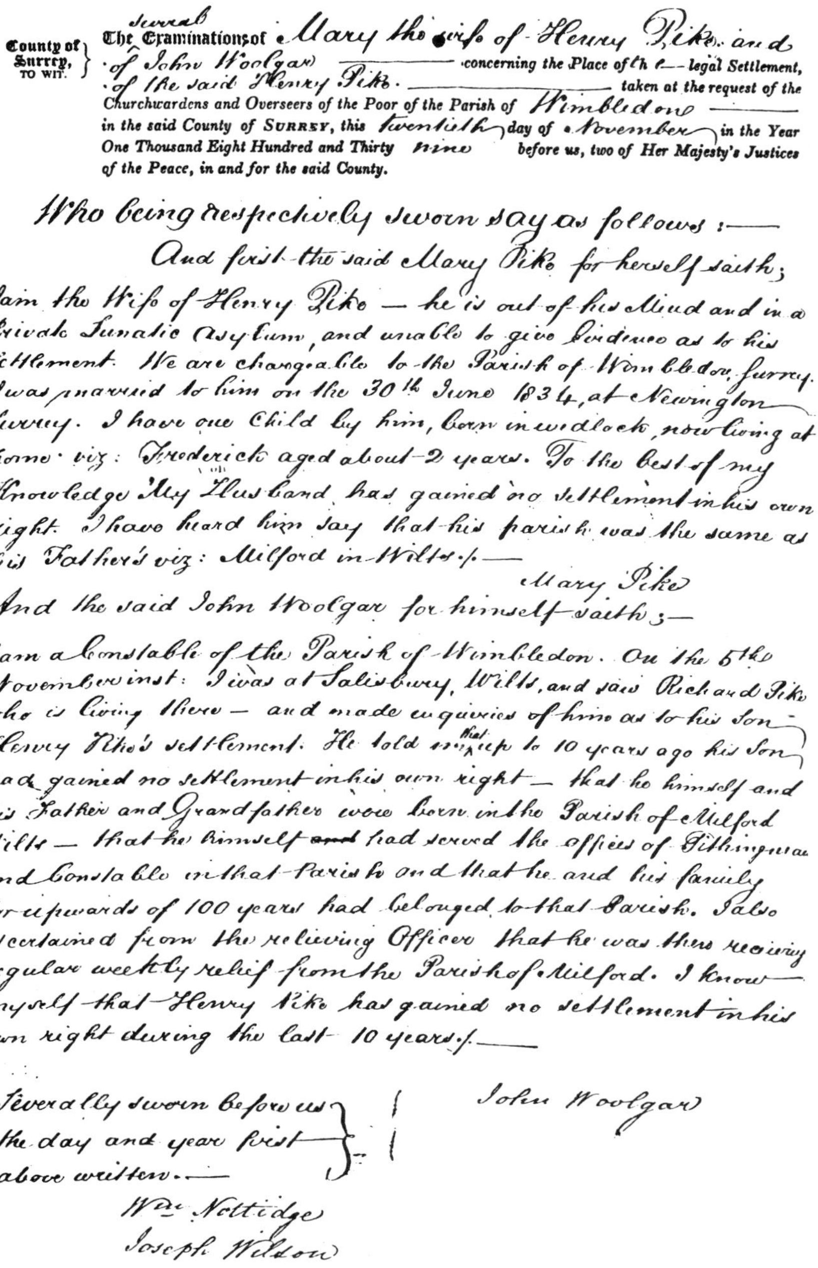

County of Surrey, TO WIT. } The several Examinations of Mary the wife of Henry Pike and of John Woolgar concerning the Place of the legal Settlement, of the said Henry Pike. taken at the request of the Churchwardens and Overseers of the Poor of the Parish of Wimbledon in the said County of SURREY, this twentieth day of November in the Year One Thousand Eight Hundred and Thirty nine before us, two of Her Majesty's Justices of the Peace, in and for the said County.

Who being respectively sworn say as follows:—

And first the said Mary Pike for herself saith;

I am the Wife of Henry Pike — he is out of his Mind and in a Private Lunatic Asylum, and unable to give Evidence as to his settlement. We are chargeable to the Parish of Wimbledon Surrey. I was married to him on the 30th June 1834, at Newington Surrey. I have one Child by him, born in wedlock, now living at home viz: Frederick aged about 2 years. To the best of my Knowledge My Husband has gained no settlement in his own right. I have heard him say that his parish was the same as his Father's viz: Milford in Wilts./—

Mary Pike

And the said John Woolgar for himself saith;—

I am a Constable of the Parish of Wimbledon. On the 5th November inst: I was at Salisbury, Wilts, and saw Richard Pike who is living there — and made enquiries of him as to his Son Henry Pike's settlement. He told me that up to 10 years ago his Son had gained no settlement in his own right — that he himself and his Father and Grandfather were born in the Parish of Milford Wilts — that he himself ~~and~~ had served the offices of Tithingman and Constable in that Parish and that he and his family for upwards of 100 years had belonged to that Parish. I also ascertained from the relieving Officer that he was there receiving regular weekly relief from the Parish of Milford. I know myself that Henry Pike has gained no settlement in his own right during the last 10 years./—

Severally sworn before us the day and year first above written.— }

John Woolgar

Wm Nottidge
Joseph Wilson

12 Surrey JPs examine the wife of a pauper living in Wimbledon, 1839.

when analysing this source that as freemen tended to come from the more prosperous trades and crafts, they do not constitute an accurate cross-section of contemporary society.

Having obtained lists of the migrants, local historians should work out why they had moved. Their decision could have been influenced by local factors such as the availability of jobs or land and the social structure of the community. They should also look at the background of these people. This can be done by collating the names with records which indicate the amount of land held or which note occupations.

The modern period

The beginning of this period coincided with a time of renewed population growth, a rise that was far more dramatic than any previous surge. In the century from 1750 to 1850 the population of England almost tripled and it continued to grow thereafter. Only in the second decade of the twentieth century did the momentum slacken.[32] It did so because, as the traditional checks were overcome, a Malthusian catastrophe was avoided. Much of the rise in the population was caused by urbanization as towns grew with the expansion of industry. Many of these townspeople had come from the countryside, drawn to the towns by the prospects of a better life which they seemed to offer.

Even though there were three-quarters as many more villagers in 1851 than there had been in 1750, there were 5.5 times as many town dwellers. Nationally, the rural population peaked at 8.6 million in 1861; it then declined to 7.2 million in 1901 as families died out or emigrated and were not replaced in sufficient numbers.[33] The agricultural depression of the last quarter of the nineteenth century had an effect too. Many farmers, unable to make a living, gave up and joined the exodus from the countryside.

Even if the population rise from 1750 to 1850 was less steep in the countryside than in the towns, the numbers were not easily absorbed.[34] The period, therefore, was one of hardship for many people, especially small-holders, labourers and cottagers. The situation was particularly severe in the first half of the nineteenth century, a period when the population rose more rapidly than it had done in the preceding 50 years, though the problem was masked during the course of the French wars by the demand for soldiers. The problem was worst in the South and East, in areas where no alternative forms of employment to farm work existed. In the North and West, notably in the vicinity of industrial towns, farmers had to pay more in order to prevent their work-force from leaving, although many of them still did. For the majority of the rural population their lot only eased in the second half of the nineteenth century when numbers declined.

Within this overall framework, the demographic experience of individual

13 An open village: Steeple Aston (Oxfordshire).

14 A closed village: Turville Park (Buckinghamshire).

communities varied greatly. In general a distinction can be made between the population trends in open and closed villages. Differences between rural communities, based on landownership patterns, were already apparent before the middle of the eighteenth century but they became increasingly sharp in the subsequent period. In closed townships control over access to land, accommodation and jobs enabled landowners and farmers to limit immigration, even to the extent of leaving themselves short of labour. A few essential workers, notably those employed to tend the animals and look after the game, were housed in the village but many day labourers, especially harvest workers, had to be hired from nearby open parishes.

Open villages grew more rapidly than the norm. Migrants were still attracted to them, particularly if they were centres of rural industry. Such places continued to flourish in the late eighteenth and nineteenth centuries in spite of the growth of industrial towns, offering a means whereby some of the surplus numbers in the countryside could be absorbed. In communities like these a large proportion of the work-force could be engaged in non-agricultural pursuits. Increasingly divorced from the land, they formed a rural proletariat, almost entirely dependent upon industrial work for their employment, though many of them would have supplemented their income by labouring on the farm at critical times of the year. This trend can be discerned in villages like Wigston Magna (Leicestershire) in the late seventeenth century but it continued to develop over the course of the next 150 years or so.[35]

Sources on population

Because of the lack of any reliable set of national statistics, it is difficult to calculate precisely the population of eighteenth-century England, although the broad trends are certainly known. In Scotland a national census was taken in 1755 and because the evidence suggests that it was an accurate one, it can be used with confidence.[36] In England the only censuses that were made were occasional local listings, much in the tradition of earlier ones.

Most local historians still have to rely upon a disparate set of documents which list individuals. Rentals and surveys provide names of tenants (and perhaps freeholders) but they are subject to the same problems as before. Indeed, with the growing diversification of occupations in the countryside and the expansion of a landless class of labourers, omissions were more numerous. The land tax returns from 1786 also record names of occupiers of land, including cottage holders, and therefore give a general indication of the size of the population. Unfortunately, the widespread use of the formula 'Joe Bloggs and others' to describe the inhabitants of sets of cottages makes it impossible to arrive at an exact total. After 1798 the assessments cannot be used for demographic purposes because all small-scale owners, those whose property was valued below £1.00, no longer had to pay the tax. Luckily, by this time we have the national census figures.

Parish rates provide other lists of occupants and include a wide section of the local community: a church rate of 1769 for Great Bookham states that it had been levied on all occupiers of houses and lands in the parish. This was not true, of course, because the poor were exempt.[37] To estimate the size of this last named group, one should look at the accounts of the overseers of the poor, count up the number of people (by household) in receipt of poor relief and add them to the first total. Having done this, a multiplier has to be used to convert the figure into an overall population.

From the parish registers trends can be discerned and their causes explained. Unfortunately, the growth of Methodism in the late eighteenth century had a far greater impact upon the quality of the registration than the old nonconformist sects had had at an earlier date. Like old dissent, Methodism found its greatest success in places where the Anglican church was weakest – in large parishes with scattered townships, in open and industrial communities and in towns. It failed to gain much of a foothold in closed villages unless the dominant landowner was sympathetic to it.

Migration

Studies concerned with the mobility of the rural population in the first 100 years of this period are also affected by problems of registration. At least Lord Hardwicke's Marriage Act of 1753, by insisting that dissenters should use the parish church, makes it possible to explore the effect of marriage on migration patterns. It is easier to chart too, because the printed forms, authorized by the act, had spaces in which the couple's residences were entered. The new baptismal and burial books, introduced in 1813 as a result of George Rose's act, similarly demanded this information.[38]

Of the other relevant parish records, settlement papers become more important as a source. As the problem of poverty intensified, especially during the French wars and the critical years afterwards, parish officers became more vigilant and more likely to enlist the support of the magistrates to remove illegal immigrants. Apprenticeship lists and freemen's rolls were still kept, but in general they are less comprehensive.

To these traditional sources must be added the national census returns. In 1841 only a general impression of mobility among the rural population can be gained because the enumerators merely had to find out if a person had been born in the county of residence or not. From 1851 onwards the place, as well as the county, was recorded. Inevitably, some people could not remember exactly where they had been born and it was not unusual for the county alone (or even the country) of birth to be given. Errors in transcription occurred too and this makes some places hard to find.

Apart from revealing the distances individuals had travelled from their original home, the censuses also show some of the stops on the way. This can be inferred from the places where a couple's children were born. Of course, the birth of a child in a particular place does not always indicate residency there. William and Eliza Hopkins, both born in Market Lavington (Wiltshire), had clearly moved from there to Great Bookham (Surrey) between the birth of their six-year-old daughter, Louisa, and their three-year-old son, Charles. The birth of their 11-month-old son, Alfred, at Market Lavington suggests a visit back to the old home rather than a permanent move.

Many people still did not move far, though the censuses show some migrants travelling across the country, perhaps in a series of stages. One aspect of long distance migration that increased in the nineteenth century was that of overseas emigration. Many labourers saw it as an opportunity to make a better life for themselves, while the authorities welcomed it as a means of getting rid of surplus population. Some emigrants had their fares paid for them out of public or charitable funds and thus evidence might appear in the records of the administering bodies, notably in the minutes of the Poor Law Guardians.[39] It also can be found in the growing volume of personal papers, as more people kept diaries or wrote to one another. On 17 April 1827 John Howells, an Albrighton farmer, noted in his diary that his son, Peter, had set out for America. Eleven days later he recorded his departure from Liverpool and on 21 June the receipt of his first letter from him.[40]

Summary

In the study of local demography the national censuses of the nineteenth century mark a watershed in our knowledge of the subject. Before then the sources do not permit us to make an accurate assessment of the size of the population either in the locality or at a national level. The local listings that were made are few and far between. Most local historians, therefore, are forced to use parallel documents, records which contain names or numbers of people, from which some idea of the total population can be formed. To do so, assumptions have to be made (like the average size of the household or the proportion of the population under a certain age) and dubious arithmetic tentatively employed.

Many local historians may feel that the problems outweigh the possible benefits and that the results gained, which might be wildly inaccurate, are not worth the trouble of collecting them. This would be a mistake. Many of the developments that have occurred only become intelligible when put into a demographic context. At the very least, the sources allow us to discern the broad outlines of what was going on and to relate the experience of our own community to that of others elsewhere. Moreover, through a combination of local and national records many of the factors which impinged on the size of the population can be looked at and their relative importance in shaping the history of individual communities assessed.

CHAPTER FOUR

Earning a living

Until well into the present century most people living in the countryside derived some economic benefit from agriculture. Freeholders obtained an income from those who farmed their land, even if they did not exploit it directly themselves. However, many did: apart from small owner-occupiers, large landowners kept a portion of their property in hand, though the amount fluctuated according to interest or economic circumstance. The upper classes often appointed a bailiff to supervise the operation but farmers normally worked the land themselves, using members of the family and outside labour to help them. They therefore gave employment to tens of thousands of people in the countryside, a number of whom had specific skills and occupations.

A large number of trades- and craftsmen also relied upon agriculture for their livelihood. Many jobs, like those undertaken by blacksmiths, wheelwrights and millers, were directly related to farming or the processing of agricultural products. Other groups – textile- and leather-workers, for instance – were often organized on an industrial rather than on an agricultural basis. Yet more people provided goods and services to the rural community.

The jobs that villagers did were not mutually exclusive and there was considerable overlap. Small farmers, unable to support their families on the proceeds of their holdings, hired themselves out as agricultural labourers for part of the year. Conversely, many labourers had perhaps an acre of land or at least rights of common, thereby giving them the means to keep an animal or two. Numerous craftsmen had smallholdings, normally of a pastoral nature. Involvement in a dual economy was commonplace, with participants dividing their time between agriculture and some craft or industrial employment. In many instances it is difficult to discern the more important element of the two.

The realization that work patterns in the countryside were far more complex than had hitherto been assumed, has been a major advance in the study of rural life. Local historians should be aware of this diversity so that they can more readily identify the varied activities practised by members of their communities in the past. This exercise should go beyond the mere listing of occupations and ought to include an investigation into the ways in which the strands of economic life were organized and integrated with one another. In particular, they should examine the documentation for answers to questions on the nature and size of the local work-force.

On a practical note, readers ought to read this chapter in conjunction with comments made elsewhere in this book and in its companion volume, *Farming: Sources for Local Historians*, to gain a proper appreciation of the issues involved and the sources which can be used.[1] The chapter on social structure, for instance, provides details of the various constituent groups which made up the farming community, while in the book on farming, the chapters on farming practices, tenure and the work-force give additional information. Emphasis here is therefore placed on those aspects of the topic which have not already been fully discussed, with special attention being given to the range of jobs to be found in the countryside and their relative importance to the rural work-force.

The Middle Ages

The surveys and extents which, together with entries in the manor court rolls, give us the names of peasant farmers and the amount of land they held directly of the lord, indicate the groups of people who drew an income from agriculture. As such, they should provide us with evidence of the varying fortunes of the peasantry, revealing those members who could provide comfortably for themselves and their families from their holdings, those who could just about make ends meet and those who needed supplementary sources of income to eke out an existence. Although on average ten acres of land seem to have been required for subsistence, the amount varied according to local circumstances.

Because of the looseness of areal measurements like virgates and yardlands, as well as the largely hidden but extensive practice of subletting, the size of each group cannot be determined with any certainty. One can state with confidence, however, that as pressure on land grew in the twelfth and thirteenth centuries, the number of smallholdings increased and with it the proportion of the population who had to find secondary employment. After the mid-fourteenth-century crisis conditions improved: with land more readily available, families were able to gain access to it or to expand their holdings.

Many peasant farmers employed outside labour and stray references to them appear in surveys and manor court rolls. Because they have not left any accounts, we have to turn to the records of demesne farming for the bulk of our information on the agricultural work-force. A certain proportion of the work was performed by tenants, who held their land partly in return for labour services. Also employed were the *famuli*, full-time workers often resident on the demesne, and casual labourers, hired by the day for specific tasks or as additional hands at critical times of the year.

Although the amount of work done by each group varied from place to place and fluctuated over time, the long-term trend was towards the greater use of paid labour. As the population rose in the twelfth and thirteenth centuries, competition for jobs reduced the comparative cost of hiring workers, and meant they worked better too. Thus, in many extents the tenants' obligations are listed and valued, with each service or task priced for commutation purposes. Details of changes, as well as information on the tasks carried out by the various groups of workers, can be found in the manorial accounts. The charge section contains references to payments made by tenants for commuted services, while the discharge includes entries recording the wages of the hired work-force. The *famuli* were normally paid partly in cash and partly in kind. Casual workers were invariably paid in cash.

Among the *famuli*, who were normally appointed for the year, were the skilled workers, men who acted as shepherds, ploughmen, carters and the like. Apart from casual work, day labourers tended to be given routine jobs like weeding, winnowing and threshing. Whenever they replaced tenant labour, they generally took over the weekly works first of all. Lords were less willing to commute the seasonal boon-works because at peak times of the year they needed as many hands as they could get and had to pay higher rates to them.

From the accounts we also learn of the crafts- and tradesmen who provided essential services for the agricultural community. At Petworth (Sussex) in the year 1347–8 smiths, glaziers, masons, carpenters, plumbers and thatchers all carried out jobs on the demesne. Like the labourers, craftsmen were paid by the piece or day. From the latter, wage rates can be worked out and if possible, variations between different crafts discerned.[2]

Before they became fixed in the late thirteenth or early fourteenth century surname evidence can be used to pin-point those individuals who were doing particular jobs. An examination of records which list names (surveys, extents, rentals, manor court rolls and tax returns) reveals many examples of people with agricultural or craft specializations. Among the occupations suggested by the names listed in a survey of the manor of Ardleigh (Hertfordshire) in 1222 are those of shepherd, carter, smith, carpenter, cooper, plumber, weaver, presbyter and merchant.[3]

Women and children also appear in the record. In the peasant economy the family, normally comprising parents and their children, operated as a team. Everyone worked as soon as they could and continued for as long as they were able. Boys did odd jobs such as running errands, scaring crows or picking stones. Later they might tend the animals or help to bring in the harvest – more adult work but not at the full rate of pay. At Petworth in 1347–8 two lads who spent four days digging earth and fetching water, received 6d apiece, 2d less than labourers would have been paid.[4] Girls are not so frequently mentioned in the accounts; they were associated with their mothers at home, though in adolescence (like their mothers) they were involved in field work, especially at critical times of the year. This gender division was established at an early age, as children of one sex became more closely linked with one parent rather than the other. The evidence heard at coroners' inquests, for instance, indicates considerable discrepancy between boys' and girls' accidents and the places where they occurred.[5]

By the time they had reached adolescence, children had acquired a number of skills and were ready to join the work-force. Even if some of them continued to live at home, it was common practice for teenagers to move out and board with their employer. Most boys went to farms as *famuli*.[6] Others were apprenticed to a master craftsman. Girls entered domestic service or, if working on a farm, were involved in brewing, milking and making dairy produce.

Women played a crucial role in the peasant family economy. Apart from having charge of the household, they performed other tasks that complemented the work of their husbands. Wives were most closely engaged in activities in and around the home. While their husbands worked out in the fields or pastures, they were occupied in the yard, garden or croft. There, they grew vegetables, herbs and fruit and kept pigs and poultry. They also made dairy products, brewed ale and spun wool. At peak times of the year they helped out in the fields, undertaking such tasks as planting, weeding, gleaning or binding.[7]

If necessary, women hired themselves out as labourers. Typically, they carried out the lighter jobs on the farm, such as those listed above. Among the items of expenditure recorded in the manorial account of Petworth for 1347–8 is one for 21d, the wages of various women employed to plant 2 quarters and 3 bushels of beans in the garden.[8] Some accounts indicate that they also did tasks traditionally associated with men, even heavy ones such as ploughing and reaping.[9]

Late fourteenth-century presentments of women workers who infringed the terms of the Statute of Labourers of 1351 confirm this picture. This measure, like the slightly earlier Ordinance of Labourers, was drawn up in an attempt to maintain control over labour in the aftermath of the Black Death and the records provide much material on wages, jobs and migratory work. The information is recorded on assize and other indictment rolls (except for those which were determined at the quarter sessions) and these can be consulted at the Public Record Office, Chancery Lane.[10] The documents show that, apart from mowing, women were fully involved in all kinds of harvest work. (Mowing, though the most highly paid task, was also the most strenuous one.) The evidence also suggests that women were being paid at the same rate as men.

Apart from their involvement in agriculture, the rolls reveal other economic activities in which women were engaged. In particular, they emphasize the importance of the brewing and textile industries as sources of employment.[11] Brewing, spinning and weaving could be carried out at home and offered the flexibility that was especially important to wives. At certain times of the year, however, they had to help their husbands, since that work took precedence over any other job in the household. Whenever extra hands were needed in the field, women had to abandon whatever they were doing and join in.

Ale-making fitted perfectly into the routine of the domestic economy. Most women possessed the necessary skills, while the product could be made by using tools and equipment readily available. Demand was localized and constant so quick profits could be made without too much effort. Production, furthermore, could be tailored to economic circumstances and the time available, and could therefore be raised and lowered at will.[12]

Historians know a good deal about the brewing industry because it was highly regulated. Control was based upon the assize of bread and ale of 1266, which imposed standards of quality and price. In the countryside those found guilty of breaking the assize were presented at the manor court, along with those who sought licence to brew. In effect, virtually all brewers were brought before the court for one reason or another and thus the rolls provide the local historian with an excellent source of information on the trade, its organization and personnel.

Men might also be involved in brewing and textile manufacture, though their activities spanned the whole range of industrial endeavour. Outside agriculture, the production of cloth provided the greatest number of jobs and few regions of the country were without a textile industry of some size. Leather-working was also widespread, as were woodcrafts, though concentrations occurred in woodland districts. These areas tended to attract other industries which, like iron smelting and glass making, required large quantities of timber as fuel. Where local deposits could be exploited easily, mining enterprises were established.

For local evidence of industrial activity a number of sources can be examined. Surnames are instructive, especially if they relate to a number of processes within a single industry. For the late fourteenth century the occupational details recorded in the poll tax returns of 1379 and 1381 should be used. Crafts- and tradesmen, as well as others carrying on some industrial activity, regularly appear in manor court rolls, often for work-related offences. Church court depositions often give the names and residences of the parties involved and of the witnesses. From the evidence presented at coroners' inquests we not only learn about the variety of jobs in medieval England but also gain an insight into occupational practices and organization.

Where plant was used, documentation appears in surveys and extents, in rentals and in admissions entered in manor court rolls. References can be found to wind- and water-mills, fulling mills, charcoal pits, coal and iron mines, stone quarries, forges and furnaces and the like. Manorial accounts give details of particular operations if the enterprises were kept in hand, though if farmed out, only income from rents or royalties will appear. Of particular value are the various administrative records of the royal forests, for they provide material on the industries which had established themselves within their boundaries.

If the availability of raw materials in the forests drew industry to them, so did the type of husbandry being practised there. Pastoral farming was less labour-intensive than mixed farming, giving peasants the time to dovetail their industrial work into their agricultural routine. Mining apart, much could be done in winter and at other slack times of the year. In the Forest of Inglewood (Cumberland) early fourteenth-century accounts show that licences to burn charcoal for part of the year were more common than those for a full year.[13]

Evidence of dual economy can be obtained from surveys and rentals, as well as an impression of the groups of people involved. Peasant charcoal-burners, for instance, often appear as smallholders, engaged in their industrial occupation on a part-time basis. At Rugeley (Staffordshire) a thirteenth-century rental lists two men named Collier, the one holding an acre of land and the other $2\frac{1}{2}$ acres. A third at Longden held a messuage and a curtilage. Men like this worked in the Forest of Dean too, but this was a highly industrialized area, and surveys and accounts suggest that many charcoal-burner smiths employed servants and labourers. Some workers were wage earners and details of their pay may appear in manorial accounts, if the lord had not farmed out the enterprise. Others were independent operators and they appear in the records leasing plant and paying for licences.

Peasant craftsmen seem to have benefited from the combination of occupations. In medieval tax lists they often appear to be reasonably prosperous by peasant standards; they feature regularly in the lists and often are not among the lowest categories. For the late Middle Ages, wills can be used. Apart from the references to plant and equipment, the bequests indicate the wealth of the testator, whether in the form of real estate, moveable goods, money or debts. They also provide evidence of the way in which a trade or a craft was passed on from one generation to the next, showing, for instance, the existence of family dynasties in a particular trade or craft.

The early modern period

In the early modern period agriculture continued to provide the bulk of the income for most of the rural population. As noted in an earlier chapter, many farmers prospered in the years of rising food prices and experienced an improvement in their standard of living. Thereafter (from the mid-seventeenth century), falling demand had an adverse effect, especially on the smaller farmers. A growing number of them were forced to look for additional sources of income, even if they did not lose all contact with the land. For the majority of the population, the hundred years after 1550 had been the critical time with a drop in real income and a worsening in their quality of life.

Economic pressures therefore had the effect of increasing the size of the labouring sector of rural society. Some changes occurred in the nature of the agricultural work-force, though essentially progress was evolutionary, continuing developments that had taken place in the late Middle Ages. On many estates residual labour services survived but in general they were light, if not commuted. In practice, too, tenants often sent a labourer to do the work for them.[14] In consequence, virtually all the extra-familial labour requirements on the farm were met by hiring workers. As in the Middle Ages, they might be full-time employees – the successors of the *famuli* – comprising skilled workers, as well as young men and women in their late teens and early twenties. Apart from these servants in husbandry, there were the day labourers, taken on for the day or task.

Rural crafts and industries provided other job opportunities, often, as before, coupled with work in agriculture. For smallholders and labourers it offered a vital source of extra income, while for larger farmers it was a profitable way for them or members of their household to utilize the slack times of the year. Although a long-established practice, industry's contribution to the well-being of rural society was probably more greatly appreciated during this period. In particular, the authorities saw it as a means of securing additional jobs and alleviating distress. Various schemes were propounded, the value of which lay in the fact that they were labour-intensive and therefore useful as a means of employing the poor. As many of the projects were concerned with the manufacture of goods hitherto made abroad, the country, it was argued, would benefit too.[15]

Rural industries were probably more prominent than they had been in the Middle Ages owing to the industrial developments that were taking place in villages and unincorporated market towns. Entrepreneurs often ignored the traditional urban centres, seeking to free themselves from guild restrictions and take advantage of cheaper labour in the countryside. This did cause some tension but the growth of rural industry was not necessarily inimical to the urban economy. In many ways the two complemented each other. Urban merchants often organized the business and controlled the trade. Many of the rural workers were less skilled than their urban counterparts, so they tended to concentrate on the initial stages of manufacture and the production of cheaper goods. This left the really valuable work, the finishing processes and the manufacture of high quality commodities, to the townspeople.[16]

Apart from the availability of raw materials and the type of farming being practised, the pattern of landownership was also an important factor in the siting of an industry. Thus, in populous open field villages in the east Midlands, in which strong seigneurial control was lacking, a framework knitting industry developed in the seventeenth and eighteenth centuries, even though mixed farming was the dominant form of agriculture.[17] In such communities the origins of a proletarian work-force can sometimes be discerned.

With regard to the documentation, on a general level contemporary topographical accounts often discuss the economic life of an area, noting any particular specializations that occurred. The details can then be filled in by extracting occupational data from other sources. Early parish censuses provide the best source of information. Although few and far between, they can also be used in a general way as examples of the possible pattern in similar communities elsewhere. At Swinderby (Lincolnshire) a listing of 1771 shows a fully functioning agricultural village with farmers, labourers and associated crafts- and tradesmen.[18] There is no sign of any by-employment. This might be expected in a mixed farming parish with a dominant landowner but the general tendency of writers, when noting jobs, merely to record primary occupations, weights the evidence against it. Similarly, they do not tell if the person was unemployed or not.

Occasional references to the status or occupation of an individual appear in parish registers and in many there are periods when a full coverage is given. Much, of course, depends upon the industriousness of the incumbent. All social groups are included, even if some tend to be under-represented. As a result, the picture gained should be a fairly accurate one, especially as the growth of nonconformity was not yet a serious problem to registration.

Estate records, like their medieval counterparts, provide evidence of economic activity. Accounts record the number and type of workers – men, women and children – employed on the demesne. In late seventeenth-century Kent Sir John Knatchbull only used day labour but the skilled men, if not servants in husbandry, were still given almost continuous work. The other labourers were employed on a casual basis, though at critical times of the year the work-force more than doubled.[20] The accounts may also include references to industrial concerns, especially the exploitation of timber and mineral resources. Separate industrial accounts were also drawn up. The Foresters and Charltons, two gentry families from Shropshire with mineral extraction and processing interests, both kept specific accounts for their enterprises. When the names of operatives are compared with rentals, surveys and leases, a considerable overlap, denoting the practice of dual economy, emerges. In particular, many farmers were employed in carrying services, thereby making good use of their horses and carts.[20]

Sets of apprenticeship indentures provide evidence of the range of crafts in a community, as well as any specializations, though they are less numerous and informative than urban examples. Many workers did not serve their time, picking up their skills – often simple and repetitive – as they went along. On the other hand, references to a particular craft, like the metalworking indentures of the Black Country, do reveal the existence of specific rural industries. Pauper indentures may do the same but the 'apprenticeships' were less likely to be genuine ones. Evidence of the work done by paupers also

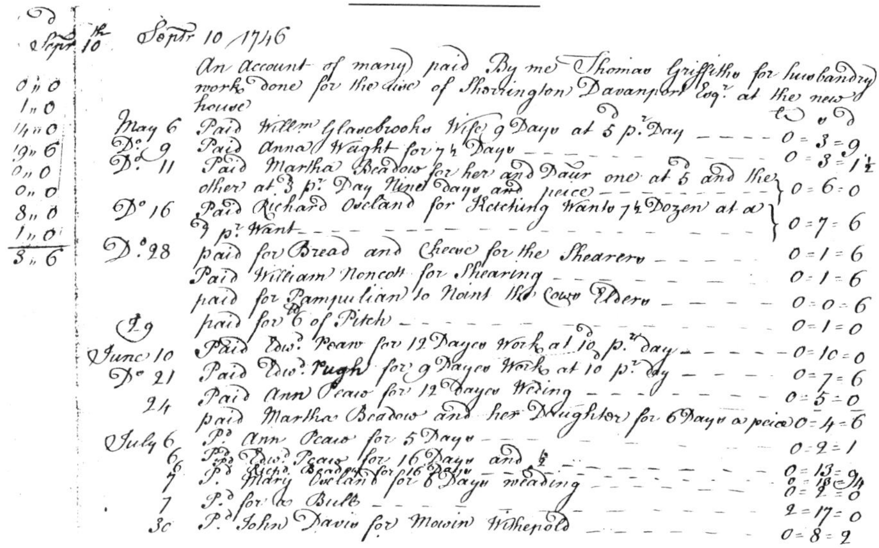

Sepr 10 1746

An Account of money paid By me Thomas Griffiths for husbandry work done for the use of Sherington Davanport Esqr. at the new house

May 6 Paid Willm. Glasbrooks Wife 9 Days at 5 p. Day ---- 0 = 3 = 9
Do. 9 Paid Anna Waight for 7½ Days ---- 0 = 3 = 1½
Do. 11 Paid Martha Beadow for her and Daur one at 5 and the other at 3 p. Day Nine days and peice ---- 0 = 6 = 0
Do 16 Paid Richard Ocland for Ketching Wants 7½ Dozen at a 9 p. Want ---- 0 = 7 = 6
Do. 28 paid for Bread and Cheese for the Shearers ---- 0 = 1 = 6
Paid William Noncott for Shearing ---- 0 = 1 = 6
paid for Pampulian to Noint the Cows Udders ---- 0 = 0 = 6
29 paid for 6 of Pitch ---- 0 = 1 = 0
June 10 Paid Edw. Peare for 12 Days work at 10 p. day ---- 0 = 10 = 0
Do 21 Paid Edw. Pugh for 9 Days Work at 10 p. dy ---- 0 = 7 = 6
24 Paid Ann Peare for 12 Days Weding ---- 0 = 5 = 0
paid Martha Beadow and her Daughter for 6 Days a peice 0 = 4 = 6
July 6 Pd Ann Peare for 5 Days ---- 0 = 2 = 1
6 Pd Edw. Peare for 16 Days and ½ ---- 0 = 13 = 9
6 Pd Richd. Beadow for 16 Days
7 Pd Mary Ocland for 8 Days weading ---- [illegible]
7 Pd for a Bull ---- 2 = 17 = 0
30 Pd John Davis for Mowin Withepold ---- 0 = 8 = 2

15 Payments to labourers for work done on the Davenport estate in Shropshire in 1746.

appears in the account of their lives made in their depositions to the magistrates in settlement cases.

Freemen's rolls, though an urban source, list inhabitants from the countryside who had gained their freedom. When first-generation townsmen became free, moreover, rural crafts may be revealed through the record of their fathers' occupations. Corporation minutes, too, might mention rural craftsmen and traders, most commonly in connection with trading at markets and fairs. If, at the same time, an individual bought or sold a horse, his or her name was entered in the toll book. Surviving books, especially those recording sales at the weekly market, indicate that a wide range of people from the countryside went to town to do business. Included in their number were women, who typically came to market to sell agricultural goods such as dairy produce or poultry, or a variety of handicraft products.[21]

Much information can be obtained from legal and quasi-legal records such as those taken at the manor, church, piepowder and equity courts; at the quarter sessions and assizes; and at coroners' inquests. Not only do they provide a record of the occupations of the people involved, they may also describe industrial organization and work practices. The local regulation of the economy lay largely in the hands of the Justices of the Peace, but cases were also heard at the manor, piepowder and equity courts and at the assizes. Because they often give background details, the depositions made by suspects and witnesses are of particular value.

The depositions tend to provide more accurate information on occupations than do quarter sessions and assize indictments. The latter are somewhat suspect, since it was in the interest of the defendant and the plaintiff to enhance their own social standing, while belittling that of their opponent. In all legal proceedings, the course of justice (and any punishment that ensued) was influenced by the status of the individuals concerned. The depositions also reveal that many people, especially from the lower classes, changed jobs regularly and in a casual fashion. In a quarter sessions case heard in Wiltshire in 1606 a suspected horse thief described himself as a painter, although he had kept a barber-surgeon's shop in the Smithfield Market at London. The man further deposed that he was travelling about looking for work. Such people were in effect vagrants but they are not described as such in the indictments because it was a proscribed occupation.[22]

Probate records are another source from which historians can gain an insight into the local economy. Of course, because they were taken after death, they may not fully represent the scale and scope of a person's activities at the height of his or her career. From the lists of goods it is clear that some people were retired: there are many examples of yeomen with a single cow or one or two sheep and no corn. Yet many people, if they were able, continued in work. Death, in any case, might come suddenly and unexpectedly. It should also be noted that the records deal with a socially selective group; they do include labourers in their number, for instance, but they were not typical members of their class. To obtain as accurate a picture as possible of the range of an individual's interests, both the will and the inventory should be examined. Reseachers can be misled if they merely look at only one or the other.[23]

As in the Middle Ages, wills can be used to see how economic resources were transferred from one generation to the next. In my own studies of Albrighton (Shropshire) and Rushock (Worcestershire), wills, taken in conjunction with parish registers, have helped me to identify family dynasties working at a particular occupation over several generations. By recording details of real estate, wills complement the information on moveable goods found in the inventories. They might also list the debts owing to and by the testator, in which case they might not be noted in so much detail in the inventory, if written down at all. These debts, when given in full, provide much of value, indicating the goods being traded, the people involved and the geographical extent of a person's economic connections.

Both wills and inventories often record a person's status or occupation, though the two are sometimes at variance. If in doubt, the lower rank should be taken, which is normally the one given in the inventory. Appraisers in general had a less inflated opinion of the deceased than the latter, as testator, had had of him- or herself. Sometimes, the disparity was due to a genuine difference in perception: when John Williamson of Edgley (Shropshire) made his will in October 1692 he styled himself a weaver, and indeed the appraisers

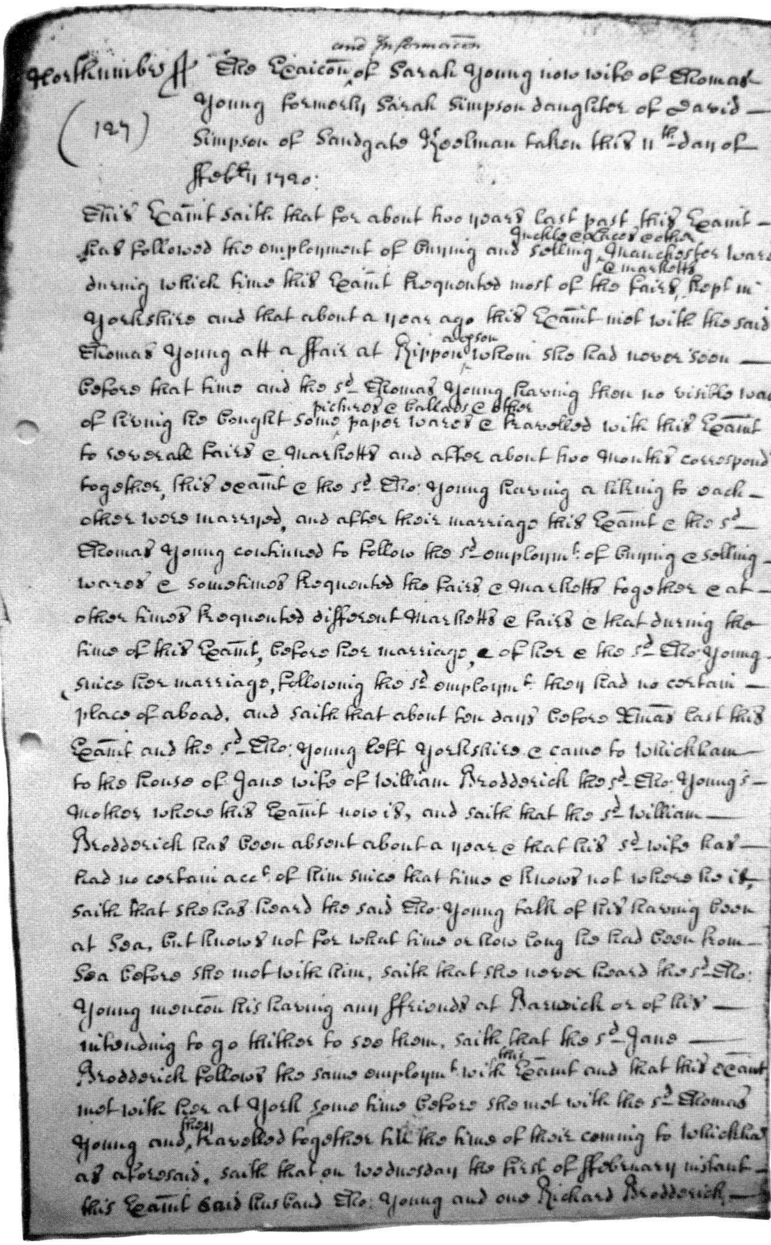

and Information

Northumbr ss The Examination of Sarah Young now wife of Thomas Young formerly Sarah Simpson daughter of David Simpson of Sandgate Keelman taken this 11th day of Febry 1720:

(127)

This Examt saith that for about two years last past this Examt has followed the employment of buying and selling huckle backs etc Manchester wares during which time this Examt frequented most of the fairs & marketts kept in Yorkshire and that about a year ago this Examt met with the said Thomas Young att a Fair at Rippon alias Dobson whom she had never seen before that time and the sd Thomas Young having then no visible way of living he bought some pictures & ballads & other paper wares & travelled with this Examt to severall fairs & marketts and after about two months correspondce together, this Examt & the sd Tho: Young having a liking to each other were marryed, and after their marriage this Examt & the sd Thomas Young continued to follow the sd employmt of buying & selling wares & sometimes frequented the fairs & marketts together & at other times frequented different marketts & fairs & that during the time of this Examt, before her marriage, & of her & the sd Tho: Young since her marriage, following the sd employmt they had no certain place of aboad, and saith that about ten days before Xmas last this Examt and the sd Tho: Young left Yorkshire & came to Whickham to the house of Jane wife of William Broddrick the sd Tho: Young's mother where this Examt now is, and saith that the sd William Broddrick has been absent about a year & that his sd wife has had no certain acct of him since that time & knows not where he is, saith that she has heard the said Tho: Young talk of his having been at Sea, but knows not for what time or how long he had been from Sea before she met with him, saith that she never heard the sd Tho: Young mention his having any ffriends at Barwick or of his intending to go thither to see them, saith that the sd Jane Broddrick follows the same employmt with this Examt and that this Examt met with her at York some time before she met with the sd Thomas Young and they travelled together till the time of their coming to Whickham as aforesaid, saith that on Wednesday the first of February instant this Examt said husband Tho: Young and one Richard Broddrick —

16 Examination of Sarah Young, petty chapman, at the Northumberland Quarter Sessions, 1720.

of his goods found a loom in his house after his death. Nonetheless, they called him a yeoman, taking into consideration his dairy herd of 35 head; his corn, malt, cheese and bacon in store valued at £42; and his growing corn worth £21.[24]

This example illustrates that while cases of dual occupation can be identified from inventories, weighing up the two in terms of the value of appraised stock and equipment is an imperfect device. In October John would have been concentrating on his farm and in any case he may have sold his woven cloth as soon as he had made it. Nonetheless, the agricultural material does provide a good basis upon which to assess the status of those farmers who were engaged in some form of secondary employment. At the same time, it indicates the range and extent of the farming interests of rural crafts- and tradesmen and labourers.

In general, rural craftsmen (with some obvious exceptions) worked from their home. They may have had to share the living space with other members of the family, but it was not uncommon for them to set aside or add a room for work. Metalworkers, for instance, had small forges attached to their houses. The work-place can usually be identified in the inventory from the list of goods, tools and equipment to be found in it. It was often called a 'shop', that is, a workshop not a retail outlet, although goods were sold there. During this period, retail outlets, as we would define them, also became more widespread. To traditional tradesmen such as bakers, butchers and ale and beer sellers, inventory evidence adds grocers, mercers, haberdashers, drapers and the ubiquitous general storekeepers. From the list of goods appraised we can see the type of stock they possessed and the scale of their activities. As much of the business was done on credit, both for purchases and sales, it is important to examine the list of debts included in either the will or the inventory.

Married women did not have a personal estate separate from their husbands so they did not make a will or leave goods to be appraised. We can, however, look at the economic resources of spinsters and widows (especially the latter). With regard to spinsters, much is hidden from us because they generally worked within the household. Sometimes, however, the documents give us an indication of the means whereby they earned their income, referring to an animal or two or a spinning wheel or other pieces of equipment. A major source of income for spinsters seems to have been the lending of money out at interest, generally from a lump sum already bequeathed to them. Widows, on the other hand, often took possession of their husband's enterprise, especially if there were no grown-up son. They were then faced with the problem of coping with the business. The choices open to them were to run it themselves; get a man to do it for them by remarrying or appointing a 'manager'; or lease it out. Depending upon their attitude, as well as upon personal and economic circumstances, individual widows made their own choice.

The modern period

In the long term, economic developments led to a decline in the number of people who earned a living in the countryside. In agriculture farmers were affected by the continuing trend towards larger units, as holdings were amalgamated and farms put in the hands of more substantial tenants. Changes had an impact upon the work-force too. Mechanization reduced the labour requirements and did away with many of the unskilled repetitive jobs. Thousands of labourers moved away, either attracted by higher wages in towns or better prospects in the colonies, or forced there by lack of opportunities at home.

Rural industries also suffered. Increasingly, industry became town based, with a full-time labour force, working in large units, operating the new and improved power-driven machines. This was the antithesis of the old rural handicraft industries. Because they were largely carried out in the operatives' own homes on a part-time basis, they offered the participants a great deal of flexibility and choice. This system, though geared to the rhythm of the countryside, made it difficult for operatives to compete effectively with urban factories and in the end they succumbed. As the manufacturing towns expanded, they swallowed up villages, converting them into suburbs or urban districts.

However, it would be wrong to overestimate the pace of change. In agriculture, small farmers, although undoubtedly in decline, proved to be a tenacious group. Family pastoral farms remained more viable than those in mixed farming areas, though even here they survived in some number throughout the nineteenth century. Farm labourers, too, fared better than they had expected. Some of the improved agricultural techniques were labour-intensive and offered them more employment. Although there were anti-machinery riots in the early nineteenth century, mechanization made slow progress. With labour cheap, many farmers did not see the need to spend money on machinery, especially if greater unemployment meant a rise in their poor rates. When machines eventually replaced manual labour it was as much a result of labour shortages as the desire for improved efficiency.[25]

Handicraft industries continued to flourish in the countryside for some time too, sustaining many households until around the mid-nineteenth century. Even though these industries declined thereafter, they lingered on in some places for a while longer, as certain families kept up old practices.[26] As before, they were a feature of pastoral regions or populous open villages in mixed farming areas and gave work to many men, women and children. Initially, the work, carried on in the traditional part-time way, was integrated into the routine of the farming year. However, the growth in population in the century after 1750 reduced the number of people who could combine a craft with an agricultural holding, even if the industry remained home-based. Increasingly, the operatives comprised landless workers, solely dependent upon their earnings from industry. At Thurlstone (West Riding), a weaving community in the Pennines, this development had occurred by the opening years of the nineteenth century. There were other villages, notably those growing up around newly developed coal mines, quarries and iron foundries, which were purely proletarian.

When studying the impact of such developments on their own community, local historians will invariably turn first of all to the national censuses of the nineteenth century. The earlier returns only give generalized information; between 1801 and 1821 they merely record total numbers working mainly in agriculture, manufacturing industry and crafts and other occupations. It was only in 1831 that farmers were distinguished from labourers, but at least the figures give an impression of the occupational structure of a particular parish and provide data for a study of general developments. From 1841 onwards a much more thorough analysis is possible because information on occupations was recorded for each individual. As with other sources, we have to take the evidence on trust, for they do not tell us if they were unemployed or if they had other jobs. For the most recent returns – those remaining closed because of the hundred years' rule – printed abstracts can be consulted but these only summarize the contents by registration district, not by parish.

Six sets of detailed returns (1841–91) are now available for research. As noted above, this was a critical time for many rural communities. In some villages, especially those of a largely agricultural character, the work-force shrank. In others, notably where a handicraft industry had developed, the proportion of people working solely at non-agricultural pursuits increased. At Long Buckby (Northamptonshire) 131 men and boys were involved in shoemaking in 1841 and 273 ten years later. In 1851 a further 50 women and girls were employed.[27] An indication of the farming interests (or lack of them) of these workers can be seen by checking the names against those appearing in estate surveys, leases and rentals, parish rate books and especially in the tithe award. Within this period a peak in activity was often reached, with later returns showing a decline in numbers as the industries failed to meet the competition of large-scale factory production.

The origin of the people who made up the work-force can be seen in the data on place of birth. In craft villages many came in from outside, attracted there by the prospect of work. A number brought with them skills learned elsewhere and the names of the places from which they had emigrated can be illuminating. Shropshire miners, for example, were in demand wherever the longwall system was being used or developed. Even farm labourers had exportable skills and were actively sought in areas where they were needed. Requests often appeared in local newspapers: in an advert in the *Newcastle Courant* on 5 September 1845 a southern farmer asked for a labourer adept at working with the Aberdeen corn scythe.[28]

The census returns reveal the involvement of whole families in handicraft production. In industries such as framework knitting, children began to do basic tasks at an early age, graduating to more complex and more physically demanding work as they grew older. From the ages noted in the returns we can see the children passing through the various stages. In Buckinghamshire and Bedfordshire, where lace-schools had been established to teach children the necessary skills, about one-fifth of the lacemakers in the 1851 census were under the age of 15.[29] The work that women did was also recorded. This is in marked contrast to the situation in agriculture, in which the wives of agricultural labourers were only irregularly assigned an occupation. Yet we know from documents such as farm and estate accounts and labour books and vouchers that, as in earlier periods, women continued to undertake fieldwork.[30] They inform us that children were employed too, even after the introduction of universal education in 1870. Researchers should read the comments, as well as the list of absences, in the log books of rural schools at harvest time.

The censuses remain a valuable source of information on farmers and the agricultural work-force. They often note the acreage of the farms and the number of workers employed there. Open parishes tended to have more agricultural labourers living there than there were jobs on the farms, whereas in closed parishes the opposite was the case. Other entries refer to many of the specialized jobs done on the farm. Even the census abstracts from 1901 onwards are of value for they divide the work-force into shepherds, horsemen, cowmen and labourers. The returns also chart the decline in the practice of living-in farm servants. There, these workers were generally entered as agricultural servants to distinguish them from day labourers and from the figures we can see a steady fall in their number.

During the nineteenth century the government took a great deal of interest in the work-force and a number of enquiries were carried out to examine pay and conditions in agriculture and industry. The authorities were particularly concerned about the employment of women and children; a number of reports specifically looked at this aspect of labour and others contain information on the subject.[31] Some of the enquiries were nation-wide but many were concerned with a particular area and are therefore of less value to local historians living elsewhere. Clearly, too, not all communities in an area will be covered, though the information may well have a more general relevance. As the workers spoke for themselves (even if their comments have been selected by middle-class commissioners), the account is likely to be an accurate one. In their depositions the workers describe in detail such matters as wages and conditions of work, the organization of the industry and the involvement of other members of the family.

To complement these documents a number of other sources can be used. As before, estate papers provide much information. The records of families like the dukes of Sutherland who had extensive industrial and mining interests, tell as much about industrial development as they do about agriculture. In particular, there may be sets of indentures drawn up to accompany an agreement made between the proprietor and a lessee or group of workers. These range from the terms made with a harvest gang to a contract sealed with a lessee of a coal mine. In this period, too, there is a greater range of business records to be examined.

Among commercial records those of fire insurance companies are of particular value. The papers of some firms like the Sun Fire and the Phoenix stretch as far back as the early eighteenth century. These have been deposited at the Guildhall Library, London. The policy registers include information on agricultural and industrial buildings; the materials used in their construction; and their contents, often in terms of plant, equipment and stock. If the premises being insured by the owner had been leased out, the name and occupation of the tenant is normally given. Some buildings still have a firemark on them, while other marks have been collected by local museums. From the policy number written on the plaque, one can get back to the original records. Because local agents tended to send up a batch of policies at one time, one reference often brings to light other local examples in a consecutive sequence. Once the name of the agent is known (this is written in the margin) the registers can be quickly scanned for further local policies. In this way the lack of a comprehensive topographical index can be overcome, though there is one for the period up to 1732.[32]

To a certain extent the information in the fire insurance records compensates the local historian for the loss of probate inventories as a source. Auction records provide a similar service, especially those of disposal sales listing the goods to be sold off. As these included such items as stock, tools, equipment and machinery, they tell us much about the scale and nature of the enterprise, whether agricultural or industrial. Apart from the auctioneers' own archives, local newspapers should also be searched. Auctioneers regularly placed advertisements to inform the public of forthcoming sales and often listed the lots.[33]

Another commercial source that can be used is the trade directory. Local directories were first made in the eighteenth century but early ones tend to be more concerned with the local gentry than with industry and commerce.[34] As the nineteenth century progressed more consideration was given to economic activity and therefore it received greater prominence. The data is either classified by trade or by surname. In the second half of the nineteenth century the Post Office published directories which list inhabitants and their occupations street by street. The arrangement of the information for villages, however, is often very loose. Indeed, one often has to look for it under the nearest town.

The compilation of directories appears to have been a profitable venture for many were published. For local historians they provide a readily accessible source of information on occupational structure, one which enables them to look at any changes and developments that occurred over time. In particular, they have a longer time span than that of the national censuses

BANSTEAD is a parish, in Epsom union and county court district, hundred of Copthorne and Effingham, West Surrey, Winchester bishopric, Surrey archdeaconry, and North-East Ewell deanery, 2¼ miles from Sutton station, on the road to Reigate, 16 from London by railway and 15 by road, and 3 from Epsom and Ewell. The downs are celebrated for the fineness of the turf, and noted for coursing, hunting, &c. The prospects upon these downs are very extensive, including views of London, Windsor Castle, and the surrounding country for many miles. Here are many good residences. The church of All Saints contains several fine specimens of pointed arches, and has a handsome tower, surmounted by a lofty spire, which is seen for miles round. The living is a vicarage, valued at £310, with residence, in the patronage of the Earl of Egmont, and held by the Rev. William Lewis Buckle, M.A., of Lincoln College, Oxford. The parish contains 5,518 acres, and a population in 1861 of 1,461. Here is a National school. Part of Banstead is in Kingswood ecclesiastical district.

PRIVATE RESIDENTS.

Aubertin Mrs. Mary
Buckle Rev. Edwd. M.A. Wilmot cot
Buckle Rev. Wm. Lewis, M.A. [vicar]
Burnell George, esq
Cooke John, esq. Bentley lodge
Durrell Timothy James, esq. Can hatch
Egmont Earl of, Nork park
Fitzroy Capt. William, Banstead place
Flower Capt. Lamrock
Goslett William, esq
Hohler Henry, esq
Hudson Geo. Fredk. esq. Little Burgh
Hudson Mrs. Tadworth court
Lambert Benjamin, esq. Well house
Lambert John, esq. Garratt hall
Maudslay Thomas, esq. Banstead park
Mullens Duncan, esq. Walton lodge
Nevins Robert Thos. esq. The Cottage
Robertson John, esq. The Cottage
Woodman John, esq
Wright Misses, Pound villa

COMMERCIAL.

Beall William, butcher
Brown Percival, farmer
Collett Mrs. Eleanor, linendraper
Cooper John, builder & parish clerk
Dibden T. C. artist
Dimbleby John, *Woolpack inn*
Dumsday Mrs. Jane, grocer
Farnborough Thomas, farmer
Field Robert, wheelwright
Forsdick Benjamin, *Tangier*
Griffin William, carrier
Hardy Lewis Thomas, farmer
Hardy William, miller
Harrison George, farmer, Chapel grove
Haydon Henry, butcher
Henton Edward, farmer
Lashwood William, blacksmith
Lucas James, blacksmith
Marter Joseph, carpenter
Masters Talbot, *Surrey Yeoman*
Richardson Thomas, house & estate agent, & agent for the Guardian fire & life office
Risbridger George, farmer
Russell George, grocer
Saunders John, farmer
Selsby James, grocer & post office
Sharp Wm. Jno. steward to T. Alcock, esq
Steer George, farmer
Steer Henry, farmer
Taylor William, plumber
Terry Henry, brickmaker
Wheeler Richard Edward, tailor
Wood John, timber merchant

POST OFFICE.—James Selsby, postmaster. Letters dispatched at 6.10 p.m. The nearest money order office is at Epsom
INSURANCE AGENT.—*Guardian*, Mr. T. Richardson
Police Station, Duncan McDonald, sergeant (& 12 men)
Parish Clerk, John Cooper
National School, John Taylor, master; Mrs. Hannah Taylor, mistress
CARRIER TO LONDON.—William Griffin, tuesday & friday, to 'Catherine Wheel,' Borough, & 'Cross Keys,' Gracechurch street, returning same days

17 Post Office Directory, Surrey, 1862: Banstead.

and are not restricted to census years. Compilers were selective in the people whom they listed, however. No mention is made of labourers and many handicraft workers were excluded. Moreover, town centres were covered more thoroughly than the suburbs and villages. The accuracy of the material also has to be assessed. While there were reputable firms like Pigot's, Slater's and Kelly's which had national coverage and employed local agents to update their lists, there were also unscrupulous firms, locally based, who did little more than copy the information gathered by others.

Parish registers should also be consulted, especially as post-1812 baptismal and burial registers have spaces in which occupations can be written. In rural parishes with a prominent industrial work-force, however, nonconformity was often strong. Here, one needs to examine chapel registers too. After 1837 the problem is eased because occupational details were entered on to the new civil registration forms. For other pre-census documentation one should look among the quarter sessions records of the eighteenth century for militia papers, which record the occupations of able-bodied men aged between 18 and 45. They are of particular value as a source of evidence of occupations in rural areas.[35] From a set of Northamptonshire returns made between 1762 and 1786 we learn that most villages had one or two craftsmen and that in a few over half of those liable for military service were involved in some form of non-agricultural pursuit for at least part of the year.[36]

For more recent developments local historians have a number of sources which add a personal touch to the account. They should talk to the older inhabitants of the community, especially to those who grew up and worked in the village. They will often describe a way of life and a manner of doing things that has long gone. To their reminiscences, should be added the evidence of old photographs, letters and diaries. With the onset of compulsory education, working-class literacy improved and as a result we know of their experiences at first hand. Other items of interest can be found in local newspapers, including photographs, eye-witness accounts and reports of economic activity.

Summary

Because most people until comparatively recent times earned a living from the land, the documents tend to emphasize this aspect of the economy. Information can readily be found on farmers, the size of their farms and the type of farming they practised. We can also learn of the people who worked for them and the terms and conditions of their employment. Even rural craftsmen formed a part of the same community; many of them were related to the farmers and agricultural labourers, even though they tended to establish long-term associations with a particular occupation. Moreover, they frequently held a small agricultural holding, generally of a pastoral nature as it required less attention.

18 Women harvesters in Norfolk at the end of the nineteenth century.

19 A Buckinghamshire wheelwright's yard in the late nineteenth century.

The same sources also reveal the existence of industries in the countryside, some small-scale and supplying a local market but others integrated into the national economy. Here, too, there was a link with agriculture for many of the operatives were farmers and smallholders, working part-time in industry. It has only been in the last 200 years, a time when the pace of industrial progress has accelerated, that this association has been broken. The traditional handicraft industries survived for a time, even increasing their output and expanding their numbers before eventual decline. By the mid-nineteenth century, however, the work-force had largely become an industrial proletariat, divorced from the land and with little connection with traditional rural life. Their plight is graphically described in the depositions they made before the commissions established in the nineteenth century to investigate contemporary working conditions.

CHAPTER FIVE

The peasant world

Until recent times life was a struggle for the majority of people living in the countryside. Most laboured long hours at jobs which were not only tedious and physically demanding but were also badly paid. Because of the casual nature of much of the work, many did not have security of employment either and sought to eke out a living by piecing together scraps of work as and when they could find them. As a result, villagers devoted a good deal of time and energy to matters of a practical nature and such considerations were often uppermost in their thoughts. Nonetheless, in spite of the harsh reality of everyday existence, there were opportunities for relaxation and recreation. Indeed, the endemic underemployment in the countryside provided periods of enforced rest for many people. Festivals and rituals were scattered throughout the calendar too, occasions when the community could come together and reaffirm its corporate identity. By providing scope for 'letting off steam', these occasions helped to reduce social tensions and prevent dissent. Inevitably, changes occurred over time; after the Reformation the number of feast-days decreased, as did the sense of communal solidarity. Although one should not exaggerate the pace of this development or its comprehensiveness – it did vary regionally and according to type of community – society tended to become more fragmented and divided along class lines.

For centuries the church acted as a focal point for the community. Physically, the building dominated its surroundings, while the activities which went on in its precincts were many and varied. It had a major impact on the mental outlook of the villagers, providing them with an explanation for natural phenomena and events, as well as a guide to the way they should conduct their lives. It did not eliminate superstition, however, and for centuries it had to contend with popular belief in magic which offered an alternative view of the world. During the course of the seventeenth century the propertied and educated classes, influenced by the scientific revolution, adopted a more rational approach which was reflected in the decline in prosecutions for witchcraft. Nonetheless, even if growing educational opportunities had the effect of making more people receptive to enlightened ideas, superstitious practices proved to be remarkably resilient among the majority of the population.[1]

The populace at large had long had its own rituals and ceremonies, performed to commemorate or influence events or to maintain social cohesion. From the late seventeenth century, however, the gulf separating popular culture from that of 'polite' society widened. This split was reinforced by the use of the law to redefine certain traditional customs (such as gleaning) as crimes.[2] At all levels the law favoured the privileged over the poor and was often used as a means of class control. Status was important and it therefore benefited the plaintiff or defendant to enhance his or her own social position, while denigrating that of the other party. This did not mean that ordinary villagers could not obtain a fair hearing and their readiness to go to law suggests a certain amount of confidence in the judicial process.

Beliefs

Although there have been many changes in the pattern of worship in individual parishes, the Reformation undoubtedly had the greatest impact, breaking, as it did, the unity of Western Christendom. In the English countryside, however, it was not presaged by an appreciable rise in opposition to the established church.[3] There then followed a series of changes, sometimes violent and extreme, which made the mass of the population ready to accept the compromise offered by the Elizabethan Settlement of 1559. Of course, some continued to adhere to the old religion, while others wanted more radical reform. The latter had their chance in the Interregnum period.

Geographically, Catholic sympathizers remained numerous in the North and the West, though most of them outwardly conformed and did not support militant action. In contrast, the South and the East contained many centres of radical Protestantism. Some influences cut across this regional divide. The quality of the incumbent was important, for an active and 'godly' minister might prevent dissent taking a hold. On a general level, closed parishes tended to be staunchly Anglican as, there, recusants could be weeded out more easily. Conversely, recusancy flourished in villages where the squire was sympathetic. In this way, communities of Roman Catholics were able to survive. Nonconformity throve in open villages, and especially in large parishes with scattered settlements. The inhabitants of outlying townships were not only less easy to control but often felt deprived of proper spiritual provision. Market centres or villages where industry had developed often became centres of dissent; apart from outgrowing the facilities of the established church, they contained workers who were attracted to the more radical views of the nonconformists. The Methodists were to make many converts in such communities.[4]

Of the sources that can be used to study the spiritual life of a community and the religious beliefs of its members, the most personal one is the probate will. Before the Reformation the importance of the Catholic Church can be seen in the number of bequests it received from testators – money for the maintenance of the fabric of the church or gifts such as vestments, ornaments, books and furnishings.[5] Testators also laid aside money for masses to be said for their souls. The preambles were often positively Catholic in content, whereas, thereafter, the form of words varied according to individual belief. Thus in 1598 Henry Slyfield of Great Bookham (Surrey) revealed his Protestantism in the emphasis he gave to the death of Christ and to justification by faith. Catholic wills tend to refer to the Virgin Mary and the whole Company of Heaven.[6] Analysed *en masse* a set of wills reveals the religious make-up of a community and any developments that occurred over time. At Willingham (Cambridgeshire) under the radical Lancelot Ridley, Protestant preambles were being written as early as the 1540s.[7]

Bequests made to the church appear in the churchwardens' accounts. One might also find inventories of church goods; lists spanning the Reformation are particularly valuable for they offer graphic evidence of alterations in the form of worship. Change cost money and this is reflected in the record of expenditure. At Yatton (Somerset) under Edward VI (1547–53) images were removed, stone altars and the rood screen taken down and walls white-washed. Fitments, vessels and vestments were sold but prayer books and plain furniture had to be bought. Other expenses were incurred under Mary (1553–8) to re-establish the original state of affairs and again under Elizabeth to undo them once more.[8] In the mid-seventeenth century further upheavals rent the church, with government policy moving from high church Anglicanism under Charles I, to radical Protestantism in the Interregnum and back to Anglicanism at the Restoration. Churchwardens' accounts record these shifts, though in practice the local impact was often not as great as might have been expected. From an examination of inventories of church goods and items of expenditure listed there it can be shown that parishioners frequently were unwilling to adjust and consequently resisted change.[9]

The periodic visitations made by bishops, archdeacons and bodies with jurisdiction over peculiars provide us with further information of the state of the church locally, dealing, as they do, with such matters as the structure of the church, clerical standards and the moral and spiritual well-being of the laity. Typically, they tend to concentrate on instances of abuse. During the sixteenth century these records help us to discern the progress of religious change. Visitations became more formal; churchwardens were asked specific questions and as a result the bishops could more effectively monitor the local situation.[10] In sees like Ely, with large puritan followings, however, they were ineffective for the churchwardens failed to present people holding views with which they were in sympathy.[11] Later developments such as the separation from the Anglican Church of the nonconformist groups and their

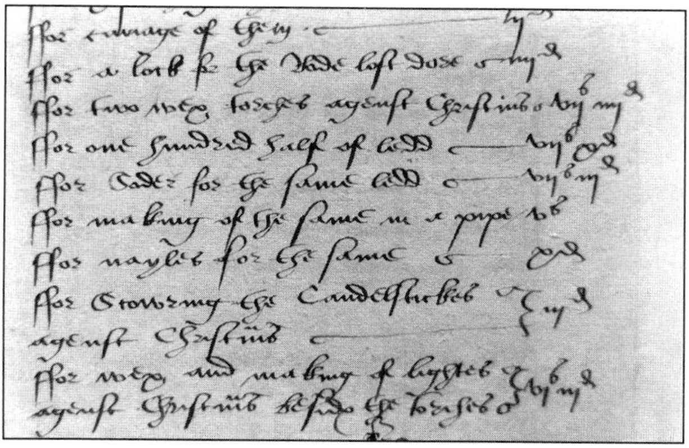

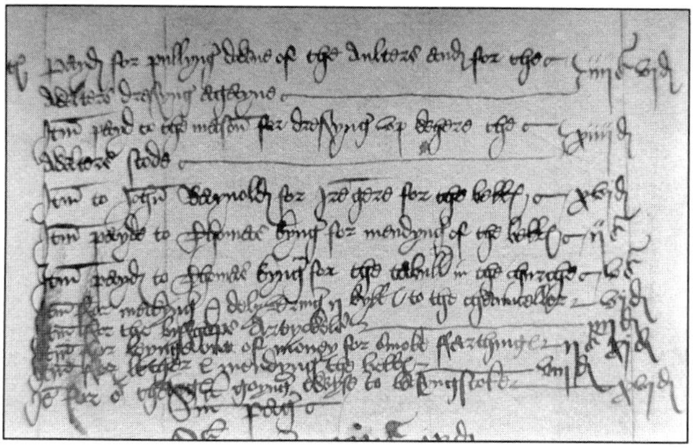

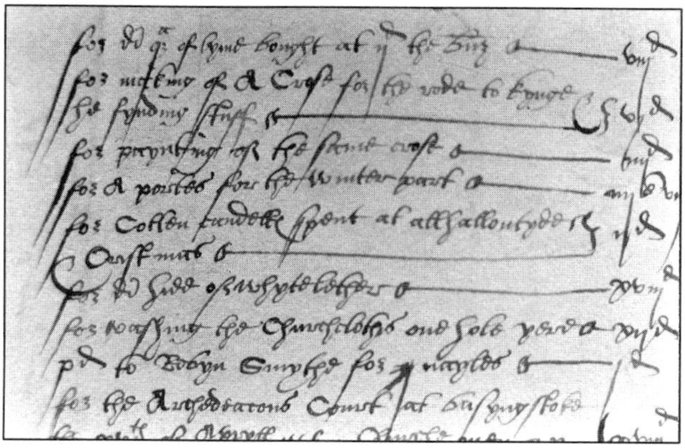

20–22 Churchwardens' accounts for the parish of Crondall (Hampshire) taken in the reigns of Henry VIII, Edward VI and Mary. They include entries describing the physical changes that occurred in the parish churches.

subsequent fragmentation into sects should also be recorded there, as should the later progress of Methodism and its offshoots.

Members of the laity accused of moral and doctrinal lapses were traditionally dealt with at the archdeaconery or consistory courts. If found guilty, depending upon the magnitude of the offence, they were punished by a fine, public penance or excommunication.[12] In the files the depositions are of particular value as they record much incidental material.

At the Reformation religious unorthodoxy increasingly came within the jurisdiction of the secular courts because of the statutes passed to implement the various changes. Many cases were heard at the quarter sessions and assizes. In Middlesex one of the most regular items of business conducted by the Elizabethan magistrates was the prosecution of Catholic recusants.[13] The church courts were abolished in 1642 and much of their work was done by the county committees, who set about ejecting unsuitable clerics and prosecuting the ungodly. They returned at the Restoration but never regained their former authority; while they had a role in the maintenance of uniformity, the records of quarter sessions and the assizes are much better sources.

Initially, most recusants were Catholic, although some radical Protestants refused to accept the Elizabethan Settlement. The latter grew in numbers in the early seventeenth century, especially after the introduction of Arminianism, with its emphasis on ritual and ceremony, during Charles I's reign. In the more favourable climate of the Civil War and Interregnum periods Protestant sects of all types proliferated. The passing of the Clarendon Code in the 1660s, designed to impose religious uniformity, led to renewed prosecution of Protestant nonconformists. The Toleration Act of 1689 eased matters, although dissenters were affected by the Occasional Conformity Act of 1711 and the Schism Act of 1714.[14] Fortunately, the statutes were soon repealed (1718) and nonconformists were treated with increasing toleration as the eighteenth century progressed. Even Roman Catholics benefited, though they had to wait until 1791 before a measure of toleration was formally granted to them.

A high proportion of nonconformists did not make a complete break with the Anglican Church. They still used the baptismal, marriage and burial services and attended church at other times too. Consequently, references to them appear in the parish registers.[15] Even if they held themselves aloof, the parson might include in the book a list of their names or memoranda of their activities. Some dissenting congregations did maintain separate records, largely registers, minute books and accounts. For Dedham (Essex) a minute book of the Presbyterian *classis* survives for the years 1582–9.[16] As conditions improved in the late seventeenth century, dissenters were able to worship more openly and erect their own meeting places. This encouraged them to keep their own records and these need to be looked at by local historians. Many have been deposited at the PRO, Chancery Lane, while others have been placed in the care of county archivists.

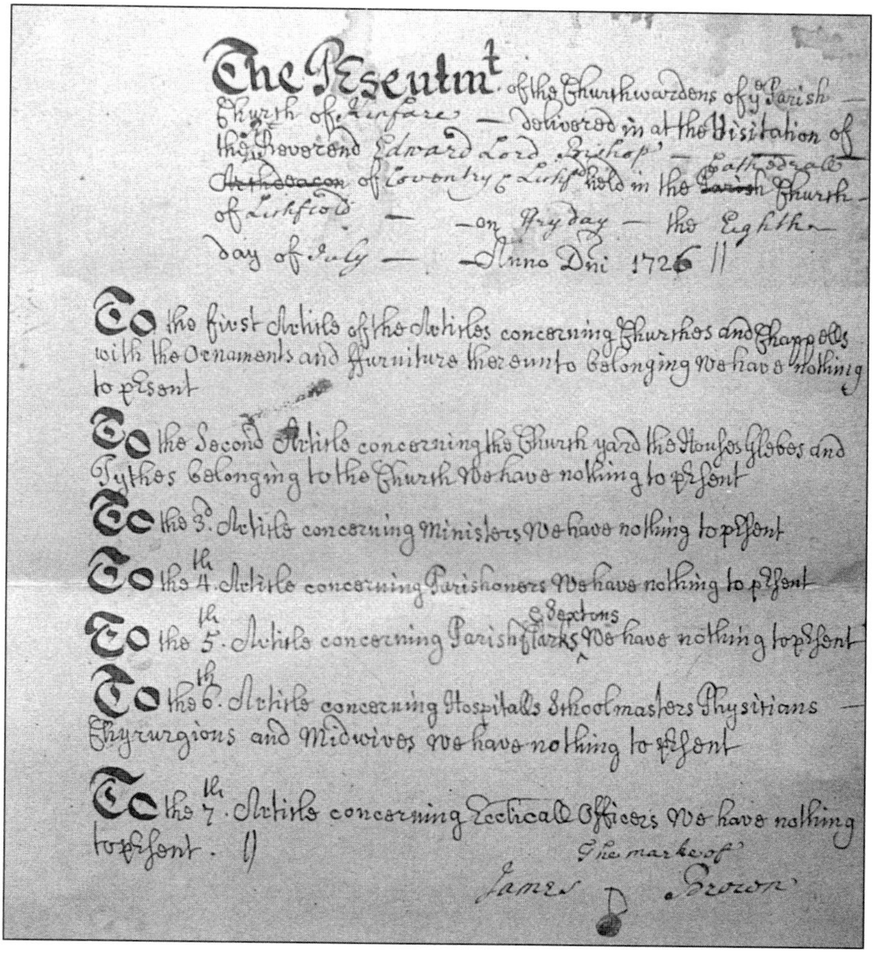

The Presentmt of the Churchwardens of ye Parish Church of Kinfare — delivered in at the Visitation of the Reverend Edward Lord Bishop — Cathedrale ~~Archdeacon~~ of Coventry & Lichf held in the ~~Parish~~ Church of Lichfield — on Fryday — the Eighth day of July — Anno Dni 1726 ||

To the first Article of the Articles concerning Churches and Chappells with the Ornaments and furniture thereunto belonging we have nothing to present

To the Second Article concerning the Church yard the Houses Glebes and Tythes belonging to the Church we have nothing to present

To the 3d. Article concerning Ministers we have nothing to present

To the 4th. Article concerning Parishoners we have nothing to present

To the 5th. Article concerning Parish Clarks & Sextons we have nothing to present

To the 6th. Article concerning Hospitalls Schoolmasters Physitians Chyrurgions and Midwives we have nothing to present

To the 7th. Article concerning Ecclicall Officers we have nothing to present. ||

The marke of
James D Brown

23 Bishop of Lichfield's diocesan visitation of 1726: presentments of the churchwardens of Kinver (Staffordshire).

Apart from diocesan visitations, one or two nation-wide surveys were made of religious affiliation. The *Liber Cleri* of 1603 and the Compton Census of 1676 (referred to pp. 15 and 52) give numbers of communicants, nonconformists and (Catholic) recusants in parishes in various dioceses. While they pin-point those places of widespread opposition to the established church, detailed local research suggests that the figures tend to underestimate their numerical strength.

In the nineteenth century two other national censuses were taken. The first, ordered by the House of Commons in 1829, surveyed all non-Anglican places of worship in the country. Although all the originals were destroyed in the fire at the Houses of Parliament in 1834, enrolled copies have survived among the records of the Clerk of the Peace in several counties (and others may turn up elsewhere). For Lancashire there exists a printed copy. Inevitably, because they depended upon the conscientiousness of the persons taking the poll (the incumbent, churchwardens or overseers), as well as upon their knowledge of the parish, some returns are more accurate than others. Moreover, the material may be couched in vague terms or written down in insufficient detail for a distinction between the various sects to be made.[17]

Nonetheless, the source provides valuable evidence of the distribution of Roman Catholics and nonconformists in a county. The returns also give the date of erection of all chapels built after 1800 (though many congregations were still meeting in private houses). Comments made by the compiler often add to the value of the material, enabling the researcher to see behind the statistics to the people involved. The continuing connection with the Church of England is brought out in a number of entries. At North Scarle (Lincolnshire) there was a Methodist meeting house with 52 members but almost all of them occasionally attended the parish church.[18]

Comparisons can also be made with the religious census of 1851, the originals of which may be consulted at the PRO, Kew. The census was taken on Sunday 30 March and recorded attendance at all religious services held that day, as well as the average size of the congregation over the previous 12 months.[19] Also collected were details of endowments, pew-rents and the number of available seats. Although the figures were subject to the same sort of errors as affected the census of 1829, the general pattern is clear. Contemporaries were shocked: well over one-half of the population of England and Wales had not gone to any church at all, and about one-half of those who had done so, had worshipped in a nonconformist chapel. Even if they had wanted to, all the people who had attended a service that Sunday could not have been accommodated in an Anglican church. In spite of a certain amount of building and extension, the Church of England was still paying for past architectural and spiritual neglect.

From this census we can see that a large proportion of the population was not even formally involved with religious worship. By then parishioners had a choice. In earlier generations the appearance at church of those with a similar attitude probably owed more to custom and the law than genuine belief. They are the ones who appear in the court records and provide a counterpoint to the genuine piety of men like Richard Gough whose firm belief in the omniscience of God pervades the history of his parish written *c.* 1700.[20]

Visitations and church court records indicate that church attendance was less than total in the Middle Ages but only at the Reformation did the law become involved. The Act of Uniformity (1559), for example, declared that every one should regularly attend their parish church.[21] People still stayed away: in a visitation of 1599 it was found that at Great Bradfield (Essex) no more than 20 to 40 people celebrated Easter communion out of an eligible population of up to 200.[22] Elsewhere in Essex attempts were made to tighten up conformity by prosecuting at the church courts those who had not taken communion. At Terling, the last two decades of the sixteenth century saw numerous indictments for this offence.[23]

Some of the population were recusants but many stayed away through negligence or even obstinacy. At one archdeaconery visitation the churchwardens at Terling presented Thomas Mead who 'doth very negligentlye and wilfullye absent himself from churche and amongeste the rest upon sundaye last being requested to come in he obstinately refused and went his way.'[24] In the village, as elsewhere, a large proportion of the people prosecuted for non-attendance came from the lower classes. They may have been baptised, married and buried there but for many, church-going was a rather casual affair. In the Oxfordshire peculiars of Dorchester, Thame and Banbury churchwardens' presentments are full of complaints concerning indifference or hostility to the church.[25]

Church services were often disrupted. In 1598 a Cambridgeshire man was charged with indecent behaviour at the Ely consistory court for his 'most loathsome farting, striking and scoffing speeches.'[26] Actions such as these ensured that church services were not always conducted with reverence or respect. Keith Thomas, in his book, *Religion and the Decline of Magic*, notes that 'they jostled for pews, nudged their neighbours, hawked and spat, knitted, made coarse remarks, told jokes, fell asleep, and even let off guns.'[27] It was not uncommon for individuals to heckle the preacher, either to raise a laugh or to hurry him up. Once released, some headed straight for the alehouse.

Many were ignorant about the basic tenets of Christianity, making them susceptible to superstitious beliefs. Even Richard Gough at times acknowledged the role played by the supernatural in human affairs. For the uneducated, acceptance must have been even more wholehearted. Research done on this topic, examining records, local customs and folklore, suggests that among such people belief in magic lasted well into the nineteenth century.[28]

Within the sphere of popular culture references abound to rituals that would enable individuals to perform such feats as foretelling the future, warding off disease or influencing the weather. For greater certainty people had recourse to so-called 'cunning men', whose services included healing the sick, finding lost goods, fortune-telling and divination. Examples of their art can readily be found among the records of the church courts. In the treatment of illness, liturgical elements were often included as part of the spell. At his trial in 1590 James Sykes of Guiseley (West Riding) confessed that he had cured horses by writing prayers on a piece of paper which were then hung

24 Trial of a witch in seventeenth-century England: a woman is ducked in a mill pond.

around the creatures' necks.[29] Incantations and special props were part of the stock-in-trade of all cunning men. To discover the identity of a thief a sieve and a pair of shears were commonly employed as divining tools.

Such beliefs are also represented by the persecution in the Tudor and Stuart period of witches – people deemed to be using black magic, generally against their neighbours. In ecclesiastical law witchcraft was a form of heresy and could be dealt with at the church courts. Among the articles of enquiry included in visitations of the late sixteenth and early seventeenth centuries was one asking churchwardens to note the presence of witches.[30] Suspects found guilty normally performed some public penance. Acts of 1547, 1563 and 1604 brought witches within the jurisdiction of the secular courts; they were sometimes tried at quarter sessions but more likely at the assizes. The measures, which laid down severe penalties, were aimed at those witches who had caused death or injury to humans or damage to their property.[31]

Local historians need to look at the files of the various courts. In his study of witchcraft in Essex Dr A. Macfarlane found little overlap among the records, leading him to conclude that accusations made in court formed only a small proportion of actual suspicions. Peak years occurred in the 1580s and 1590s, reflecting the general concern felt at the time over a real perceived threat. Thereafter, apart from an outburst in 1645, the number of prosecutions declined.[32] This pattern mirrors the situation in the country as a whole: by the Restoration the number of cases had fallen dramatically as those in authority ceased to prosecute for the offence. Ordinary people, however, remained hostile and without recourse to law occasionally took matters into their own hands. Some of these incidents were reported in local newspapers.

Educational provision

For centuries an elite group of village children obtained a classical education either at a cathedral school or later at a grammar or public school. Others (from the late seventeenth century) attended dissenting academies, institutions which came to rival the established schools because of their up-to-date curriculum. A number of students went on to university or to one of the inns of court. Their schools tended to be located in towns and cities and in the villages a network of elementary schools developed over the centuries to cater for most rural schoolchildren. It is this aspect of education that will be dealt with here.

We know from references to unlicensed masters in church records of the presence of teachers in medieval villages, but chantry chapels were more important centres of education. Apart from religious instruction, the priests probably gave some help with reading.[33] Suppressed under Henry VIII and Edward VI, their records can be found at the PRO, Chancery Lane. Most villagers had to rely on their parish priest or curate. The quality of the teaching, if provided, was generally poor, given the peasant background of many of the clerics.[34] Expenditure connected with their teaching activities might appear in churchwardens' accounts. References to scholars should also be listed in manorial accounts and court rolls since the sons of bondmen could only go to school if the lord permitted it and was paid a fee.

The real expansion of lay education came in the early modern period, partly due to the Protestant emphasis on the value of self-study of the scriptures. Most schoolchildren in villages went to petty schools where spelling and reading were taught and perhaps writing and counting too.[35] Some schools had endowments and were set up as charities. Others, through the encouragement of the Society for Promoting Christian Knowledge (1699), were funded by public subscription. The society aimed to spread Christianity among the poor and stressed moral and religious training and social deference.[36] Many schools continued to be run as private ventures. Such an institution was kept by one Twyford at the Warren House in Myddle

(Shropshire). According to Gough, he 'lived in good repute and taught neighbours' children to read, and his wife taught women to sew, and make needle workes.'[37] These ventures varied enormously in quality, ranging from well-run establishments down to the squalid dame schools, which offered little more than a child-minding service.

The rural mass received little or no instruction as parents could not afford to allow their children time off from work. In any case many of them felt little desire for literacy. Documents signed with a mark were acceptable at law and on the rare occasion when they might need to have a letter written, they could always find someone to do the job for them.[38] Village scribes were often at work drawing up probate wills and inventories, for instance, and individual hands can frequently be recognized when examining a set of documents.

Much of the information is located in diocesan archives because of the church's supervisory role. From 1559 all teachers had to obtain a licence from the bishop, which named the location of the school and often the type of instruction to be given. Entries might refer to an intention 'to teach grammar', 'to write and read the vulgar tongue' or 'to teach young children'.[39] The evidence, unfortunately, is not always precise or consistent; apart from inevitable omissions, statements might be vague, while successive licences for a village school might refer to different criteria.

Subscription books, also to be found among the diocesan records, provide further information on schoolmasters. These were introduced as a result of a canon of 1604, requiring all candidates for a teaching licence to subscribe to the royal supremacy, the Thirty-nine Articles and the Book of Common Prayer. In 1662 this obligation became part of statute law with the passing of the Act of Uniformity. As the licensing process was tightened up too, the documentation for the late seventeenth century becomes more comprehensive.[40]

For the details visitation records can be used. After 1571 they regularly asked for information on schoolmasters and the educational facilities in each parish. In a visitation of the diocese of York made by Archbishop Herring in 1743, 379 of the 645 parishes possessed a school of one sort or another.[41] We also learn of the standard of the education that was being offered, especially where the masters were incompetent or negligent. At Woodbridge (Suffolk) in 1677 Philip Candler, master of the free school there, was presented for not ensuring that his pupils went to church on holy days. Five others were accused of keeping a school in the parish, although not allowed by the ordinary, and of not teaching the catechism to the children.[42]

For endowed schools, foundation deeds and written constitutions provide an indication of the aims of individual establishments and the curricula they were expected to follow. As boards of trustees were set up to administer the endowments and other affairs of the school, their minutes, if extant, should contain material on schoolmasters, pupils and the curriculum. The

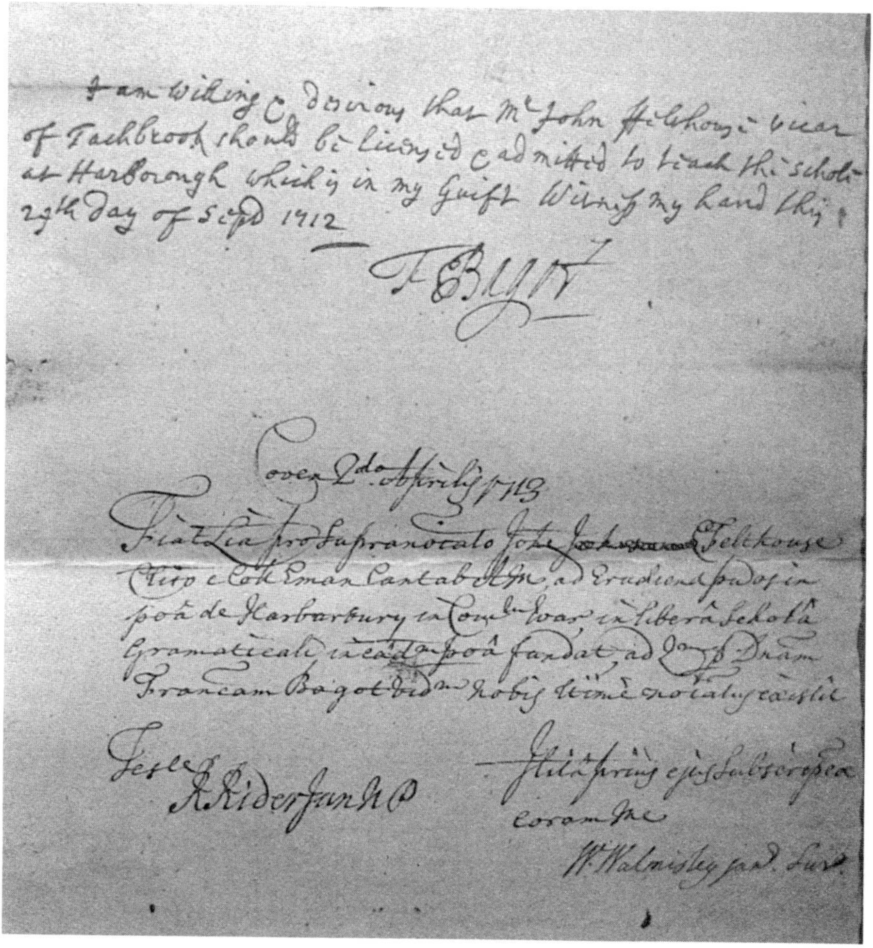
I am willing & desirous that Mr John ffieldhouse vicar of Tachbrook should be licensed & admitted to teach the schole at Harborough which is in my Guift Witness my hand this 29th day of Sept 1712

25 Licence for Mr John Fieldhouse, vicar of Tachbrook, to teach at a school in Harborough, 29 September 1712.

nineteenth-century reports of the Charity Commissioners also contain much of interest. They often provide details concerning the foundation and running of these schools, especially noting any disputes and other interesting features.

Stray references to schools and masters appear in other classes of record and local historians should come across them during the course of their researches. Many schoolmasters made wills and had their goods appraised in inventories. Those who charged fees often taught in a room in their house and the contents should include items of school equipment and books.

Documents in which occupations may appear should also be examined for references to teachers. Maps, deeds, vestry minutes and manor court rolls may mention schoolhouses.

In the late eighteenth and early nineteenth centuries rapid population growth brought the subject of mass education into prominence. A number of expedients were tried, the aims of which were similar to those of the SPCK. These ideals were typified by the Sunday School movement of the 1780s.[43] When the Weybridge Sunday School was established in 1794 the regulations stated that two persons were to be appointed, a master and a mistress who were deemed capable of teaching the children to read and of giving them instruction in their catechism and the first rudiments of their religion.[44] These schools proved a success; some extended their activities to weekday evenings or, as at Weybridge, became day schools.

Other day schools based upon a monitorial system were introduced, providing an education for poor children at little cost. Their development was mainly due to the activities of two bodies, the (largely) nonconformist British and Foreign School Society and the Anglican National Society for Promoting the Education of the Poor in the Principles of the Established Church.[45] The societies not only built schools, but also established institutions for the training of teachers. Apart from local material which should include minutes and accounts, a good deal of local information can be obtained from the central archives. Among the records of the BFSS, housed at the West London Institute of Higher Education, are bundles of correspondence with local schools and committees, reports by the society's inspectors and applications from people seeking admission to the society's training establishments.[46]

In 1833 the two societies received £20,000 from Parliament, the first step in a process which was to see the state becoming increasingly involved in education as the nineteenth century progressed. In 1839 the Committee of Council on Education was established, to be followed by various Diocesan Boards of Education.[47] The reports of their inspectors provide illuminating evidence of the conditions in schools, in particular highlighting the poor state of many rural institutions. As government grants increased, the Education Department was able to exert greater control over the schools.[48]

The government's concern for education can also be seen in the various commissions it set up. The first, a survey of elementary schools, was made in 1816. Incumbents were asked to furnish the information and the findings were published in the *Digest of Parochial Returns*. The material, arranged by county, provides details of the capacity of the schools, distinguished by type. In 1851 an enquiry into the state of education in England and Wales formed part of the religious census of that year. The few surviving returns are in the PRO, Kew. For places not covered, the printed reports contain much useful local data.[49]

The population censuses from 1841 onwards should also be looked at for material on education. The number and age of the children described as scholars can be used to discover what proportion of them attended school and between what ages. When related to the data on occupations, the social groups who made use of it can be assessed, as can the adequacy of the local provision. In addition, the returns refer to schoolhouses and teachers, topics which were also noted in commercial directories.

In 1870 Forster's Education Act added an element of compulsion into the voluntary system. In parishes with no school or none which could be brought up to the required standard, School Boards had to be set up with power to raise through the rates the necessary finances to build and maintain one.[50] Attendance was made compulsory by acts of 1876 and 1880.[51] In the countryside attendance had always been a problem, notably at critical times of the year. Older children often resented being kept on at school. In her account of her childhood in the Oxfordshire hamlet of Juniper Hill, Flora Thompson writes, 'It must be remembered that in those days a boy of eleven was nearing the end of his school life. Soon he would be at work; already he felt himself nearly a man and too old for petticoat government.'[52]

For anyone wishing to examine the situation locally school log books provide them with the best source of information. The first ones were written in the decade before the 1870 Education Act but essentially they provide a record of the developments that occurred after this landmark in elementary education. Written from the point of view of the teacher rather than that of

26 Children in a Warwickshire school have an object lesson.

the management committee, as the earlier minutes had been (and continued to be), they provide an invaluable insight not only into all aspects of school life but also into village affairs in general. The involvement of members of the community can be shown and, in particular, the role played by the incumbent and other local worthies. At Great Bookham (Surrey) in the 1870s entries reveal that the rector regularly visited the school, while his daughers taught needlework to the girls there.[53]

When we look at entries in the log books and reflect on the subjects taught and the way in which they were presented, we perhaps should not be surprised at the negative attitude adopted by many children. Yet the 1870 Act must be considered a success for by the end of the nineteenth century virtually the whole population of the country had achieved a basic level of literacy.[54] To assess the extent to which the situation had improved, a number of earlier records can be studied and a calculation of the levels attained at different times made.

The increasing number of books in circulation in the early modern period, especially cheap chap-books aimed at a popular market, suggests a sizeable reading public.[55] While the readership of such books included working people, the data cannot be quantified. Documents which contain signatures or marks, on the other hand, do provide us with hard evidence on literacy rates and enable comparisons to be made over time and between different social groups and regions of the country. Although a simple test, experts

27 Extracts from the log book of Bookham First School in the late nineteenth century.

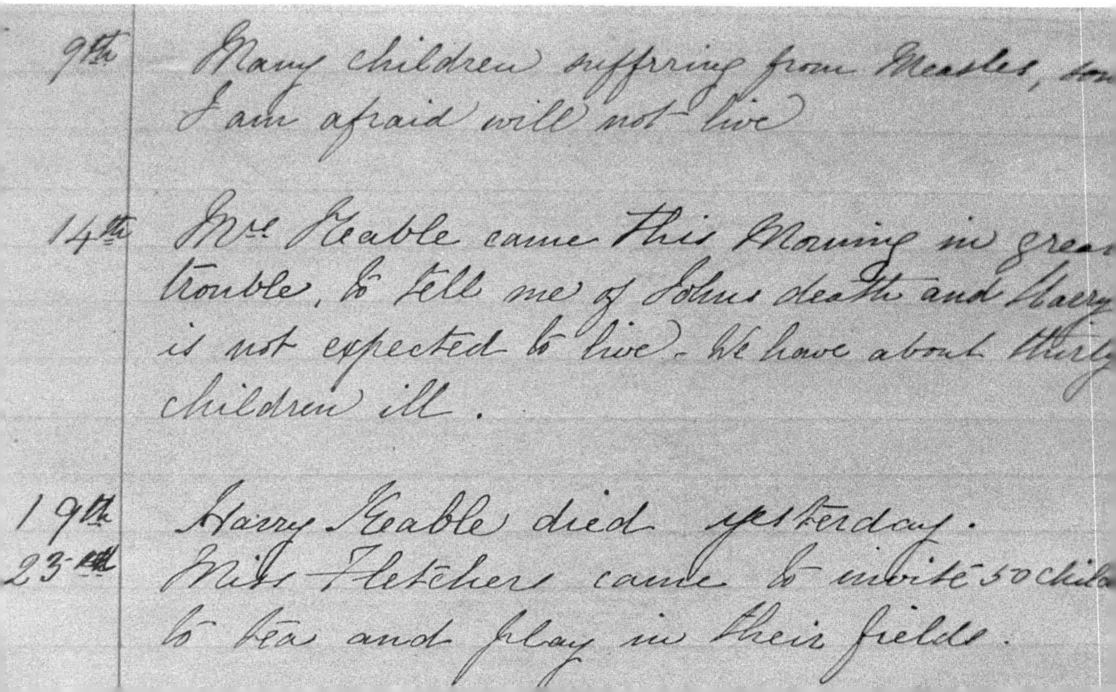
9th Many children suffering from Measles, som
I am afraid will not live

14th Mrs Keable came this Morning in grea
trouble, to tell me of Johns death and Harr
is not expected to live. We have about thirt
children ill.

19th Harry Keable died yesterday.
23rd Miss Fletcher came to invite 50 chil
to tea and play in their fields.

agree that it is a valid one: reading was taught before writing and those who could sign their name would already have acquired a basic level of literacy.[56]

Probate wills are one source that can be used, though as they were invariably written at the end of a person's life, when he or she might be incapacitated or senile, they tend to underestimate the number of people who could sign their name. Conversely, as testators were a socially selective group, the results are not truly representative. Results drawn from a sample of Norwich diocesan wills (1633–7) show that virtually all the gentry and clergy were literate; that tradesmen and yeomen might be; and that husbandmen, labourers and women overwhelmingly were not.[57] A similar survey can be made of the signed depositions of witnesses taken at church courts, at the assizes or at the quarter sessions, sources which have the advantage of not being drawn up on the deponent's death bed. In his analysis of the Northern Circuit assize depositions for the years 1640–1750, R. A. Houston found the initial pattern similar to the one just referred to, with subsequent improvements in literacy rates being made among most occupational/status groups over time.[58]

The Protestation Oath of 1642, though it does not provide as much occupational data, covers all social classes (excluding women). Work done by David Cressy, utilizing the information from the less reliable Vow and Covenant (1643) and the Solemn League and Covenant (1644), as well as evidence from the Protestation Oath, reveals that the literacy rates were higher in towns than in the countryside and that there were considerable regional and parochial differences. Overall he estimated that only 30 per cent of rural males were literate.[59]

With the passing of Lord Hardwicke's Marriage Act in 1753 we have a source which is both comprehensive and long-lasting. Husbands and wives were required to sign the register and thus the records provide us with a mass of information not only on literacy rates for all social classes but also on differentials between males and females. Analysis of the material suggests that while overall female illiteracy declined in the late eighteenth century, very little change occurred in the rate for males. In the earlier nineteenth century progress was both more uniform and more pronounced, although these general trends conceal considerable local variation.[60]

Recreation

In the Middle Ages the social life of the community was centred on the church. The holidays were often Christian festivals, occupying an important place in the calendar alongside festivities associated with the agricultural year. These occasions were marked by feasting, dancing, sports and drama. In particular, rituals, plays and processions catered for the villagers' love of spectacle. Plays often had a religious motif and were run by the church. Medieval churchwardens' accounts regularly contain references to items used by the mummers: the church at Eversholt (Bedfordshire), for instance, possessed 'playing coats' and 'playbooks and garments'.[61] Because medieval churches had no pews plays were often performed there. Secular themes were also touched upon, especially in plays performed by parish guilds.

Other celebrations took place on saints' days or at events like the Beating of the Bounds at Rogationtide. Of particular importance were the parish feasts or wakes, normally held on the patronal day of the church. Evidence of the costs incurred may appear in churchwardens' accounts. They certainly record items associated with church ales, social events run by the wardens to raise money for the church. At these gatherings, the food and drink were supplied by the wardens.[62] Other 'ales' were associated with such rites of passage as baptism, marriage and death.[63]

At times the situation got out of hand. Aware of the possibility, bishops periodically sent out injunctions against events like these which posed a threat to good order. Evidence of their concern can be found in their registers. In 1223 Bishop Poore ordered that marriages 'be celebrated reverently and with honor, not with laughter or sport, or in taverns or at public potations or feasts.'[64] Often positive action had to be taken and many cases heard at the church courts arose out of an excess of good cheer at a community function. From the records we learn of the activities that formed an essential part of the festivities. Boisterous events such as bull-baiting, wrestling and football regularly led to trouble, while many drink-related cases appear. Other offenders were those who misused the sabbath by playing games or frequenting the alehouse when they should have been in church. Cases of fornication were also heard, perhaps committed on festive occasions when young people met members of the opposite sex. During the May Day celebrations, for instance, trips to the woods to collect flowers and shrubbery for the house decorations provided them with the opportunity.[65] Fines for *leyrwite* (fornication) and *childwite* (giving birth to a bastard) were paid to the lord and therefore appear in the manor court rolls.

References to games turn up in the record. Whenever scuffles broke out, many of the protagonists were punished at the court. Fines were also imposed on individuals who played bowls, football and other games when they should have been engaged in archery practice. Coroners' inquests provide another source of information. In one incident, a man watching a bull being baited was killed when the animal broke free and ran over him.[66]

The attitude of the authorities to popular recreation was ambivalent. The church, as we have seen, was worried about the opportunities for drunken and licentious behaviour, especially if it profaned the sabbath day or a religious festival. On the other hand, church ales did bring in a good deal of money. Manorial lords (many of whom were clerics) were similarly concerned about the general unruliness of such occasions. Nonetheless, they probably recognized their value as a safety valve and their accounts are full of references to gifts of money and goods that they had given.

In the late sixteenth and early seventeeth centuries additional pressure came from the Puritans, who saw sports and festivities[67] as ungodly distractions, leading people away from religion and the pursuit of a sober, industrious life. However, most people (from the court downwards) were unsympathetic to their views, and in 1618 James I published the Declaration on Sports, a document that was reissued in an extended form under Charles I in 1633.[68] It not only allowed people to participate in certain sports on Sundays after church service, but also permitted the holding of parish feasts. The Puritans were able to impose their views on the rest of society during the Commonwealth period but overall their success was limited by popular attachment to leisure pursuits.

The Reformation did have some impact on the number of festive dates in the calendar; fewer saints' days were kept and church ales were not held so regularly. Nonetheless, wakes and other feasts retained their vitality. At Myddle (Shropshire) Richard Gough wrote of John Hall, that he 'was a weaver and a common fidler, who went abroad to wakes and merriments.'[69] The continuing importance of events like these is revealed in the county histories that were being written at the time. In Northamptonshire 198 of the 290 parishes investigated by John Bridges (mainly between 1719 and 1724) certainly possessed wakes and in only 11 of the others had they definitely ended.[70]

Evidence can be obtained from personal and estate records (diaries and commonplace books, correspondence and accounts), though as most were kept by the clergy and the gentry, they give a picture of events from the outside. Some participated – many references indicate a social mix at bull-baiting and cock-fighting matches or at boxing and wrestling bouts – but often in a way which emphasized their social superiority. They provided the bull, organized the football and (more likely) the cricket teams, and paid for the harvest supper.[71] At least these pastimes offered some form of interaction among the classes and an opportunity for working men with a talent to shine and gain status in the community. Richard Gough *c.* 1700 wrote that 'Thomas Jukes was a bauling, confident person; hee often kept company with his betters, but shewed noe more respecte than if they had beene his equalls or inferiors. Hee was a great bowler, and often bowled with Sir Humphrey Lea att a Bowling Greene on Haremeare Heath.'[72]

A good deal of socializing went on at periodic fairs, which were used by villagers as outlets for their goods. This convivial atmosphere was not new; people had always met old acquaintances there, gossipped over a pint in the market tavern and watched the entertainers drawn there by the crowd. In the early modern period, however, their commercial importance slowly declined and the recreational element came into greater prominence. By the mid-eighteenth century, the time when William Owen published *An Authentic Account . . . of all the Fairs in England and Wales*, many had become trivialized. This is revealed by the number of centres said by Owen to specialize in toys, trinkets and pedlary ware.

Town histories and chronicles record the type of amusements and recreations on offer on these occasions. From them we learn of circus acts and sideshows, bull-baiting and cock-fighting and sports such as wrestling, boxing and cudgelling. At Shrewsbury the chronicler wrote that on 24 June 1590 'there was a scaffold put up in the cornemarket . . . which an Hongarian and other of the queenes . . . players and tumblars usid and excersisid them selves in sutche maner of tumblynge and turninge as then the licke was never seene in Shrewsberie before.'[73]

Outside the festivals, villagers amused themselves as best they could in the little time they had available. They told stories, sang or made music and, above all, frequented the alehouse. Naturally, there had been alehouses before but they seem to have come into their own in the Tudor and Stuart period. The central role of the church and the regular 'ales' of earlier times probably account for the change. Literary works like Gough's *History of Myddle* reveal the English predilection for alcohol, a vice which cut across all social groups. 'Richard Eaton', he records, 'was a drunken, debauched person a great and intimate companion of Mr. Hall, of Balderton, a good benefactor to the ale-sellers.' Some women in the parish were as bad as the men: William Cross and his wife, for instance, were both 'overmuch addicted to drunkennesse, and . . . went dayly to the alehouse.'[74] Nonetheless, alehouses tended to be male preserves, even if many were run by women. There they could forget their cares and relax in congenial company.[75]

Few parishes have a Gough to inform us of the foibles of our predecessors but much can be gained from the records. For a time the church courts continued to hear cases of drunkenness and tippling at the time of divine service. More commonly, guilty parties were taken to the quarter sessions. Magistrates became involved in the legislative process through the Licensing Act of 1552 which ordered alehouse keepers to obtain a licence from them and seal a bond for the good order of their establishments. As a result, grants of licences and the prosecution of proprietors of illegal premises appear in the quarter sessions files. Because of confusion over the wording of the Act many semi-permanent licences were given, but in James I's reign the principle of annual licences was established.[76] The added information makes it easier for the local historian to chart the changes that occurred within his or her community. More colourfully, the quarter sessions records also contain petitions concerning disorderly alehouses.

Apart from the beer and good company, alehouses had additional activities. The sources already quoted reveal that a variety of games were played, of which dice, backgammon, marbles and shove-halfpenny are among the best known. Card games grew in popularity as cheap printed packs became available. Other facilities were provided too. One publican in the North Riding owned a 'common football for the young men of the town to play with' and another in Somerset kept balls, bowls and cudgels. Many had sets of quoits and some built bowling alleys.[77]

Other recreational references appear in these documents, perhaps as a result of theft, riot or slander. An entry in the Middlesex quarter sessions files records that on 20 March 1576 a hundred people had assembled to play 'a certain unlawful game, called football' and caused 'a great affray, likely to result in homicides and serious accidents.'[78] In a matrimonial case heard at the consistory court of Winchester in 1567 a witness deposed that she had been in the company of 'youth which were playing at the football a mile off.'[79]

From the late eighteenth century onwards popular recreations came under renewed attack, though they still enjoyed mass support and their demise was a gradual one.[80] Indeed, a few survived (if in an attenuated form) into the present century, late enough to be photographed and to be recalled by people still alive. The gentry, who in the past had tacitly, or even openly, supported the events, now tended to turn against them. In particular, wakes weeks and pleasure fairs or mass games like football were more widely seen as threats to law and order and inducements to licentiousness and idleness. In this, they were supported (for their own reasons) by industrialists and evangelicals. Moreover, opposition to blood sports like bull-baiting and cock-fighting grew (though not against the upper class pursuits of hunting and shooting), as it did against combat sports such as boxing and cudgelling.

Quarter sessions records become more informative as the authorities more actively sought to ban the gatherings or to curb the excesses at those that did take place. In 1778 the Nottinghamshire magistrates tried to bring the wakes under control by threatening to withhold licences from publicans who supported them. At these gatherings, they asserted, 'Diverse Riots and Disorderly doings frequently arise by Persons Assembling and Meeting together to be guilty of Excessive Drinking Tippling Gaming or other unlawful Exercises'.[81] Action was also taken against pleasure fairs and later against hiring fairs. In late eighteenth-century Essex the magistrates closed down a large number of unchartered fairs.[82] In the same way, disorderly alehouses were more carefully regulated, though the 'pub' retained its importance as a social centre.

Events were recorded in local newspapers, a source which becomes increasingly valuable as the period progressed. Inevitably, they gave prominence to the sensational aspect, concentrating on instances of tragedy and outrage. Ordinary gatherings only gained greater attention in the mid-nineteenth century when they had been brought into line with middle-class taste. Thus, the *Oxford Chronicle* of 7 May 1870 contained an item on the recent May Day celebrations, in which it was noted that 'on the 2nd. the town was live with children carrying garlands, with a view to obtaining the customary "copper". Many children from neighbouring villages also brought garlands, which they exposed at the doors of houses, singing appropriate songs.'[83] Newspapers also carried advertisements for forthcoming attractions, as did posters and handbills.

Antiquarians continued to gather material of social and historic interest and their compilations, as before, include references to customs and recreations. In Victorian times an interest in folklore developed and, as a result, efforts were made to unearth picturesque and quaint local customs and to record them for posterity. Some customs were revived, often shorn of their rougher elements and with fanciful bits added. Others were described, perhaps imperfectly because the passage of time had blunted the memory.[84]

Some festivals such as those at Christmas, Easter and Whitsun remained to provide an essential time of relaxation during the working year. As they were celebrated by almost everyone and associated with respectable institutions, they escaped the condemnation heaped on plebeian pursuits.[85] In 1897 the *Hampshire Chronicle* painted a charming picture of the childrens' Boxing Day treat which had been organized by the village elite of Shawford.[86] Another important occasion was the annual Club Day feast, often held at Whitsuntide. In many communities it filled the place once occupied by the wake but as the feast day of the local Friendly Society, it was much more acceptable. The authorities were in favour of institutions that encouraged thrift and self-help.[87] Nonconformists, too, were prominent in establishing a respectable alternative culture to the traditional popular one. As R. W. Malcolmson notes, the list might include brass bands, public recitations and lectures, lantern shows, tea festivals, railway excursions, reading clubs, temperance halls, Bands of Hope, concerts and plays.[88] For evidence of these activities local historians can look at the documentation generated by the bodies themselves or at the reports printed in the newspaper.

The attack on popular games such as football, boxing and wrestling obviously did not lead to the extinction of these sports, but they were transformed. Instead of the communal events of the preceding period, clubs were formed and rules introduced. In this way, the sports were shorn of their excesses and brought under greater control, making them more acceptable to polite society. Certain games like cricket and golf might be more exclusive than football, for example, but working people still were able to participate in them.

As standards improved and fixtures with other clubs were arranged, the top sides began to attract a large following. By the end of the nineteenth century the phenomenon of mass spectator sports had emerged. It is clear from the size of a number of professional football grounds, for instance, that they were built to accommodate a far larger crowd than they do today. This meant that most people were involved in recreational pursuits in a passive rather than an active way.

The development of organized sport provides the local historian with a good deal of information. Clubs kept minutes and accounts and corresponded with others. They may also have preserved the names of players and results, as well as photographs of teams. Games were reported in the local paper – and even in the national ones if the team had a first-class fixture list.

Crime in the countryside

Communal action

Until the nineteenth century and the development of a professional police force, the prevention and detection of crime was largely a matter for the community as a whole. In the Middle Ages all males over the age of 12 had to enter a tithing, a group of some 10 to 12 members jointly responsible for each others' actions. At a view of frankpledge they presented anyone who had committed an offence.[89] Although the organization survived the medieval period, by then it had become a formal body and no longer fulfilled its original purpose. Community control was still exercised but through the medium of an 'elected' jury who presented offences to the court.

Similarly, villagers reported to the church courts anyone acting immorally or intemperately. They even took matters into their own hands, showing their disapproval of deviant behaviour by subjecting culprits to the humiliating custom of 'rough music'. Essentially, this comprised a noisy demonstration outside the offender's house, but he might also be carried straddled across a pole or burnt in effigy after a procession and ritual ceremony. It was often used to censure 'unnatural' marriage practices – against domineering wives, old men who married young women and husbands who beat their wives excessively. Those who misused their authority or had flouted local custom also suffered.[90]

Members of the community stood as guarantors for miscreants, pledging

28 The old lock-up at Harrold (Bedfordshire).

29 Two Tudor miscreants spend their time in the stocks.

for their attendance at court or for their good behaviour, or sat on the court baron and leet juries which dealt with offenders brought before them. These jurors tended to become a socially selective group, for the elite featured prominently among them.[91] Consequently, the documentation generated by the courts not only informs us of the incidence of crime in the locality but also of the identity and social standing of the active members of the community.

The tradition of communal action persisted and can be seen in the number of local associations for the preservation of law and order that were formed in the late eighteenth and early nineteenth centuries. Often they appointed their own policemen. Some were created to fight the rising tide of poaching but most dealt with a wide range of crimes. Surviving documentation, which is not plentiful, consists mainly of minute, account and rule books, and occasional references in local newspapers.[92]

Individuals took the initiative too. Apart from bringing a private suit to court, they could raise a hue and cry to enlist the support of their neighbours in the pursuit of a criminal.[93] They might also widen their enquiries by having descriptions of suspects and stolen goods 'cried' in nearby market towns. Even if these procedures indicate the community's willingness to help victims, in the last resort the latter had to do much of the work themselves. In this respect wealth had an influence on an individual's ability to bring a criminal to justice.[94] Information on private actions appears in the papers of the courts which heard the cases. Of particular value are the depositions of witnesses and suspects since they provide an account of the crime and subsequent investigation.

Similar details are included in the files of the equity courts at Westminster, to which many people in the early modern period took their complaints.[95] Each court had a certain emphasis – the Star Chamber dealt with criminal affairs, especially those that threatened the peace – but they were all involved in a variety of cases. The format of the proceedings was virtually the same in each court; statements were made by the plaintiffs and defendants, often backed up by further evidence in the form of rejoinders and replications as both sides sought to answer the points raised by the other party. The evidence of witnesses was presented, normally as answers to set questions which may also appear in the file, but perhaps as affidavits. The name, status and age of each witness is given, providing additional information which can be examined. While the material is related to the case in hand, much incidental detail is included and this greatly increases the value of the source.

Law enforcement agencies

In the Middle Ages tithingmen (also known as headboroughs and chief pledges), as the heads of tithing groups, obviously had some concern for law enforcement. By Tudor times the office had merged with that of the parish constable. Judicially, the latter could intervene in cases of misdemeanour and take charge of felons until they could be brought before a magistrate. The parish constable was also required to present people accused of various offences to the chief constable of the hundred.[96] These lists, filed among the quarter sessions papers, provide evidence on a range of offences, though some constables were more thorough than others. Constables' accounts, kept locally, should also be examined for an indication of the varied tasks they performed.

Neither the tithingman nor the constable were professionals. Often chosen from among the wealthier inhabitants of the community, they probably had little aptitude for the job and in general were less worried about their duties than with alienating their neighbours. The system was plainly inadequate and by the late eighteenth century matters had come to a head. Though lawlessness in towns was the primary focus of attention, there were problems in the countryside too, as is reflected in the formation of a number of rural private law-enforcement associations. For the country as a whole the key date is 1839, the year that an act was passed allowing magistrates, if they chose, to establish a police force in their counties. In 1856 the County and Borough Police Act compelled them to do so.[97]

From the documentation local historians can examine the process whereby these forces were established and administered. The reports of the national inspectors, deposited with the Home Office papers at the PRO, Kew, contain much local detail. In the county, material is normally to be found among the quarter sessions records since the magistrates supervised the force. In Surrey it has been filed with the county council records. Minute and order books

30 The Hampshire constabulary in the nineteenth century.

and the reports and correspondence of chief constables deal with general matters, including information on costs, i.e. the erection or modification of buildings for use as gaols and police stations, the purchase of equipment or the payment of salaries. They also contain information on individual policemen, recording those who were to be appointed, promoted, moved or dismissed, together with the reasons for the decision, if applicable.

Personal details can be filled in from examination and appointments books. We know, for instance, that Robert Cole, a 20-year-old and a native of Helion Bumpstead (Essex), was appointed to the Surrey constabulary on 25 March 1851.[98] He was 6ft 1in tall with black hair, brown eyes and a dark complexion. Originally a labourer, he had previously worked for his father in his home village. In October he was transferred from Crowhurst to Nutfield and thence to Leigh three months later. He resigned from the force in November 1853 to take up a Cambridgeshire post. His conduct was described as good, although fined for drunkenness in December 1852 and for dereliction of duty in March and August 1853. Individuals like Robert can also be looked for in the census returns, while commercial directories refer to constables and police houses too.

Crime and the courts

Villagers came under the jurisdiction of a number of courts. At the local level the manor court played an important role, especially if the lord possessed a court leet. It was this body that dealt with petty crime, involving actions worth less than a particular fixed sum of money (normally 40 shillings).[99] In practice, its business often merged with that of the court baron.[100] On some manors the lord had acquired the power of *infangentheof*, the right to hang a thief caught red-handed. If the manor did not have a leet, cases were heard at the hundred court or at the sheriff's tourn.[101] While thousands of manor court rolls survive from the Middle Ages onwards to provide details of the cases that were heard there, material for the other courts is much thinner.

The villagers also made use of the archdeaconery or consistory courts. Apart from suits of a religious and moral nature, already referred to in the text, the main categories dealt with involved matrimonial, testamentary and tithe disputes and cases of defamation and slander. Although many of the offences would not be thought of as crimes today, the documentation provides 'character' evidence for people accused of crimes in other courts. In particular, it highlights the dissolute way of life of some members of the criminal fraternity. It also reveals the local elite's intention to impose their moral standards on the poorer members of the community.

During the early modern period the work of these bodies was increasingly undertaken by the Justices of the Peace. Similar cases appear in the quarter sessions files, alongside offences of a more serious nature. Because of the pressure of work, however, misdemeanours and other minor transgressions were dealt with at the petty sessions as they developed in each county. Over time their powers grew, especially in the nineteenth century as various acts increased the number of offences which could summarily be dealt with by the magistrates.[102]

Early records are not very numerous; they were more casually kept than those of quarter sessions since they were not regarded as the property of the clerk of each division. Minute books are the most important source of information and surviving ones are generally those that have been preserved in private archives.[103] The documentation improves in the nineteenth century as business being conducted there grew. Certificates of each case were sent to the Clerk of the Peace who might enter the details into ledgers. From these books we learn of the crimes dealt with, as well as rates of conviction. For instance, of the 150 cases heard at the petty sessions held at Henley (Oxfordshire) in 1880, poaching constituted the biggest single category, followed by assault, petty theft and drunkenness.[104]

Offences beyond the competence of these courts were generally heard at the general eyres (during the Middle Ages), or at the assizes or quarter sessions. References to murders also appear in the coroners' inquests. Although the eyres had a limited life span,[105] the other courts operated for centuries. Apart from the coroners' court, all had civil as well as criminal jurisdiction, so the material is rather mixed. Many property disputes were heard at the eyres, while economic and social offences, as well as administrative affairs, were dealt with at the quarter sessions and assizes.

For the early modern period the records of the quarter sessions and assizes

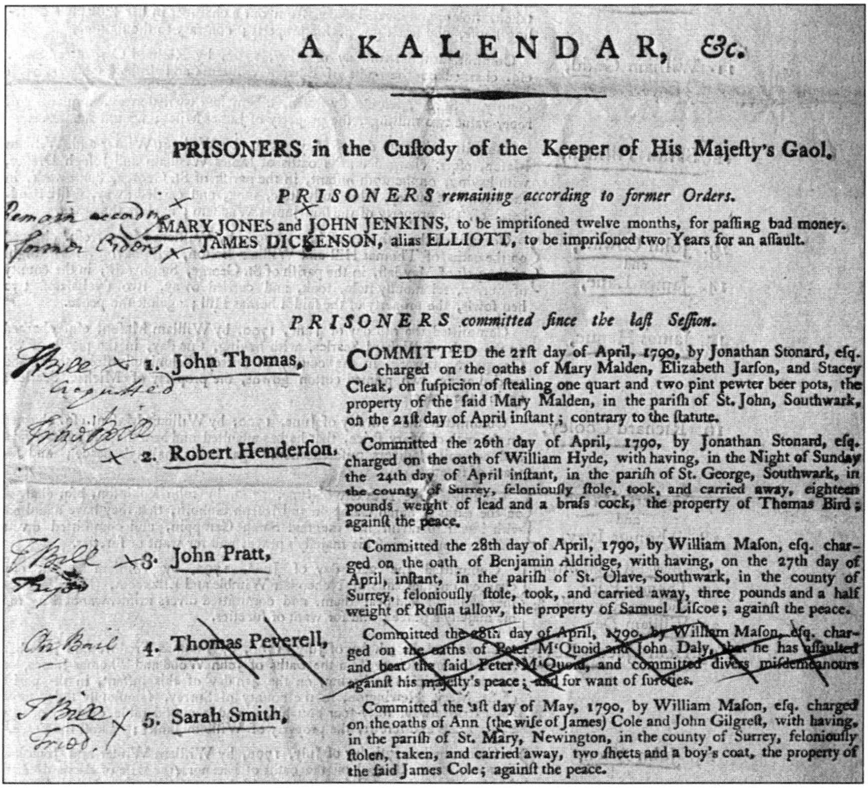

A KALENDAR, &c.

PRISONERS in the Cuſtody of the Keeper of His Majeſty's Gaol.

PRISONERS remaining according to former Orders.

MARY JONES and JOHN JENKINS, to be impriſoned twelve months, for paſſing bad money.
JAMES DICKENSON, alias ELLIOTT, to be impriſoned two Years for an aſſault.

PRISONERS committed ſince the laſt Seſſion.

1. John Thomas, — COMMITTED the 21ſt day of April, 1790, by Jonathan Stonard, eſq. charged on the oaths of Mary Malden, Elizabeth Jarſon, and Stacey Cleak, on ſuſpicion of ſtealing one quart and two pint pewter beer pots, the property of the ſaid Mary Malden, in the pariſh of St. John, Southwark, on the 21ſt day of April inſtant; contrary to the ſtatute.

2. Robert Henderſon, — Committed the 26th day of April, 1790, by Jonathan Stonard, eſq. charged on the oath of William Hyde, with having, in the Night of Sunday the 24th day of April inſtant, in the pariſh of St. George, Southwark, in the county of Surrey, feloniouſly ſtole, took, and carried away, eighteen pounds weight of lead and a braſs cock, the property of Thomas Bird; againſt the peace.

3. John Pratt, — Committed the 28th day of April, 1790, by William Maſon, eſq. charged on the oath of Benjamin Aldridge, with having, on the 27th day of April, inſtant, in the pariſh of St. Olave, Southwark, in the county of Surrey, feloniouſly ſtole, took, and carried away, three pounds and a half weight of Ruſſia tallow, the property of Samuel Liſcoe; againſt the peace.

4. Thomas Peverell, — Committed the 28th day of April, 1790, by William Maſon, eſq. charged on the oaths of Peter M'Quoid and John Daly, that he has aſſaulted and beat the ſaid Peter M'Quoid, and committed divers miſdemeanours againſt his majeſty's peace; and for want of ſureties.

5. Sarah Smith, — Committed the 1ſt day of May, 1790, by William Maſon, eſq. charged on the oaths of Ann (the wife of James) Cole and John Gilgreſt, with having, in the pariſh of St. Mary, Newington, in the county of Surrey, feloniouſly ſtolen, taken, and carried away, two ſheets and a boy's coat, the property of the ſaid James Cole; againſt the peace.

31 Calendar of prisoners in the county gaol: Surrey Quarter Sessions, Midsummer 1790.

become more numerous and easier to use (and more extensive in scope). Decisions made by the magistrates are recorded in the quarter sessions' order books and cover a number of themes. Sets of files include indictments – and presentments in the case of the quarter sessions – which list the charges and form the basis of the action to be taken. There are also recognizances, binding defendants and witnesses to appear at the court. In criminal cases the indictments give personal details of the accused: his or her name, occupation and residence. Gaol calendars provide similar material, as well as data on the crimes committed, verdicts and sentences.

In the nineteenth century county police force records provide additional information. These include charge report books and constables' order books, giving details of individual crimes and the persons involved. The annual reports made by the chief constables to the quarter sessions contain abstracts of the crimes, together with a commentary on the figures. Even better are the accompanying returns; those drawn up by the chief constable of Surrey in the mid-nineteenth century show the number of people taken into custody in each month, the nature of the offences with which they were charged and the outcome of the case. They also indicate the age, sex and place of residence of the suspects. Data from the counties is also printed in the returns and reports that appear among the parliamentary papers, which should be consulted for local material. Evidence of criminal activity, especially if of a sensationalist nature – a large-scale riot, a wave of poaching or a murder – can also be found in local newspapers.

There was considerable overlap between the assizes and quarter sessions but by convention judges of assize dealt with capital offences. Thus, assaults were heard at the quarter sessions and murder and rape at the assizes.[106] Similarly, magistrates dealt with cases of petty larceny, that is, the theft of goods worth less than one shilling, while the assize judges tried offenders accused of grand larceny, robbery and burglary. A study of the court records reveals that the general pattern of crime in the countryside was similar to that found in the towns, even if the content often differed. Indictments for theft in one form or another invariably outnumber any other offence, often a long way ahead of cases of assault. Contemporaries, nonetheless, did sense an undercurrent of violence, especially in periods of depression when social relationships were more strained than usual. As at the time of the 'Captain Swing' riots of the early 1830s, this might take the form of assault, intimidation, incendiarism or animal maiming.[107] The continuing concern about vagrants is reflected in the number of settlement cases, as well as in the prosecution of people 'with no fixed abode'.

The attack on customary practices, as property rights were redefined in the post-Restoration period, affected the urban as well as the rural population.[108] In the countryside it meant taking action against people engaging in traditional customs such as gleaning and collecting firewood. A similar attitude was taken to the catching of wild animals, even on commons and waste lands. In 1671 the Game Act was passed which in effect restricted the hunting of game to the propertied classes. The village community not only saw these measures as an attack on their customary practices but also as an affront to natural justice. As a result, people accused of such crimes enjoyed a considerable amount of public support and were not regarded as criminals but as upholders of traditional rights. In coastal districts smugglers were often treated in the same way. Court records, however, reveal a more complex picture; apart from the activities of individual villagers merely providing for their own family, gangs were regularly involved.

The documentation ought to enable local historians to analyse the types of crime committed in their localities at different times and the sort of people involved. The relationship between crime and economic conditions, for instance, is an important issue and one which requires occupational data, as

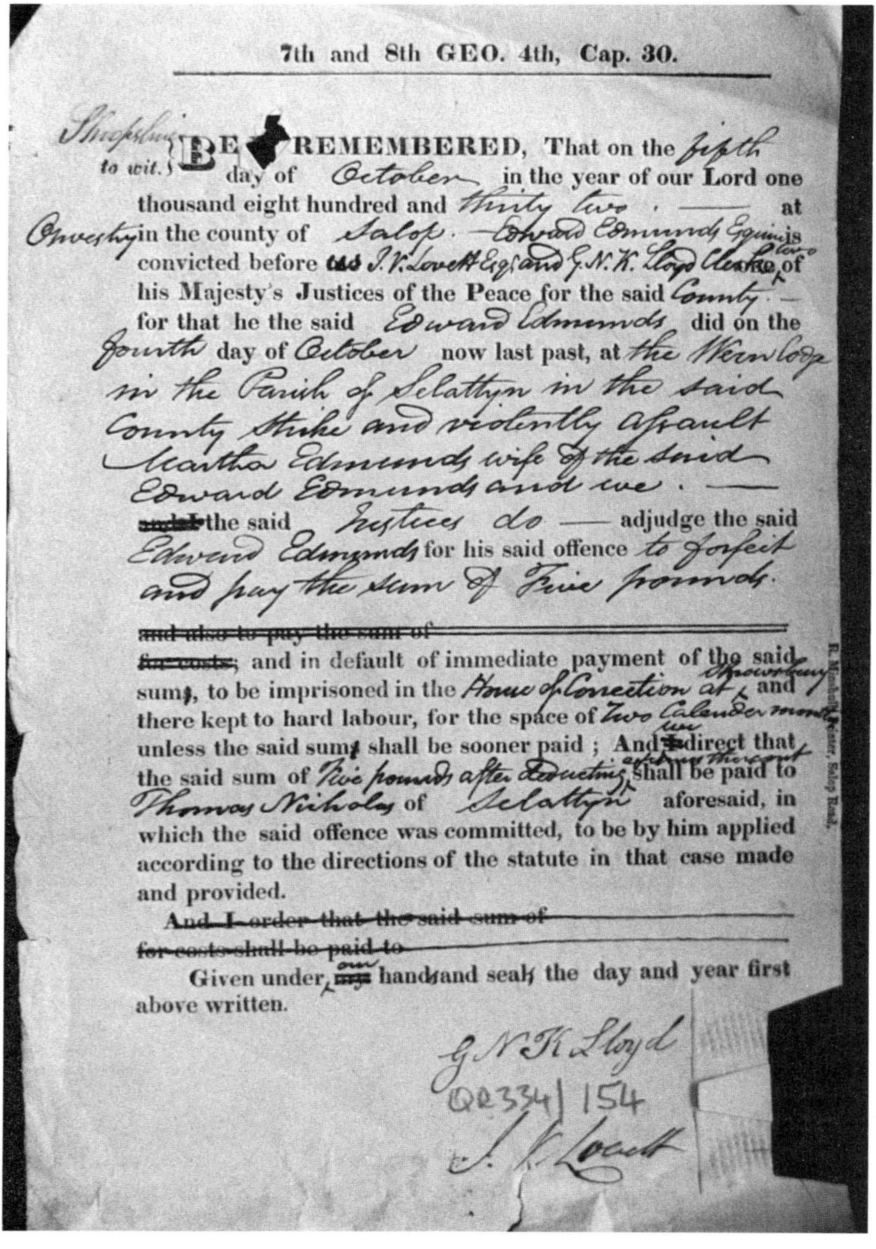

7th and 8th GEO. 4th, Cap. 30.

Shropshire to wit. } BE REMEMBERED, That on the fifth day of October in the year of our Lord one thousand eight hundred and thirty two . —— at Oswestry in the county of Salop. Edward Edmunds Esquire is convicted before ~~us~~ J. V. Lovett Esq and G. N. K. Lloyd Clerke two of his Majesty's Justices of the Peace for the said County. — for that he the said Edward Edmunds did on the fourth day of October now last past, at the Wern Lodge in the Parish of Selattyn in the said County Strike and violently assault Martha Edmunds wife of the said Edward Edmunds and we. ——

~~and I~~ the said Justices do —— adjudge the said Edward Edmunds for his said offence to forfeit and pay the sum of Five pounds.

~~and also to pay the sum of~~

~~for costs;~~ and in default of immediate payment of the said sum, to be imprisoned in the House of Correction at Shrewsbury and there kept to hard labour, for the space of two Calendar months unless the said sum shall be sooner paid; And we direct that the said sum of Five pounds after deducting all charges thereout shall be paid to Thomas Nicholas of Selattyn aforesaid, in which the said offence was committed, to be by him applied according to the directions of the statute in that case made and provided.

~~And I order that the said sum of~~

~~for costs shall be paid to~~

Given under our hands and seals the day and year first above written.

G N K Lloyd

QR334/154

J. V. Lovett

R. Mitchell, Printer, Salop Road.

32 Edward Edmunds is convicted of assault at the Shropshire Quarter Sessions on 5 October 1832.

well as information on criminal activity. Quarter sessions and assize records do in fact show that there was a positive connection and that instances of theft increased at such times. They reveal too that the poorer classes, the ones most affected, were closely involved.

Readers should still treat the evidence with care. Apart from gaps in the record, much crime went undetected, even after the creation of professional forces. One reason for this was inter-force rivalry and this was a subject which the chief constable of Surrey touched on in his report in 1855.[109] Other problems exist. A sudden rise in prosecutions, for instance, might reflect the onset of a crime wave but it might equally refer to the adoption of a 'get tough' policy or the appearance of a more zealous official. Even if taken to court, many suits, notably felonies, were thrown out. Because capital crimes included many trivial offences, grand juries were often reluctant to present or trial juries to convict. They might also reduce a charge from grand to petty larceny; in indictments the value of goods stolen was often given as just under a shilling, even if the true cost was obviously greater than this.

The occupational labels are also suspect, as are the details of residence. Individuals charged in different cases were often given different jobs and addresses.[110] Moreover, a significant proportion of the crimes, especially thefts, were committed by vagrants but as this was a proscribed 'occupation', it does not appear in the record. In this respect, the depositions of suspects and witnesses are much more accurate.

Summary

Although a number of documents can be used to examine the various aspects of social life of the peasantry discussed in this chapter, they do not tell the whole story. Theirs was largely an oral tradition, in which customs and beliefs were handed down from one generation to the next by word of mouth. Hence the importance given to the views of older members of the community – people who could speak from experience of long-established customs and practices. Depositions in legal documents invariably give the ages of the witnesses and greater respect was accorded to those whose memory of the points at issue went back many years. While we can often look at the formal actions and affiliations of individuals, we can rarely discover the reasoning behind their actions or find out what they were really thinking. Diaries, letters and memoranda books remained the preserve of the upper classes until well into the nineteenth century, although some were being written by larger farmers at an earlier date. Oral evidence allows us to reach back into the late nineteenth century and so gain a first-hand account of life conducted at a different pace to our own. Unfortunately, such reminiscences often record events and customs that had already undergone considerable modification and to retrieve an even earlier world we need to look at the documents.

CHAPTER SIX

Family and neighbourhood

From time immemorial the family has formed the basic unit of social organization in England and as such has exerted a considerable influence on its members. Although upper-class children were often reared by others and then sent away to school or to the home of someone else, most youngsters spent their formative years within the family circle. There, they learned certain habits and modes of conduct, essential for living harmoniously within a community. In earlier centuries, moreover, the influence of the family was stronger than it is today. Apart from their immediate relatives, individuals had readier access to a network of kinfolk in general. The family was much more important as an economic unit too. Such considerations make it essential for us to discern the structure of the historic family and its links with the wider world. Similarly, basic features of family life – birth, marriage and death – must be looked at, as well as other important themes such as child rearing, the daily household routines and inheritance customs.

Vital events

The Middle Ages

For the Middle Ages manor court rolls are the most informative source and a number of studies of medieval communities have been based upon them. As an indication of what can be done, Dr Z. Razi's book, *Life, Marriage and Death in a Medieval Parish: Economy, Society and Demography in Halesowen 1270–1400*, should be consulted. Dr Razi contends that the range of business heard at the court was so wide that most inhabitants appeared there at some time or another and this makes the source a very representative one. In the context of the family the main value of the rolls lies in the amount of personal information they contain. Because many of the social and economic activities on the manor were centred on the family, kinship links and relationships can often be studied.

To organize the material effectively each reference to a person should be put on a separate slip of paper. The total number of entries will often run into thousands, but once completed the piles of slips can be shuffled about in various ways and the information on individuals entered on to composite forms. This process, similar to later family reconstitution exercises involving parish registers, is laborious but it does ensure that the subjects' activities can be examined in the round and their links with others established. The time needed to sort out the information can be shortened if the material is put on to a computer.

Unfortunately, young children are poorly covered in medieval records and this affects the analysis of important aspects of family life such as fertility rates and size of family. Few references to them occur in manor court rolls since, as dependants of their father or guardian, they had little scope for individual initiative. Many died before they reached their teens, a time when youngsters began to play a more active part in communal life. At the age of 12, for instance, boys entered a tithing group.[1] As a result, the names of adolescents appear more regularly in the rolls. The poll tax returns of 1377–81 also list adolescent taxpayers, even if they are under-represented there. Young women, in particular, are conspicuous by their absence.[2]

Wills, on the other hand, do include references to children of all ages. Of course, one cannot be certain that everyone was listed or named individually, and older children, as heirs or administrators, were more likely to be mentioned than their younger siblings. When Ranold Burner of Leatherhead (Surrey) made his will in October 1485 he bequeathed 'to evere on of my chylder xx^{s}', but only John, as one of his executors (the other being his wife), was specifically named.[3] Because the will-making sector of the community was a somewhat selective group, estimates of family size based on this source are not necessarily true for all classes.

Manor court rolls reveal that young people from various social groups were actively involved in the land market, either on their own initiative or with their family's support.[4] Although often too small to support a family, their acquisitions did enable them to contemplate marriage before their parents' death. Such considerations seem to have affected the age at marriage. To work this out is a somewhat complicated business involving certain assumptions, especially that there existed a close connection between the acquisition of land and marriage. At Halesowen Dr Razi calculated that in the early fourteenth century men married between the ages of 18 and 22. In the more favourable climate of the late fourteenth century the age was even lower.[5]

Examples like this suggest that England in the Middle Ages did not conform to the typical north-west European pattern of marriage, characterized by late weddings and a high proportion of celibates.[6] Some historians have not been convinced by the evidence, criticizing the methodology, the number of people affected and, indeed, the typicality of Halesowen.[7] The poll tax returns of 1377–81, because they record both married and unmarried people, can provide a check but they are inconsistent on this point: some indicate a high age at marriage and numerous bachelors, while others suggest the opposite.[8] In fact, many young people could only attain an independent position after a number of years. Apprentices had to serve their time and establish themselves in a trade. It took servants even longer to acquire a little capital with which to set up home and, if women, to augment their dowry and perhaps pay their *merchet* (marriage) fine to the lord.[9]

Eventually, one of the partners died. More often than not it was the husband, though the dependent position of married women had the effect of masking the prior deaths of wives. They did not leave wills or do much business in court independently of their husband. The death of a tenant was reported to the manor court and from the rolls the date, and therefore an indication of the deceased's age and the duration of the marriage, can be obtained. The deceased's *heriot* (death duty), normally the best beast or good, was also noted.

The customs governing the transmission of the deceased's personal and real estate to the heir (or heirs) varied both regionally and according to the manner in which property was held. Freehold land tended to devolve to the eldest son (primogeniture), although in some areas, notably in East Anglia and Kent, it was split up among all the sons (partible inheritance). A large proportion of unfree property was subject to partible inheritance, but the practice of Borough English, inheritance by the youngest son, was widespread and this increased the amount of land descending to a single son. If there were no sons, custom generally dictated that all the daughters inherited equally.[10] Changes in the system were possible: at Bookham (Surrey) in 1339 the manor court rolls record that the tenants successfully petitioned their lord, the Abbot of Chertsey, to end the custom of Borough English and replace it by primogeniture.[11]

The custom on a particular manor can readily be seen by examining the way in which property passed from one generation to the next. Manor court entries record the deaths of tenants, the naming of the heir or heirs and the admission of the latter to the property. The rolls might also contain memoranda describing the manor's customs, though these are more generally to be found in separate custumals or in surveys and extents. Many wills show the system in operation, as testators disposed of their estate in accordance with local custom.

Testators also settled goods and property in a manner different from the one ordained by local custom. During their lifetime they used the manor court to make a variety of arrangements, each designed to meet the needs of the family at a particular time.[12] At the end of their life they could exercise discretion over the disposal of their estate by making a will. Wills also provide valuable evidence of the means adopted by the peasantry to provide for their non-inheriting children. Some obtained parcels of land but mostly they received money, animals or goods. To ensure that the heir fulfilled his

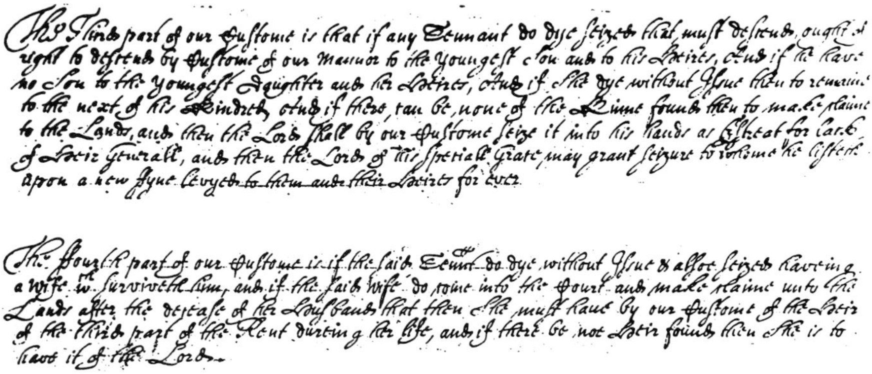
The third part of our Custome is that if any Tennant do dye seized that must descend, ought of right to descend by Custome of our Mannor to the youngest sonne and to his heires, and if he have no sonne to the youngest daughter and her heires, and if shee dye without issue then to remaine to the next of his kindred, and if there can be none of the same found then to make claime to the Lands, and then the Lord shall by our Custome seize it into his hands as escheat for lack of heir generall, and then the Lord of his speciall grace may grant seizure to whome he listeth upon a new fyne levyed to them and their heires for ever.

The fourth part of our Custome is if the said Tennant do dye without issue & allso seized having a wife which surviveth him, and if the said wife do come into the Court and make claime unto the Lands after the decease of her husband that then shee must have by our Custome of the heir the third part of the Rent during her life, and if there be not heir found then shee is to have it of the Lord.

33 Extract from a seventeenth-century custumal of the manor of Ham (Surrey) showing inheritance customs.

obligations to his brothers and sisters, the testator often added a rider to the effect that if he refused to do so, he would forfeit the estate.[13]

Special arrangements were made for the widow. By law, they were allowed one-third of the property as their dower and this overrode the claims of the heir. Manorial custom was often more generous to them: in some places in the West Midlands they were given the whole tenement for life.[14] Although this made them attractive to suitors, widows had to weigh up the benefits to be gained from remarriage against the cost of renewed dependency. Women, on becoming widows, regained their freedom of action and began once more to play an independent role in the community.[15] This is reflected in the increasing number of references to them in the manor court rolls.

The early modern period

A good deal of information can be obtained from manor court rolls but they are difficult to handle and interpret, and many local historians avoid them. They are also put off by the dubious arithmetic involved. Even those who do examine them will invariably turn with relief to the parish registers which, beginning in 1538, provide a more manageable source of information. Because the evidence is presented in a more straightforward way, family reconstitution exercises based upon them are likely to be more comprehensive and accurate, especially if augmented by material from manor court rolls and other sources such as parish and probate records. Much depends upon the quality of the registers used.

Amongst the topics that can be looked at are details concerning marriage practices: the age of the partners on their wedding day, the length of marriage, the likelihood of remarriage after the death of a spouse, and even the proportion of the population who never married. Such factors had an obvious bearing upon the fertility rate; the earlier a woman married (provided death did not intervene before menopause) the more children she was likely to bear. The stagnation of the population in the late seventeenth and early eighteenth centuries, in fact, has been partly ascribed to a rise in the age of women at first marriage.[16]

Specific information on children, especially pre-adolescents, adds to our understanding of this facet of family life. We can calculate such variables as the incidence of illegitimacy, the number of pre-nuptial conceptions, the timing of the first child and the age gaps between siblings. Of particular importance to demographers is the level of infant and child mortality, which can be assessed from baptismal and burial entries. In the early modern period one child in five or six died before the age of one, often in the first few days, and a further 10 per cent never attained the age of 10.[17]

The high level of child mortality adversely affected the general expectancy of life. Once past the dangerous early years, the individual's chances of survival improved. Adults reaching the age of 30 could expect to live until their late fifties, accidents and epidemics notwithstanding.[18] Some people lived much longer. According to the register, Margaret Brook of Albrighton (Shropshire) was '115 and odde' when she was buried on 1 November 1641.[19] Nonetheless, a large number of people died in their prime. This meant that fewer people than today lived to see their grandchildren, while many children lost one or both of their parents before they had grown up. It also made remarriage commonplace – in the seventeenth century one-quarter of the people marrying had done so at least once before.[20]

An analysis of the registers helps us not only to discern fluctuations in population levels but also to account for it. The debate surrounding population growth in the late eighteenth and early nineteenth centuries, for instance, can only be resolved by the multiplication of local studies in which the vital events of the community are carefully examined. Some demographers have attributed the rise to a fall in the mortality rate brought about by such factors as advances in medicine and hygiene, the lower morbidity of certain infectious diseases and better nutrition. Others have put it down to a rising birth rate, the outcome of a general lowering of the age of women at marriage. Improved economic prospects, it is said, encouraged early marriage and with it an increase in fertility.[21] Modern research, involving a close scrutiny of parochial records such as parish registers, vestry minutes and the accounts of the overseers of the poor, has also refuted the idea widely held by contemporaries, that population growth was an inevitable consequence of poor law relief, especially the operation of the so-called Speenhamland system.[22] In this scheme, the amount given varied according to the price of bread and the number of children in a pauper's family.

Certain points have to be borne in mind when examining registers, so that allowances can be made for them. All calculations of age, for instance, are based upon the close relationship between the date of baptism with that of birth. The high mortality rate of new-born babies did, in fact, promote speedy baptism. At Great Bookham (Surrey), where both births and baptisms were recorded in the registers at the turn of the seventeenth century, the median difference in days was nine, with a range of nought to 92.[23] Unfortunately, there were some late registrations. One entry in the Bulkington (Warwickshire) register notes: '25 Jan. 1771 Mary daugher of Elias and Mary Goodyer was baptized being about 2 years & half old.'[24] It should be remembered too that Baptists did not believe in infant baptism and that Anabaptists were against the sacrament itself.

As long as the people recorded in the registers formed a representative sample of the community, omissions do not affect the validity of statistics concerning age. The two relevant entries, correctly dated, are all that is needed. Defects in the record, on the other hand, can seriously impair the quality of the data on such matters as birth, death and marriage rates. Even the best sets of registers have gaps. Sixteenth-century material is especially thin, notably for the years before 1558, while in the Commonwealth period registration was particularly haphazard. Indeed, when in the years 1653–60 marriage became a civil ceremony, the clergy not only lost the right to officiate but also custody of the registers.[25] At Fetcham (Surrey) a later incumbent noted in the register that it had been 'very defective especially during the unnatural rebellion begun in 1641 till the happy restoration of our

34 The children of Henry Slyfield esq. of Slyfield Hall, Great Bookham: a brass in the Slyfield chapel in the parish church.

Sacred Liberties in the year 1660.'[26] The growth of nonconformity also had an effect, although, as noted above, for some time the problem was not a serious one as the old dissenting sects (apart from the Quakers) tended to make use of the Anglican baptism, marriage and burial services. The rise of Methodism in the late eighteenth century had a greater impact.

Baptismal records are the ones most likely to be incomplete. Infants born dead or who only survived a short time were not always registered, neither were the ones who were baptised privately. More commonly, couples moved from one parish to another and had their children baptised in more than one place. It is worthwhile, therefore, to examine the registers of neighbouring parishes.

Manor court rolls and probate wills should also be searched for the names of other children. Wills are a particularly useful source. As before, they give names and reveal details of family relationships, as well as recording inheritance customs and the measures taken by villagers to provide for their family. Parish records provide additional evidence. In particular, references to the children of poor families regularly appear in sources like overseers' of the poor accounts, parish apprenticeship papers and settlement examinations.

The correct identification of an individual is a problem that can be encountered when looking at any entry, whether of a baptism, a marriage or a burial. This is rendered more difficult by the common practice of naming children after their parents. One has to decide, for example, if an entry in the baptismal register refers to yet another child of Joe Bloggs senior, or to the first one of his newly married son, Joe junior. The name of the wife, if given, often determines the point, as does the use of the appellations 'senior' and 'junior'. More difficult to resolve are the burial entries; people with the same name and belonging to the same family did not always conveniently die in order of seniority. The obvious person is not always the correct one!

Not all marriages are easy to find either. Although people marrying by bann could use the parish church of either partner, it was customary for the ceremony to take place in that of the bride. As many husbands found their spouse outside their own community, evidence for their wedding will often have to be looked for elsewhere. Studies of the social horizons of villagers in early modern England suggest an area with a radius of 10 miles, the typical catchment area of the local market town. At Terling (Essex) in the years 1525–1700 four-fifths of marriage partners lived within 10 miles of each other and only one in eight more than 14 miles away.[28] There were variations: the gentry, for instance, developed a far wider network of social and economic contacts and often looked upon the county as their focus of attention.

The search is further complicated by marriages authorized by licence since they did not have to be celebrated in the parish church of one or other of the partners. They are often recorded as such in the registers and from the evidence it appears that some parishes were popular venues for such unions. At Donington (Shropshire) more than three out of every five couples married

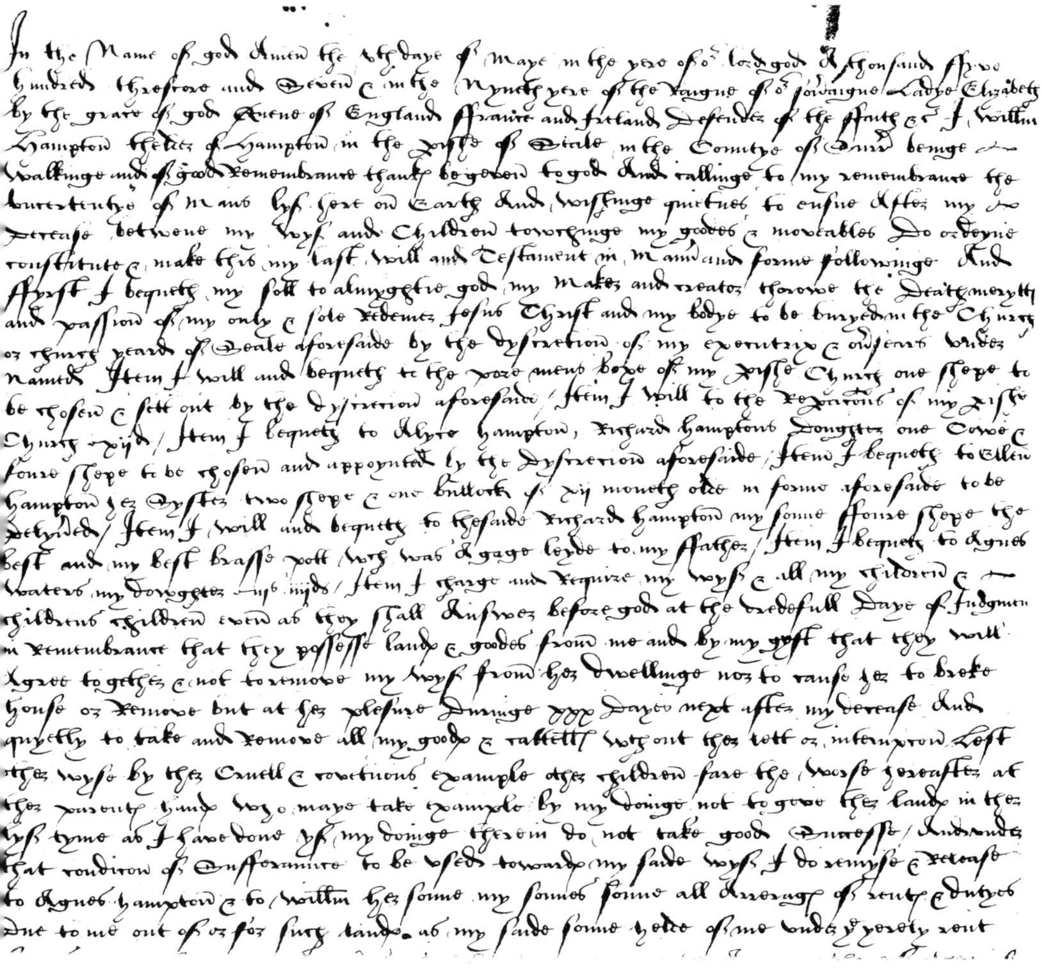

In the Name of god Amen the vth daye of Maye in the yere of o[ur] lord god A thousand fyve
hundred threscore and seven & in the Nynth yere of the raygne of o[ur] sov[er]aigne Ladye Elizabeth
by the grace of god Quene of England fraunce and Ireland defender of the faythe &c I Willm
Hampton the elder of Hampton in the p[ar]ishe of Seale in the Countye of Surr' beinge
walkinge and of good remembraunce thankes be geven to god And callinge to my remembraunce the
uncerteintye of mans lyfe here on Earth And wysshinge quietnes to ensue After my
decease betwene my wyfe and Children towchinge my goodes & moveables Do ordeyne
constitute & make this my last will and Testament in manner and forme followinge And
ffyrst I bequeth my soll to almyghtie god my maker and creator thorowe the deathe merytt
and passion of my only & sole redemer Jesus Chryst and my bodye to be buryed in the Church
or churche yearde of Seale aforesaide by the dyscretion of my executrix & overseers under
named Item I will and bequeth to the pore mens boxe of my p[ar]ishe Church one shepe to
be chosen & sett out by the dyscretion aforesaide Item I will to the reparacons of my p[ar]ishe
Church xijd Item I bequeth to Alyce Hampton Richard Hamptons Doughter one Cowe &
foure shepe to be chosen and appoynted by the dyscretion aforesaide Item I bequeth to Ellen
Hampton her syster two shepe & one bullock of xij monethes olde in forme aforesaide to be
delyvered Item I will and bequeth to thesaide Richard Hampton my sonne foure shepe the
best and my best brasse pott which was a gage leyde to my ffather Item I bequeth to Agnes
waters my Doughter vjs viijd Item I charge and require my wyfe & all my children &
childrens children even as they shall Answer before god at the dredefull Daye of Judgment
in remembraunce that they possesse landes & goodes from me and by my gyft that they will
Agree together & not to remove my wyfe from her dwellinge nor to cause her to breke
house or remove but at her pleasure duringe xxx dayes next after my decease And
quyetly to take and remove all my goodes & cattell without ther lett or interupcon Lest
ther wyfe by ther Cruell & contentious example ther children fare the worse hereafter at
ther parentes handes who maye take example by my doinge not to geve ther landes in ther
lyfe tyme as I have done yf my doinge therein do not take good successe And under
that condicon of sufferaunce to be used towardes my saide wyfe I do remyse & release
to Agnes Hampton & to Willm her sonne my sonnes sonne all Arrerages of rentes & dutyes
due to me out of or for suche landes as my saide sonne holde of me under the yerely rent

35 William Hampton the elder of the parish of Seale (Surrey) makes his will, 5 May 1567. There is a profession of faith in the preamble and he expresses his concern that his children will look after his wife afer his death.

there in the period 1660–1750 did so by licence.[29] Even more complicated are the clandestine marriages, which, if frowned upon by the authorities, were not illegal. Because of their irregular nature, many cases came before the church courts, especially after the Restoration. They were finally outlawed by Lord Hardwicke's Marriage Act of 1753. Henceforth, all marriages, except those of Jews and Quakers, had to take place in the parish church.[30]

In 1694 an act was passed which could have provided a wealth of statistical information on the inhabitants of every community in the country. Passed as a wartime measure, the act imposed a tax on births, marriages and deaths (on a sliding scale, according to status) and an annual due on bachelors over 25 years old and childless widowers. Only paupers were exempt. So that the tax could be administered effectively a census was taken to ascertain the size and structure of the population and thereby the numbers liable to be charged. The measure only ran for five years but in that time two copies of the lists were made in every parish each year, one to be retained by the incumbent and the other to be sent to the Exchequer. They have virtually all disappeared. The tax was very unpopular and many of the documents held locally have probably been destroyed. The Exchequer copies await discovery.[31]

The modern period

Under the impetus of the act some ministers may have become more conscientious in the keeping of their registers, but, if made, their attempts probably lapsed when the act was repealed. Over time, however, one or two reforms were brought in. In particular, the record of marriages improved as a result of the act of 1753. The banning of clandestine marriages ended one cause of under-recording, while the new registers had spaces in which the residences of the bride and groom could be entered, as well as their previous marital status. The registers of baptisms and burials were similarly modernized as a result of George Rose's act of 1812.[32] They include details of occupations and thereby help researchers to analyse the data in terms of social class. The new burial registers also had a space in which the age of the deceased could be written, thereby facilitating the study of life expectancy and mortality rates.

Such measures did little to remedy the defects of the registers as nonconformist and other sects asserted their independence, holding their own ceremonies and recording the vital events in separate registers. In 1837 the problem was largely overcome with the introduction of civil registration and with it a consolidated record of *all* births, marriages and deaths. As births and deaths rather than baptisms and burials were noted, it is an easier task to work out fertility and mortality rates. Of course, if a comparison is to be made with an earlier period an adjustment has to be made to convert baptisms into births. Marriage certificates should indicate the age of the bride and groom as this was asked for on the form. Unfortunately, many entries merely note that the parties were 'of full age'.

At the same time further details can be obtained from the national census returns of 1841 onwards. Although the ages of everyone over 15 are rounded down in five year steps in the 1841 returns, subsequent censuses give precise ages. This makes it possible to work out an accurate age profile for the whole parish and not merely that part of it which can be reconstituted from the registers. In turn, this information sheds light on other aspects of family life,

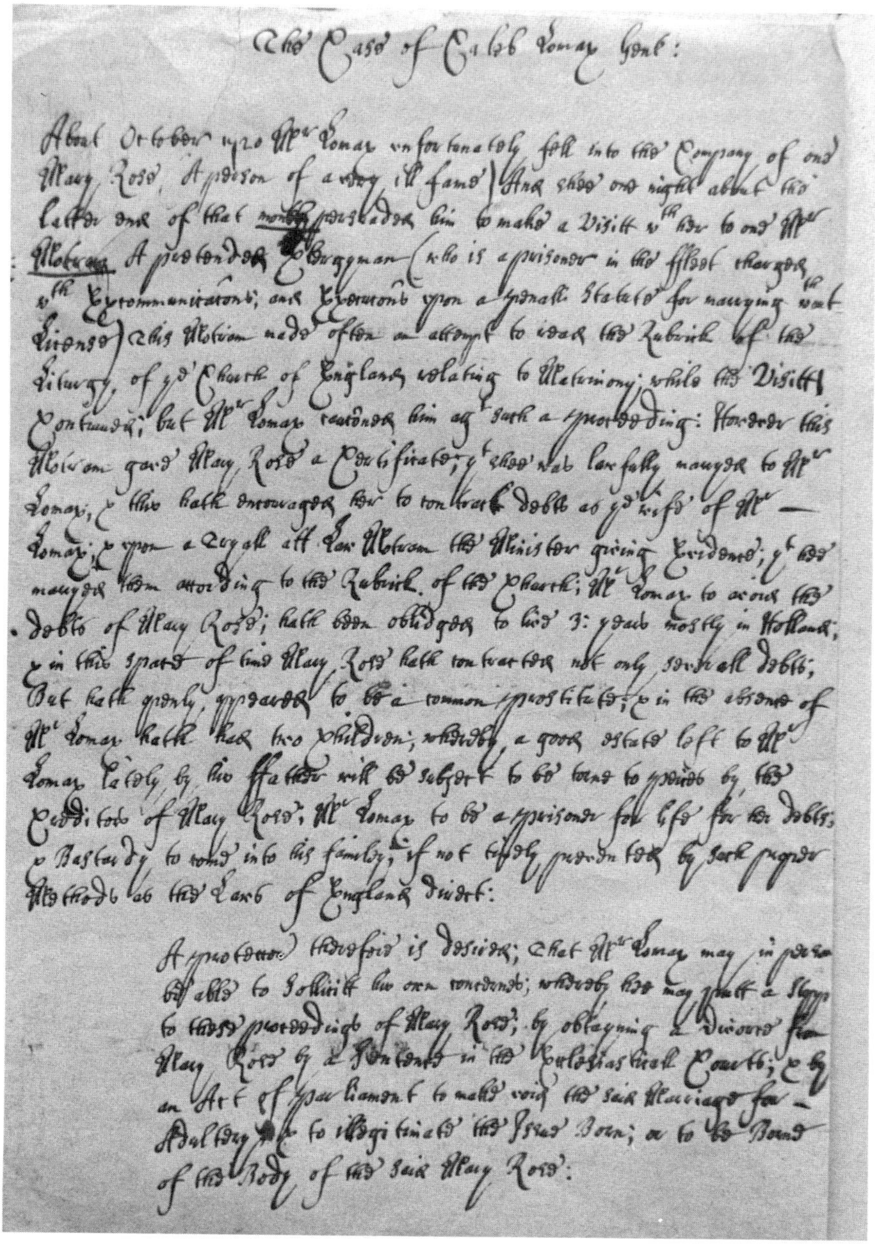

The Case of Caleb Lomax Gent:

About October 1720 Mr Lomax unfortunately fell into the Company of one Mary Rose, A person of a very ill fame) And shee one night about the latter end of that month perswaded him to make a Visitt wth her to one Mr Mokram A pretended Clergyman (who is a prisoner in the ffleet charged wth Excommunications; and Executions upon a penall Statute for marrying wthout Licenses) This Mokram made often an attempt to read the Rubrick of the Liturgy, of ye Church of England relating to Matrimony; while the Visitt Continued; but Mr Lomax restrained him agt such a proceeding: However this Mokram gave Mary Rose a Certificate; yt shee was lawfully marryed to Mr Lomax; & this hath encouraged her to contract debts as ye wife of Mr Lomax; & upon a Tryall att Law Mokram the Minister giving Evidence; yt hee marryed them according to the Rubrick of the Church; Mr Lomax to avoid the debts of Mary Rose; hath been obliged to live 3: years mostly in Holland; & in this space of time Mary Rose hath contracted not only severall debts; But hath openly appeared to be a common prostitute; & in the absence of Mr Lomax hath had two Children; whereby a good estate left to Mr Lomax lately by his ffather will be subject to be lost to provide by the Creditors of Mary Rose; Mr Lomax to be a prisoner for life for her debts; & Bastardy to come into his family; if not speedily prevented by such proper Methods as the Laws of England direct:

A proceeding therefore is desired; That Mr Lomax may in person be able to Sollicitt his own concernes; whereby hee may putt a Stopp to these proceedings of Mary Rose; by obtayning a Divorce from Mary Rose by a Sentence in the Ecclesiasticall Courts; & by an Act of parliament to make void the said Marriage for Adultery & to illegitimate the Issue Born; or to be Barred of the Body of the said Mary Rose:

36 The consequences of a clandestine marriage: the sad case of Caleb Lomax, gent., 1720.

notably on the birth, marriage and death rates. Because occupations are recorded, all conclusions can be related to social class.

The censuses also give lists of children, unlike the registers and certificates which only reveal their secrets after a search. When analysed with the age data, local historians can examine such topics as the size of families and the spacing of siblings, as well as the incidence of illegitimacy and pre-nuptial pregnancy. They can also calculate the child-bearing span of women. Censuses do have certain limitations, however. They only offer a view of a community at a single moment in time and to obtain a more dynamic picture it is necessary to study a series of returns. Moreover, they do not record the children who had left home or died, or even those absent on the census night. One therefore still has to look through the registers and certificates.

Family and inheritance

The Middle Ages

The typical English family has long been nuclear rather than extended in form. Examples of multi-generational, extended families can be found – grandparents boarding with married children or collateral relatives living in – but these are not very numerous. Only on the Scottish and Welsh borders where family composition was influenced by Celtic practices, was there an appreciable divergence from the norm. It should be borne in mind, however, that the documentation tends to be weighted in favour of nuclear families. Because life expectancy was much lower in pre-industrial England, even after the critical period of childhood, many parents did not live long enough to see their grandchildren and therefore have the opportunity to belong to an extended family.

The clearest evidence for the prevalence of nuclear families in the country from the medieval period onwards can be obtained from local censuses. For the Middle Ages we have to rely upon the occasional lists of serfs entered into manor court rolls. They tend to date from the mid-fourteenth and fifteenth centuries because, as the institution of serfdom declined, some lords decided to record the number of bond families they had at their disposal.[33] They show that even in a county like Lincolnshire where partible inheritance was practised, a system conducive to the formation of joint-family households, the peasantry typically lived in small nuclear families.[34] Local historians should not expect to find such a list in their own manor court rolls but they do at least provide a general indication of family organization against which other sources of information can be tested.

Firstly, manor court rolls can be used to good effect. In particular, family reconstitution exercises, by drawing together all references to individuals, reveal the ways in which people interacted with one another and give an indication of their personal circumstances. Numerous entries show parents of married couples maintaining an independent existence, that is, they were living in their own homes and continuing to work and do business through the manor court. They may have divested themselves of some of their land, surrendering it to the use of their son or letting it out on short-term leases, but this was often due to failing strength and fewer financial needs. Similarly, the rolls do not suggest that brothers holding joint tenancies lived in the same house.[35]

Of the other records, wills provide complementary evidence. There, the overwhelming emphasis of the bequests is on separate provision for the heir or heirs and other dependants. Even if the property was inherited by a single heir, there was little sign that he should permanently share the house with his brothers and sisters. Widows, too, were provided with the means to look after themselves. Poll tax returns of 1379 and 1381 also show that the standard family unit comprised parents and children.[36] Where grandparents or adult siblings can be identified as such from other sources, they generally appear in the lists separately as taxpayers in their own households. The pre-1334 lay subsidies provide similar evidence. Valuable material can also be found in the coroners' inquests, notably in those cases where death occurred in the home.[37]

The fact that custom favoured nuclear families did not make it the sole form of domestic organization. Orphaned children were taken in by relatives, while some adult children continued to live with their parents. When Thomas Wilkys (or Wyllys) of Blockley (Gloucestershire) drew up his will, he left his leasehold property to William Wyllys 'now dwelling with me'.[38] More commonly, aged parents had to be cared for. Manor court rolls and wills record the varied arrangements that were made, normally involving the older generation giving up all or part of their property (or other economic resource) in return for being maintained by the recipient.[39] Manor court rolls are probably the more comprehensive source because they deal with both sexes and have a wider social range. Many of the wealthier peasants, in order to make their own arrangements, probably preferred to use wills.

If at all possible, independence was maintained, with support taking the form of food, clothing and other necessities. Those who had already set up their children with property could continue to live in their own home. Others retired to a 'dower' cottage or separate annexe to the house. At Kibworth Harcourt (Leicestershire) in 1334 an entry in the manor court roll notes that Nicholas Gilbert had agreed to provide his mother and stepfather with a room three crucks in length to the west of his house, and a corner of the yard, together with two silver shillings and a quarter each of peas and wheat a year.[40] People who were incapable of fending for themselves had to be given board and lodging. Sometimes, others made the arrangements for them: after all, it was in the interest of both the lord and the community to ensure that the land was farmed properly. At a manor court held at Chobham (Surrey) in 1342 it was decided that John atte Wyle should be admitted to his mother's tenement because of her senility. In return he had to look after her.[41] Although there were many cases like this, in which a son agreed to maintain an aged parent, it was not uncommon for the person to be unrelated.

The post-medieval period

In the early modern period surviving censuses are not only more numerous (though hardly commonplace) but they also encompass a greater section of the population. They show that nuclear families were the norm for all strata of village society. From an analysis of some 100 listings, Peter Laslett has estimated that only one family in 20 was non-nuclear.[42] Even in north country parishes like Kirkby Lonsdale (Westmorland), where a listing of the inhabitants was made in 1695, a similar pattern is found.[43] On the other hand, the Scottish Border family of Graham, leaders of society in Eskdale in the late sixteenth century, were living in extended family groups.[44]

A number of households recorded in these early listings contained widows or widowers or married couples, many of whom must have been elderly people living apart from their grown-up children. At Ealing (Middlesex) in 1599 the ages of the inhabitants suggest that perhaps one in every eight or nine households comprised people who may have been in this position.[45] Taxes imposed on households (lay subsidies and the hearth tax) show the continuing independence of many parents and the establishment of new households by siblings. Widows, in particular, stand out in the hearth tax returns. Even those deemed too poor to pay were recorded because they were living in their own homes.

From 1841 the age data in the decennial national censuses allow local historians everywhere in the country to assess the situation in their own community. From 1851 a more refined analysis is possible for in that year the forms include information on marital status and relationship to the head of the household. Although the general pattern remained the same, these censuses suggest that there was a tendency, especially among the poor, for the number of extended families to grow.[46] At Long Buckby (Northamptonshire) in 1851 15 per cent of the families were non-nuclear.[47]

The censuses reveal that whatever the cause that had prompted an elderly parent to live with a married son or daughter, invariably they had lost their spouse.[48] Few examples exist of two married couples sharing the same home. Moreover, although the son or daughter might discuss matters with the parent, the formal headship of the family normally rested with the younger generation. On the other hand, where adult unmarried children continued to live in their parents' house, the latter remained the head.

Other listings can be found in Easter books, noting the payment of Easter offerings to the incumbent. As all communicants should be recorded, including relations and servants, theoretically only children under the age of 14 do not appear. Paupers seem to have been exempt, however, and the comprehensiveness of the source is further affected by the growth of nonconformity. In places like Highley (Shropshire) with good runs of material,[49] the situation can be examined dynamically but in general surviving documents are more fragmentary.

Arrangements made for the elderly continued to be recorded in wills and manor court rolls, especially in the early modern period. Individual indentures were also drawn up and become more numerous with the passage of time. To a certain extent their development had become necessary because of the decline of the manor court as a local administrative body but they took business away from it too. The formality of these documents reinforces the impression that the circumstances surrounding them were exceptional and that in the normal course of events parents were expected to live in their own home. The will which John Fletcher of Albrighton (Shropshire) made in 1618 illustrates a common reason for keeping the generations separate. In it he left his entire estate (with the exception of £60 to be given to his daughter, Alice), to his wife, Elizabeth, and his only son, William. It seems as though he envisaged William, later the vicar of Albrighton, managing the farm and providing a home for his mother. However, he added the comment, 'It is my will that yf the aforsaid Elizabeth do dislike to liue with my sonne William that then she may parte at her pleasure.'[50]

The household

Although most homes were based on the nuclear family, many households were enlarged by the presence of other people living-in. The upper classes, for instance, had their domestic and estate servants, in numbers which varied according to their wealth and status. Others employed them too, though typically in ones and twos. Many farmers had servants in husbandry living-in, as did master craftsmen their apprentices. Both tended to set up in their own homes in their mid-twenties, the one group to become day labourers, the other to pursue their trade or craft. The poor, for their part, took in lodgers or received nurse children.

The household functioned as much as an economic unit as it did a social one, a fact reflected in the government's emphasis on it as a source of taxation. Its composition was not static, however, for its personnel increased or declined over time and with changing circumstances. At its core was the husband and wife team, each with a separate sphere of influence but whose tasks overlapped to a considerable extent. To help them they had their children, though the amount of work they did was determined by their number and age. When extra hands were required, they were generally found from outside the family, either as casual labourers or as living-in servants.

The middle ages

In the Middle Ages most of the evidence for members of the household relates to the homes of the upper classes. The Domesday survey records the existence of many slaves who lived and toiled on the demesne. By the end of the eleventh century, however, the institution of slavery was in full decline and their work was taken over by resident *famuli*.[51] References to them – their number and the cost of their board and lodging – appear in manorial accounts. These records also provide material on household officers and servants, though on the largest estates separate household accounts were kept. Other members of the household who appear in the accounts were guests and non-familial children. The wardship of the latter may have been purchased by the lord in the hope of future gain but many had been sent there by their parents to be brought up in the home of another, as was the custom among the upper classes.[52]

Some manorial surveys give evidence of the other groups of people who possessed servants. References to the tenant having to bring his household with him when performing his labour services imply the use of servants as well as members of the family.[53] On the Bishop of Worcester's estates in the thirteenth century, surveys indicate that farmers with a virgate and even a half-virgate of land (15–30 acres) had full-time servants.[54] Even if particular surveys do not record this information, they can be used to ascertain the status of people who from other sources were known to employ servants. Farm servants are recorded in manor court rolls, though as the reasons for their appearances there owed more to chance than design – typically a presentment for an offence or a dispute over work or conditions – the entries are somewhat intermittent. Their actions, however, often enable them to be linked with their master. Because of the dependent nature of the relationship, the latter invariably pledged for them whenever they were accused of some misdemeanour in the manor court.[55] Much can be gleaned from a good set of records: at Halesowen (Worcestershire) a close examination of the rolls has led Dr Razi to conclude that in the early fourteenth century over two-fifths of the households employed a servant at least occasionally.[56]

In the poll tax assessments of 1379 and 1381 servants were assessed and recorded under the names of their master and other taxpayers in the household. They include some who were the sons and daughters of the head of the household. Because the tax was graded according to income, the classes who possessed servants can be discerned. Moreover, some occupations were given (more in 1379 than in 1381) and this provides additional evidence of their social distribution. In general the figures should only be treated as minimum numbers for there was mass evasion of the tax and, more to the point, much concealment of servants. In Gloucestershire the tax collectors made a second visitation and caught a considerable number of extra servants in the net. At Kempsford, where the first assessment listed some 30 servants out of a taxed population of 118, the second enquiry revealed a further 39, 19 of whom were women.[57]

References to non-familial members of the household abound in probate wills. Often a number of people received bequests, though these varied according to the individual's status and relationship to the testator. Servants were regularly mentioned, perhaps to remind the executor to pay them any outstanding wages, but also to receive gifts. Typically, they were left clothing, an animal, corn or a small sum of money, the type of bequests which were made to god- and grandchildren, nephews and nieces (see p. 132).[58] In May 1489, for instance, John Ropley of Chiddingfold (Surrey) gave a young sow to each of his three servant boys.[59]

The post-medieval period

In the early modern period the documentation becomes fuller and as a result it is easier to examine the composition of the households of ordinary people. Naturally, upper-class households are still the best documented. For some time the format of the old manorial accounts persisted but increasingly they were supplanted by books of disbursements and income, in which items were often entered as and when they were presented to the accountant. A certain amount of patience and stamina is therefore needed to extract the information on living-in servants and other members of the household. By the end of the period some landowners had begun to use special wages books, while others kept bundles of individual vouchers recording payments to servants and labourers. There may also be individual indentures of agreement made with servants over terms and conditions of work. Other evidence appears in estate correspondence and in diaries and commonplace books.

Early censuses indicate more precisely the servant-owning classes, as well as revealing other non-familial members of the household. At Ealing in 1599 the elite stand out on account of the number and range of their farm and domestic servants.[60] The distribution of the servants in husbandry can be plotted with some accuracy because the households of the yeomen are distinguished from those of husbandmen. Not surprisingly, the yeomen were better supplied, for they were wealthier and their farms were larger. They also had more domestic servants. Interestingly, there seems to have been an internal division within the husbandmen class, between those who possessed servants and those who did not. The latter seem to have been smallholders, and often little better than labourers.

Among the upper classes it was not unusual to employ servants related to the family. Often the person involved was a distant relative, perhaps from a poorer branch of the family, and as such would not be in a position to abuse the connection. Edward Vaughan, the leading figure in Ealing, had 17 employees living in his house, one of whom was his niece, Margery Bould. Among the servants of Robert Taylor, a yeoman, were an adolescent girl and boy with the same surname as his. In general, however, the servants at Ealing, as elsewhere, were outsiders.

Several foster children are recorded in the poorer households. They appear to have been foundlings and their presence at Ealing suggests one solution to a problem which must have bedevilled authorities living in densely populated areas like London. Four of the children were being wet-nursed. Typically, they shared the milk with the mother's own baby but because of the high mortality rate among infants, they may have had it to themselves. Women from the class who acted as wet-nurses clearly welcomed the opportunity to earn some extra money and perhaps the reduced risk of an early pregnancy. Prolonged breast feeding was used by contemporaries as a means of birth control.

Probate records continue to name various members of the household. Apart from wills, additional evidence can be found in inventories. From the latter source we can gain an impression of the living conditions of the servants. They mention servants' rooms and describe their furnishings, while accommodation for lodgers and other guests might also be recorded. Inventories of the upper classes with their large households have references like 'all the goods in Mr. X's room'. Many servants slept in the house, if in garrets and attics, but others were put up in outbuildings and barns. The disposition of the rooms and the number of beds suggest that they often shared both with each other and with members of the family. This medieval practice, which emphasizes the lack of privacy in homes, persisted and was often spoken about by witnesses in quarter sessions and assize cases.

As in the Middle Ages, manor court rolls may contain relevant material, though many of them are no longer as comprehensive a record of social life as they once had been. To a certain extent parochial records like vestry minutes and the overseers of the poor accounts take their place. In particular, the examination papers of paupers, produced as a result of the Act of Settlement of 1662, provide an invaluable source of information. In them the examinants gave a brief history of their lives, emphasizing the time spent as servants in people's homes. As contracts normally lasted a year, this gained them a settlement in their employer's parish. Such cases were heard before the magistrates and so the quarter sessions' records should be searched. As indicated above, depositions of witnesses in cases which came before the courts (the assizes and coroners' courts as well as the quarter sessions) are full of incidental detail about the way of life of those involved.

Records designed to secure the loyalty of the populace to their leaders, like the Protestation Return (1641–2); the Vow and Covenant (1643); the Solemn League and Covenant (1644), and the Association Oath (1696), offer other, if less reliable, evidence. In essence, they consist of lists of names of adult males, some of which note occupations and servants. Easter books refer to servants too, contributions made on their behalf being recorded under the name of the head of the household. None of these sources has a good

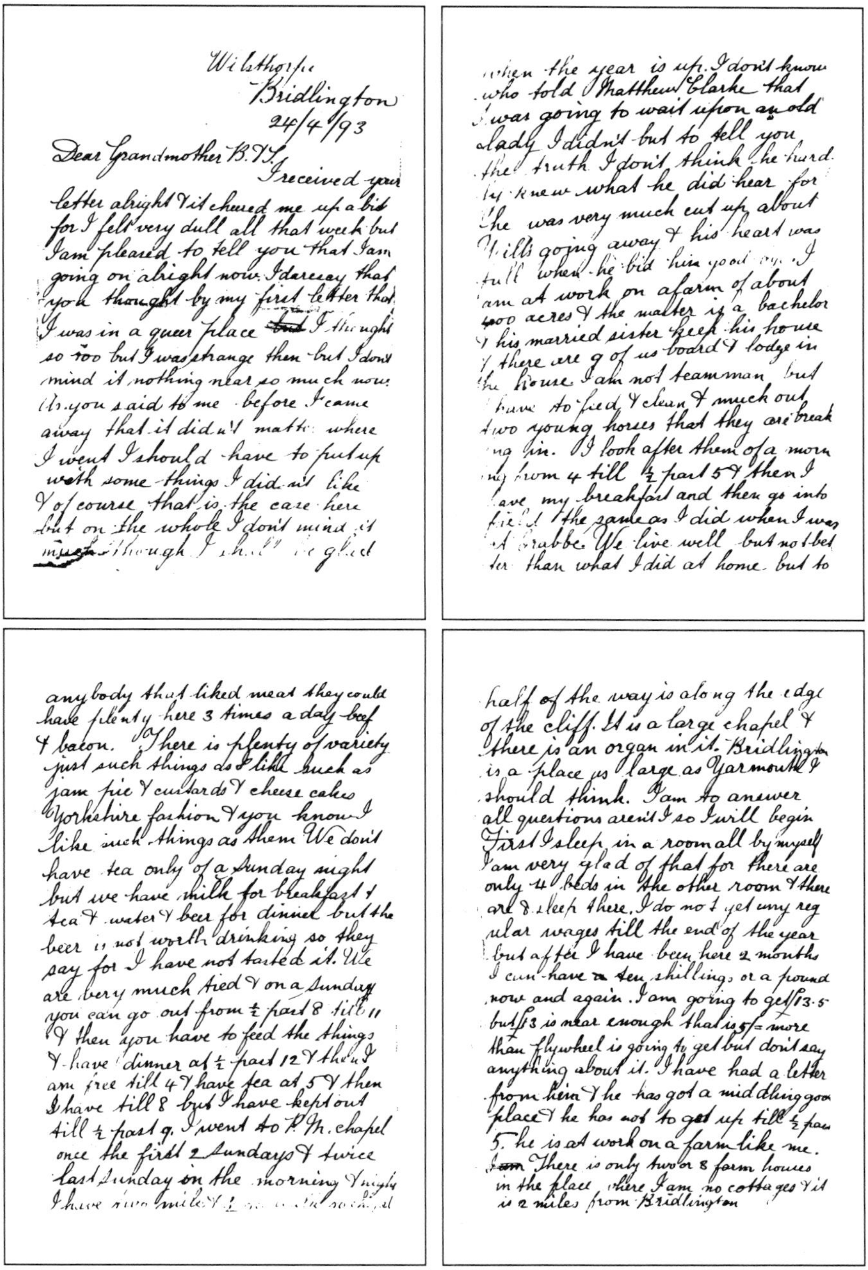

Wilsthorpe
Bridlington
24/4/93

Dear Grandmother B.T.S.

I received your letter alright & it cheered me up a bit for I felt very dull all that week but I am pleased to tell you that I am going on alright now. I dareray that you thought by my first letter that I was in a queer place ~~but~~ I thought so too but I was strange then but I don't mind it nothing near so much now. As you said to me before I came away that it didn't matter where I went I should have to put up with some things I didn't like & of course that is the case here but on the whole I don't mind it ~~much~~ though I shall be glad when the year is up. I don't know who told Matthew Clarke that I was going to wait upon an old lady I didn't but to tell you the truth I don't think he hurd by knew what he did hear for he was very much cut up about Will's going away & his heart was full when he bid him good bye. I am at work on a farm of about 400 acres & the master is a bachelor & his married sister keep his house & there are 9 of us board & lodge in the house I am not teamman but have to feed & clean & muck out two young horses that they are breaking in. I look after them of a morning from 4 till ½ past 5 & then I have my breakfast and then go into field the same as I did when I was at Crabbe. We live well but not better than what I did at home but to anybody that liked meat they could have plenty here 3 times a day beef & bacon. There is plenty of variety just such things as I like such as jam pie & custards & cheese cakes Yorkshire fashion & you know I like such things as them We don't have tea only of a Sunday night but we have milk for breakfast & tea & water & beer for dinner but the beer is not worth drinking so they say for I have not tasted it. We are very much tied & on a Sunday you can go out from ½ past 8 till 11 & then you have to feed the things & have dinner at ½ past 12 & then I am free till 4 & have tea at 5 & then I have till 8 but I have kept out till ½ past 9. I went to P. M. chapel once the first 2 Sundays & twice last Sunday in the morning & night I have two miles & ½ [illegible] to chapel half of the way is along the edge of the cliff. It is a large chapel & there is an organ in it. Bridlington is a place as large as Yarmouth I should think. I am to answer all questions aren't I so I will begin First I sleep in a room all by myself I am very glad of that for there are only 4 beds in the other room & there are 8 sleep there. I do not get any regular wages till the end of the year but after I have been here 2 months I can have a ten shillings or a pound now and again. I am going to get £13.5 but £13 is near enough that is 5/= more than Flywheel is going to get but don't say anything about it. I have had a letter from him & he has got a middling good place & he has not to get up till ½ past 5. he is at work on a farm like me. ~~I am~~ There is only two or 3 farm houses in the place where I am no cottages & it is 2 miles from Bridlington

37 A letter from a servant in husbandry, Bridlington, 24 April 1893.

coverage of the country and those that do survive can be full of gaps.

In the mid-nineteenth century the national censuses provide detailed information on the various additional people found in individual households, their relative number in the community as a whole and their distribution among the social classes. From 1851, as visitors are designated as such, temporary residents can be distinguished from permanent ones. They also help to reveal the demise of the living-in farm servant. The tendency, which had begun in the South and East in the eighteenth century, became more pronounced after 1790 as a result of problems associated with such issues as population growth, increasing corn prices and the rising cost of poor relief.[61] In effect, farmers found it cheaper to employ labourers on a casual basis than to hire servants on full board for the year. The development also reflected a change in social attitudes; as the size of farms increased, especially in mixed farming areas, the gulf between farmers and labourers widened and many farmers no longer wanted such intimate contact with people whom they deemed their social inferiors. Gradually the changes spread throughout the country, though they did not occur overnight. Even in 1881 many farm servants were recorded in the census. In parts of the North it survived much longer, as can be seen in W. M. Williams's study of the Cumberland village of Gosforth in the early 1950s.[62]

The mid-nineteenth-century censuses also suggest that the number of lodgers had increased, a rise influenced by the growth in the population. Many boarded with the poor, for the latter saw it as an opportunity to make a little extra money. If, at the same time, they were putting up an elderly parent, their houses must have been very cramped. Some of these lodgers may have been relatives but the link can only be made by studying such sources as wills and parish registers. At Great Bookham (Surrey) in 1881 one household in seven contained lodgers, mainly residing with the labourers and the poor.[63]

Kinship and neighbourliness

More so than today, the routine of village life had to be conducted in an atmosphere of neighbourliness and sociability, and naturally individuals established links with kin, friends and neighbours. Given the smaller numbers involved and the greater awareness of each other's business, antisocial behaviour was particularly disruptive, hindering the smooth running of local affairs. The amount of interaction, of course, varied from place to place according to the social and economic profile of each community. Similarly, the class to which an individual belonged influenced the range and social background of his or her contacts.

Villagers were far less concerned with their kinfolk than they were with their immediate family. Significantly, the English language is very poor in kinship terms: in particular, the word cousin was used to cover a myriad of relationships.[64] This makes it difficult for the modern researcher to discern precise family connections but it must also have caused problems at the time. Before the Reformation marriages were forbidden within the fourth degree of kinship and while people certainly knew their close relatives, beyond them they were less sure. When divorce cases came before the church courts, the documents reveal that the partners often did not know their exact blood relationship to each other. In reconstituted families a number of instances emerge of people breaking the marriage rules. Nonetheless, from the ecclesiastical court records it appears that few unions were dissolved on grounds of consanguinity.[65]

Succession to property, as recorded in the manor court rolls, is another indicator of the extent to which the peasantry knew about their wider kinship group. Normally, the 'heir' would be an obvious one, but this was not always the case, especially in times of demographic crisis. Those who owned land needed to know who would succeed them, especially if there were a failure in the main line, while others hoped to gain from such an event. After the Black Death openings for collateral branches increased. At Halesowen (Worcestershire) the court rolls reveal that immigrants were coming from other villages to make good their claim to freehold land.[66] Bondland was also involved; even if the lord theoretically had the right to take property back at the death of a tenant, in practice the 'heir' generally succeeded to it. The source can still be used in the early modern period; although many rolls ceased to be used to record administrative details, land transactions were still registered there.

A person's awareness of kinship relationships seems to have varied according to social status. The upper classes were particularly well-informed. Many constructed their own genealogical trees, while the College of Arms made periodic visitations. Kinship links can also be examined through correspondence and in the pages of diaries and commonplace books. However, for the farming community one has to wait until the eighteenth or nineteenth centuries before these sources become readily available. Nonetheless, it is clear that earlier generations of yeomen farmers had already taken an interest in their kin. In his history of Myddle, written *c.* 1700, Richard Gough not only displayed an intimate knowledge of his family, including members long dead, but also showed a considerable grasp of relationships that existed within other families in the parish.[67]

In this respect, wills provide an important source of information. When they drew them up, testators often made bequests to a number of kinsfolk, though imprecise terminology tends to obscure the particular connection. References to people living outside the village, even if the location is only occasionally given, are a further indication of contact with the wider kinship group. Their appearance in wills, however, is low when compared to members of the nuclear family.

Testators also differentiated between the two groups in terms of the goods they bestowed upon them. The bulk of the estate invariably went to sons and daughters, while many of the bequests to others were of a symbolic nature. In the main these gifts comprised animals, grain, household utensils or money. People who died unmarried or who had no children were the ones most likely to make bequests to godchildren and to nephews and nieces.[68] When Hugh Wexham, a husbandman from Roehampton (Surrey) made his will in December 1632 he left goods to various members of his family, including nephews, nieces and godchildren, as well as to a number of unidentified people.[69]

Members of the immediate family were prominent in administering the will. Wives or children were the relatives most commonly chosen as executors and after them, brothers and brothers-in-law. At Terling (1550–1699) nearly nine out of every ten executors were kin, over three-quarters of whom were wives and children. Only 13 per cent of the executors had no relationship with the testator.[70] Close relatives were also regularly used as overseers of the will, though the proportion of friends and neighbours was correspondingly greater. The latter were even more extensively employed as witnesses, availability clearly being an important factor in the choice.[71]

In pre-industrial England much use was made of kinship links in the conduct of economic affairs. Trading was a risky business and it paid to be associated with people one could trust. Toll books, recording the sale of animals (especially horses) at markets and fairs, when analysed in conjunction with parish registers and probate wills, reveal the existence of many family dynasties of dealers, incorporating fathers and sons, uncles and nephews. From the late seventeenth century, for instance, several generations of the Frizwell family of Bedworth (Warwickshire) were involved in the business.[72]

Lists of licensed badgers and drovers (dealers) found in the quarter sessions' papers similarly reveal family involvement in a trade. Quarter sessions' depositions, together with those from the assizes, provide further information. The records of Chancery and of the Court of Requests contain details of trading offences and disputes which were heard there, although for the local historian such records are something of a lucky dip. In one case *c.* 1566 it was stated that when Lawrence Pake of Dagenham (Essex) had bought seven cows from his brother-in-law, John Wright of South Weald (Essex), he had been given three more 'in token and show of the good will [Wright] then bare unto his sister' and brother-in-law.[73]

While such sources indicate the existence of kinship links in trade, they also show that people were just as likely to use their friends and neighbours. The Frizwells, for instance, formed part of a larger group of horse dealers who travelled to fairs together and did business with each other. It was not uncommon for these economic partnerships to be strengthened by marriage ties. Wills and parish registers reveal that the Frizwells were related to one or two of the other horse-dealing families in the area, and there are other

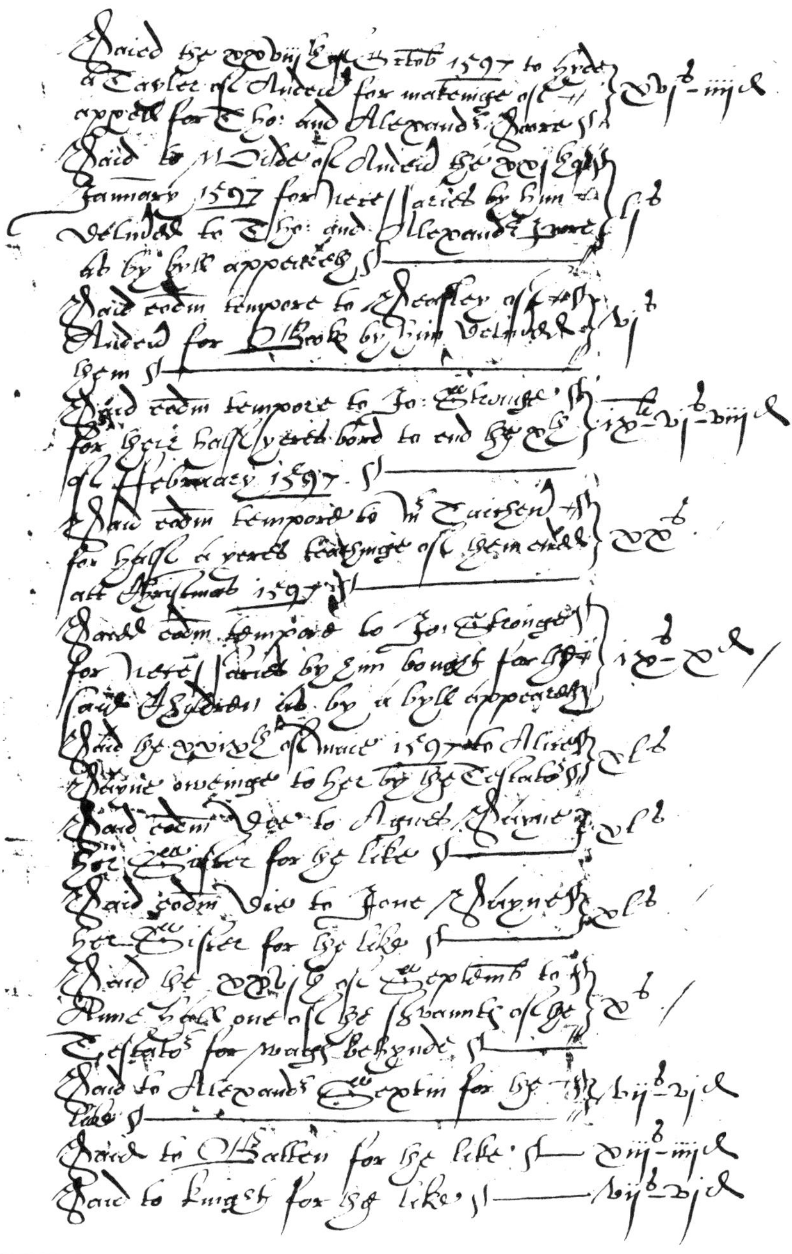

38 Administrators' accounts of the estate of William Poore of Longstock (Hampshire), an Elizabethan yeoman-farmer: costs of bringing up his children.

examples. These business connections often explain why a particular person was used as an overseer of a person's will or was associated with him in another way.[74]

When people travelled around the country, either on business or for some other purpose, they made full use of kinship links. Many examples appear in quarter sessions and assize depositions. When Richard Price, a suspected horse stealer, was examined by the magistrates at Shrewsbury in December 1606 he spoke of his movements around the country since leaving his home in London. Apart from inns, he stayed one night at the house of his wife's brother in Ludlow and spent some time with his uncle at Llanrewed in Montgomeryshire.[75] This practice can be charted much more accurately from the middle of the nineteenth century for censuses from 1851 onwards denote visitors, and often their relationship to the head of the household.

Money lending and the giving and taking of credit were other areas in which one would expect kin to be involved since trust was an important consideration. Once more, however, relatives were not alone in making this provision, for friends and neighbours were also involved. In the Middle Ages litigation over debt commonly took place at the manor court, especially if the amounts were small (as they often were). The network of credit facilities in the Tudor and Stuart village is much easier to research because it appears in a non-pathological way in probate wills and inventories. For the sixteenth and early seventeenth centuries the material is quite detailed, recording the parties involved and the nature of the debt – perhaps for money owed, an unpaid rent or wage or the balance on a commodity sold. Thereafter, the documentation becomes vaguer and less informative. Instances of the non-payment of debts also turn up in the records of the Court of Requests but, like the manor court material, they deal with disputes.

In the early modern period the practice grew of using bonds, enforceable by law, to secure debts. The form of bond employed was known as a bill obligatory or speciality (there are many examples of these in inventories and wills) and in it the debtor agreed to repay the sum by a certain date. Over time it became customary for a penal sum, greater than the principal, to be charged in the event of non-payment.[76] To provide added security creditors often asked the debtor to find one or more sureties to act as guarantors. Because the latter were liable to prosecution should the debtor default, they naturally tended to be people who knew him or her well. For the same reason, kinsfolk, friends and neighbours acted as pledges at the manor court, guaranteeing that an individual would carry out his or her obligations. They also appeared on behalf of others as compurgators in the church courts, swearing to the innocence of a defendant charged with an offence there, and stood as sureties for a person bound by a recognizance issued by a Justice of the Peace.[77]

An examination of the records of these bodies will reveal much about the status of a particular person and the circle of people with whom he or she was associated, as well as the strength of his or her kinship ties. Such links did not always take place between equals. Elite members of the community were much in demand as overseers of wills, as sureties in bonds, as compurgators and character witnesses and as pledgers since they lent a greater weight of authority to the proceedings.[78] In a hierarchical society status counted – with a powerful supporter one might even get away with murder.

Summary

Apart from a favoured few, most local historians have to wait until the mid-nineteenth century for documentation which gives direct evidence of the relationship between the immediate family and the wider kin – and neighbourhood groupings. Nonetheless, with care and ingenuity much relevant material can be extracted from the available sources. A number of local studies, already completed, have shown what can be done if the analysis is based upon a close examination of the records. They have shed a good deal of light on the nature of the English family in the past, while at the same time laying to rest some of the old preconceived ideas that used to be held on the subject.

Except on the fringes of the country people did not live in large extended family groups, preferring instead to form new households whenever they married and settled down. Indeed, a great deal of effort was made to maintain the integrity of the nuclear family. Adult siblings, even in areas of partible inheritance, lived apart, while retired parents, if at all possible, had a separate establishment. As the latter grew older and more infirm, many of them had to be taken in and maintained but such people did not form a very large proportion of the population. Apart from any other consideration, the high average age at marriage, combined with the low expectancy of life, ensured that their numbers remained low.

Although the family unit generally consisted solely of parents and their children, they often shared the home with others. Most commonly, these residents comprised servants of one sort or another and records reveal that they were spread quite widely among the villagers. In fact, the English predilection for servants had an influence on another aspect of family life. Instead of making use of their kin to help them in their enterprises, farmers, and others who needed workers, preferred to employ outsiders to do the work. In particular, the custom developed early of employing adolescents and young adults, who were normally retained for a year and who were boarded in the house or outbuildings. Certainly, individuals did associate with their kin and used them for a variety of purposes. The records reveal, however, that they were just as likely to turn to their friends and neighbours.

CHAPTER SEVEN

Rural housing

Many houses in the countryside have stood for hundreds of years, though few of them survive in their original form. Modifications have been made, with pieces added or parts pulled down or reconstructed. Much change took place in the period known as the 'Great Rebuilding of England' which occurred (depending on region) between the mid-sixteenth and eighteenth centuries. Naturally, houses varied in terms of size, structure and contents, differences which were largely based upon the wealth and status of their owners and occupiers. A basic distinction is the one that existed between 'polite' and 'vernacular' architecture. Houses of the former type were designed according to national rather than local criteria and aesthetic considerations were equally as important as functional ones. Not only were designs and features imported from outside but so too were the materials. Vernacular houses, on the other hand, were those which conformed to the customary practices of the area and which were built of local materials.

As this chapter is concerned with the homes of people who ranked below the level of the landed gentry, polite architecture will only be referred to when its styles influenced the design of vernacular buildings. It certainly did have an effect; over time some of its conventions and ideas percolated downwards to find expression in the homes of farmers and eventually in those of craftsmen and labourers. When, as a result of transport improvements in the late eighteenth and nineteenth centuries, it became easier to move bulky building materials around the country, regional variations in the physical appearance of houses were further eroded.

There are many documentary sources which can be used to examine the history of the houses and buildings of a rural community and these will be looked at in detail. The buildings themselves provide additional evidence. For dating purposes the practice, common in some parts of the country, of inserting date-stones is an undoubted help, yet they can also be misleading. At Hallaton (Leicestershire) the date 1832 on a late medieval cruck-framed house relates to the heightening of the building in brick in the early nineteenth century and not to the time when the original structure was erected. The outward appearance of a house, together with its structural features, therefore, must also be considered. The dimensions and layout of the rooms give further evidence, as do the mouldings on beams, doors and windows. Care must always be taken when looking at a house, however, because original features may have been removed or hidden behind later developments or alterations. Many timber-framed houses have been encased in brick or have had a brick façade put on the front. As the original character of a house may not always be apparent from the front, it is a good idea to look around the back, and get into the roof space, if possible.

Even to the most casual observer it is clear that in a large number of houses alterations have taken place. Some changes are obvious but others are more subtle and need to be appraised by an expert. Indeed, the study of vernacular architecture has become a highly specialized branch of local history, complete with its own journals and terminology. In many counties vernacular, or domestic, architecture societies have been established, the aims of which are to record and research the historic houses of their area. They welcome invitations to view individual properties, though, as amateurs fitting in the work in their spare time, they may not always be able to respond immediately. Local historians interested in the study of vernacular architecture should join their local society where they will be given guidance on the recognition and dating of the various features.

Owners and occupiers

When studying the history of a house it is essential to discover the names of its owners and occupiers. Apart from creating a framework around which a fuller account can be written, such an investigation makes it easier to match the premises with the documentation. Some houses can be more readily identified than others, because of their name or location, and as a rule local historians in old enclosed areas of scattered settlement have a greater chance of success than do their counterparts in erstwhile open field communities.

As always, houses situated on large estates (now or at some time in the past) are the best documented. Small freeholders were less likely to preserve their deeds and records, though there are examples of such properties with documentation going back for centuries. Where old lease- and copyhold premises have been enfranchised the survival rate may be better because the new owners had an incentive to retain written evidence of ownership. For further information on this subject, readers should look at John H. Harvey's pamphlet, 'Sources for the History of Houses', *British Records Association: Archives and the User*, no. 3 (1974).

In this type of research, one should begin at a fixed point, using a document which provides firm evidence of ownership and occupancy. For houses built before the mid-nineteenth century the tithe award (if one was made) is a good place to start. Buildings can be identified on the map, and by looking up the reference numbers on the accompanying apportionment the owners and many of the occupiers can be named. There may be some omissions in the list, notably in the record of cottagers, so that it is not always possible to pin-point the homes of all labourers and workers. Typically, at Great Bookham (Surrey) most of the inhabitants of groups of small cottages (many seemingly subdivided houses) were not mentioned by name. The three sets of cottages owned by Mary Tickner, for instance, were said to be occupied by James Elliott and others.[1] On the other hand, the occupiers of even the smallest holdings (of one acre or less) were recorded by name. If no tithe award exists for the township or parish being examined, an estate map with its associated field book could serve the same purpose. Coverage may be as complete as in the tithe map but in most cases it will be partial, its comprehensiveness dependent upon the amount of land held there.

Moving forward from the tithe award, a range of records are available to continue the chronology. First of all, one may find a bundle of title deeds relating to the property, comprising documents drawn up to accompany changes in ownership and occupancy. There could be an abstract of title too, setting out the names of previous owners, perhaps beyond the date of the earliest surviving original deed. Deeds conveying ownership reveal the names of the parties involved, while leases and court baron entries also give those of the occupiers or tenants. In this respect the problem of subletting should be borne in mind, though if licensed, it will be recorded in deeds and in the manor court rolls.

On an estate, title deeds to various properties will often have been sorted out into different bundles, neatly tied up with a ribbon or filed in separate boxes. Even if faced with a box of miscellaneous deeds, researchers may be able to identify relevant documents by looking at such details as the name of the property, its location and abuttals and perhaps an enclosed plan. Other estate records – court rolls, rentals, maps and surveys – should be used to assist in the task of identification. If the records have been transferred to a record office, it is not always necessary to look at the original deeds for information as catalogue entries, if made, may provide sufficient evidence.

Of the other nineteenth-century sources parish rating assessments are of particular value, especially as from the 1830s the names of owners as well as occupiers are recorded.[2] Even if one set of returns is incomplete, a chronology can be established by combining the information to be found in others. Once the connection has been made with the evidence contained in the base document, identification of particular properties in subsequent assessments is often quite straightforward. Apart from the names of the owners and occupiers, there are the figures in the assessments themselves which tend to remain constant over a number of years. It is true that rates did vary, as a greater or lesser income was required, but as the whole community was affected, it is still possible to discern individual houses.

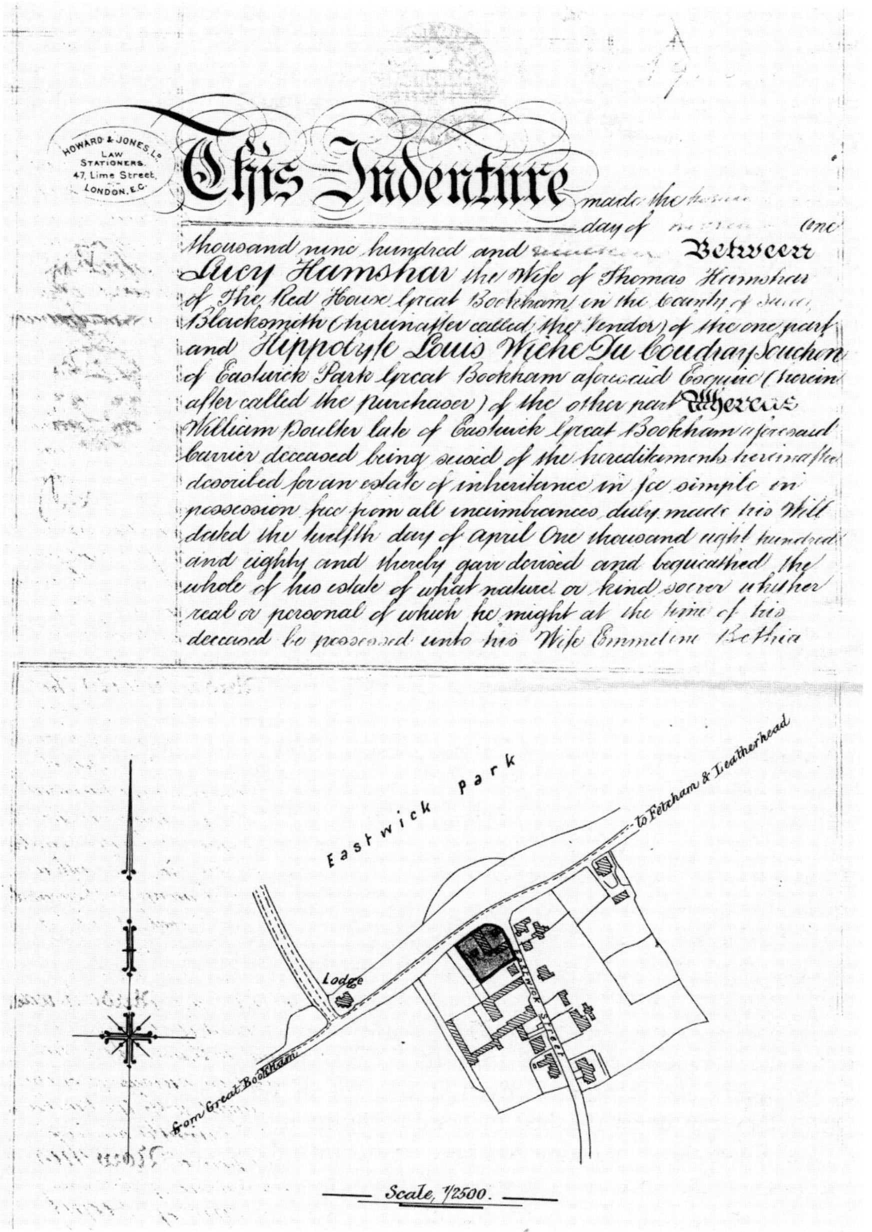

Howard & Jones Ld Law Stationers. 47, Lime Street, London, E.C.

This Indenture made the day of One thousand nine hundred and Between Lucy Hamshar the Wife of Thomas Hamshar of The Red House Great Bookham in the County of Surrey Blacksmith (hereinafter called the Vendor) of the one part and Hippolyte Louis Wiehe Du Coudray Souchon of Eastwick Park Great Bookham aforesaid Esquire (herein after called the purchaser) of the other part Whereas William Boulter late of Eastwick Great Bookham aforesaid Carrier deceased being seised of the hereditaments hereinafter described for an estate of inheritance in fee simple in possession free from all incumbrances duly made his Will dated the twelfth day of April One thousand eight hundred and eighty and thereby gave devised and bequeathed the whole of his estate of what nature or kind soever whether real or personal of which he might at the time of his decease be possessed unto his Wife Emmeline Bethia

39 Title deed showing the conveyance of 'Woodcote', Great Bookham (Surrey) 24 November 1919.

More complicated are those changes which altered the rateable value of a building, perhaps as a result of the subdivision of a house into cottages or because of an enlargement of the premises. As well as personal names, topographical references provide clues – the name of a farm or of a house, or a mention of the street or area of the parish in which the building is located. Such information, of course, helps in a general way to identify specific houses. When changes of ownership or occupancy occurred, both old and new names were normally given. Thus, at Great Bookham, William Poulter bought a cottage at Ralph's Cross in 1851–2 and in the 1852 church rate assessment it was recorded as 'late Lefever'. The occupant, George Simmons, remained the same, as did the assessment.[3]

Names, often allied to a topographical reference, also appear in sources such as parish accounts and registers and in censuses and commercial directories. Street directories, which become more numerous as the nineteenth century progressed, are very useful, since they list residents living in numbered houses street by street. They are more valuable for urban areas than for rural ones, however; because of the informal pattern of housing in the countryside, entries are often not arranged into streets. There, the information is normally presented in the same way as in the older commercial directories, namely, divided into sections comprising private residents and tradesmen. Nonetheless (as with parish rates), the name and location of a number of residences will be included in the list.

Census returns do record families by street, though not always by an identifiable house. There must have been some logical pattern for the order in which the material was entered into the books by the enumerators but it cannot always be discovered. Did they go up one side of the street before going down the other, or did they criss-cross it as they went along? At what point did they visit those houses lying behind the street frontage and did they go back to houses where there had been no answer on the first visit? Because houses were not as tightly packed in villages as they were in towns, this may not be such a problem. Much depends upon individual circumstances and the haphazard arrangement of an open village would tend to lead to greater complications than in a closed community.

Censuses have the advantage over the other sources previously mentioned because they list all classes and miss no one out because of poverty. Poor people and labourers also appear in parish records, notably in the papers relating to poor law administration, and, like any other parishioner, the place of their abode might be given. Similarly, parish registers occasionally include information of a topographical nature.

At the beginning of the twentieth century the records of the Edwardian land surveys, taken in conjunction with Lloyd George's reform of the land tax, can serve as a starting point.[4] Valuation and field books and forms 37-land all give the names of owners and occupiers of individual hereditaments (properties) which can be identified from the map references, though the marked-up maps used by the officials may be in a different record repository. Local rating assessments continued to be made and in villages with a rising population and an expanding housing stock they may give an address. From 1925 district councils were involved in the assessment but this entailed little change in the form or substance of the documents. Electoral registers become more important as a source during the course of the twentieth century. Some were drawn up in the nineteenth century but only acquire comprehensiveness with the establishment of adult male suffrage in 1918 and its extension to women in 1929.

For the period before the tithe award local historians can work backwards from this document, a practice which has certain advantages. Not only can they progress from the known to the unknown but they can also spot any developments that occurred – the building of new houses or the modification of existing ones, for example. It is easier to chart these changes too because additional houses do not have to be squeezed into the list.

One or two of the sources referred to above extend back beyond the 1830s and can be examined for names. Unfortunately, parish rates for this earlier period do not record owners, an omission which can make the identification of some houses more difficult. The holdings of the farmers are normally given, though where tenants were cultivating more than one farm the house in which they were living may not be stated. In commercial directories too, only the homes of the farmers and the gentry can be pin-pointed with any certainty.

The main source of information for the late eighteenth and early nineteenth centuries is the land tax, especially for the years 1780–1832.[5] By comparing the list of names of owners and occupiers in the 1832 assessment with those in the tithe apportionment many of the houses can be located. If parish rates survive for the intervening years, there will be a continuous run of documentation back to 1780. The returns need to be comprehensive if maximum benefit is to be gained from them. The best ones, therefore, are those which continue to list all properties, even those belonging to people who, after 1789, had compounded for their tax. As with parish rates, the amount of the assessment is a guide to individual houses. Similarly, topographical information might be included. From 1826 a brief description of the property – 'mill'; 'house and land'; 'cottage & garden'; 'Smith's Farm' – was usually given. At Great Bookham the list is arranged by area, beginning with the village and continuing through Bookham Common, Eastwick and Little Bookham Side to On the Hill and Ranmore.[6] The properties of the large landowners, however, are gathered together at the head of the return but as they were entered separately, often with a topographical reference, they too can be located. Moreover, houses like these are often recorded in estate papers.

Filling houses with named people becomes more difficult in the period before the mid-eighteenth century. Some parish rating lists and land tax assessments do exist, but generally these are scattered examples rather than an unbroken series spanning a number of years. A high proportion of early land tax returns, moreover, do not record both proprietors and occupiers but merely give a single list of taxpayers. Inevitably, farmers, as a group, are the best documented because their holdings are often named. Tax returns such as the lay subsidies of the sixteenth and seventeenth centuries and the hearth tax of Charles II's reign give names and sometimes the places in which individual taxpayers lived. At Great Bookham a Thomas Wood of Bagdon is recorded in the hearth tax list of 1664, presumably to distinguish him from his relative, Thomas Wood of Ewetrees Farm.[7]

Unfortunately, the lay subsidies caught fewer and fewer people in the tax net as the sixteenth century wore on and even the hearth tax, which often includes the exempt, is now reckoned to contain some omissions. Anyone's name, of course, may appear in the parish registers, vestry minutes or manor court rolls, while paupers are regularly referred to in the papers of the overseers of the poor. Occasionally, an entry might indicate a person's home but only in an intermittent fashion.

The shortcomings of these records emphasizes the greater importance attached to deeds and other estate records as a source of evidence in the medieval and early modern periods. This means that it is more difficult to find out the names of owners of small freeholds or the tenants on small estates than it is to discover the identity of people leasing houses and land from large landowners. However, as many members of the former groups owed suit of court in the manor in which their property lay, they should be referred to in the court rolls. They may also appear in maps and surveys which indicate abuttals – farming land adjacent to that belonging to the estate.

40 Great Bookham Land Tax assessment 1780: the Eastwick area.

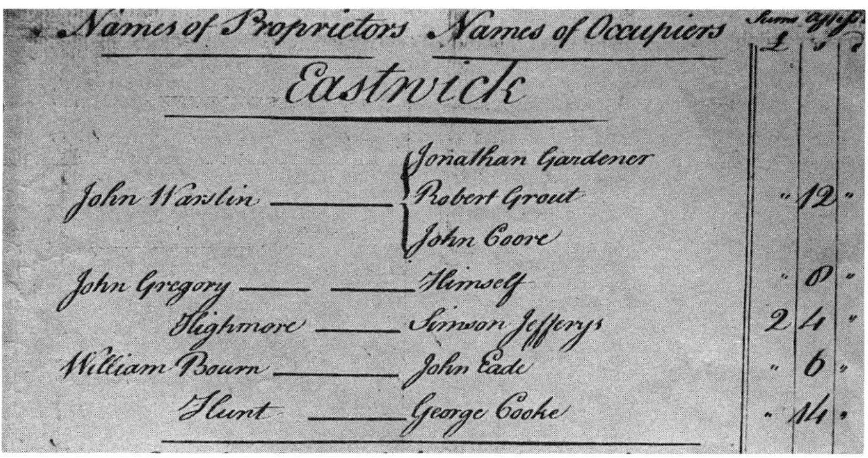

Names of Proprietors	Names of Occupiers	Sums assessed £	s	d
Eastwick				
John Warslin	Jonathan Gardener Robert Grout John Coore	"	12	"
John Gregory	Himself	"	8	"
Highmore	Simson Jefferys	2	4	"
William Bourn	John Eade	"	6	"
Hunt	George Cooke	"	14	"

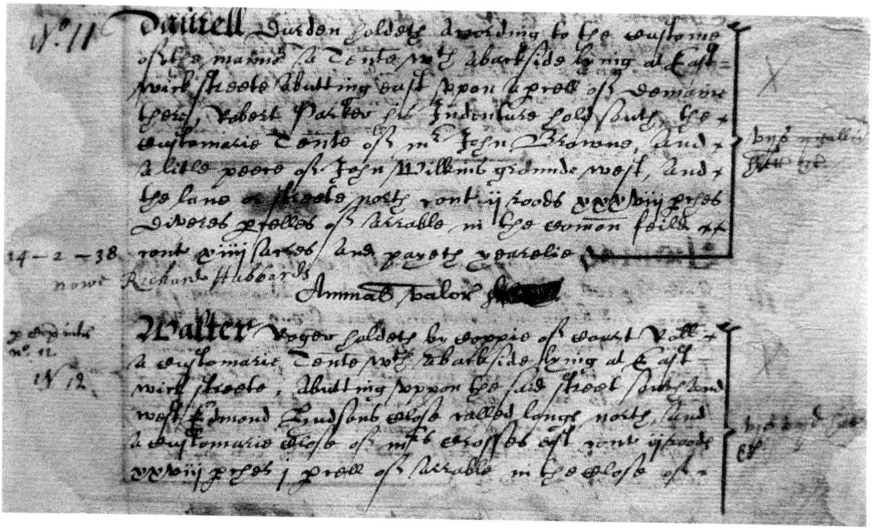

41 Extract from the survey of the manor of Great Bookham (Surrey) 1614–17.

On many large estates there will be a map, often accompanied by a field book, which can be used to locate houses on the ground. If not, a detailed survey, giving abuttals and other topographical information, will provide enough evidence to identify the homes of many of the inhabitants, even allowing for the problem of subletting. Having established a fixed point, the researcher should work forwards and backwards from it, examining estate and manorial records such as leases, rentals and court baron papers. Where copyhold property survived throughout the period the records of the court baron are particularly valuable. When a copyhold tenant died, his or her death was reported at the following meeting of the court baron and a description given of the land so held. If it was a copyhold of inheritance, the heir was named and perhaps granted seisin, should he or she come to the court in person to claim it. If it was a copyhold at will, the name of the person who eventually took the property would similarly be entered on the roll.

Medieval houses

Apart from farm servants who resided with their masters, most peasants in the medieval English countryside lived in simple single-storeyed buildings. In 1300 they were mainly one-room cells, if the details of two tax assessments for the Colchester area (1296 and 1301) have any general validity. As such structures have not survived into modern times, our knowledge of them can only be gained from excavations at deserted medieval sites like the one at Wharram Percy (East Riding). The labouring classes continued to live in such buildings in the late Middle Ages but because of the general rise in the standard of living after the mid-fourteenth-century demographic crisis, more people had homes of two rooms or more. By then, the most prosperous farmers were living in bigger houses, which, while retaining the open hall as a focus of domestic life, were built with storeyed ends.[8] The archetypal home of this sort is the Wealden house, so-called because of its south-eastern origins, but it can be found much farther afield than that.

In medieval houses the most important room was the hall, a prominence reflected in the fact that many dwellings were called hall houses.[9] It had a multitude of functions – a space for storage as well as a place to cook, eat, live and sleep – though the tasks carried on there were obviously related to the size and complexity of the structure. It often contained the only hearth in the home, an open fireplace in the middle of the room on which food was cooked and the house heated. If the house possessed a kitchen, it was normally located in the yard. In two-roomed houses a chamber was added to the hall, relieving some of the pressure on that room and perhaps serving as a private place for the head of the household.

More space was provided in houses of three units, though they were not always of equal size. The hall was frequently extended to two bays of building. At the end of such a house lay the service end, used for storage and perhaps divided into a buttery and a pantry for wet and dry goods. These rooms were entered by doors opening off a cross-passage which ran between them and the hall. If there was an outside kitchen, this was often reached via a corridor at the service end. On the other side of the hall was situated a room which came to be known as the parlour and which was generally used as a private room – perhaps a bedroom – for the head of the household.

This basic three-unit plan can be seen in many surviving buildings throughout lowland England which is perhaps the reason why it is often said to typify the medieval house. Even the houses with storeyed wings preserve this arrangement of an upper and lower end. In the North and the West a different tradition developed, that of the longhouse, in which humans and animals were accommodated under one roof. There, the cross-passage linked two entrances, one to the house and the other to the byre. Elsewhere, separate provision was made for housing animals and keeping grain. Among the most imposing monuments to medieval farming are the enormous tithe barns constructed by the Church to store the produce brought in.

Carpenters were the craftsmen in greatest demand when building a house. In addition to the wooden internal partitions – joists and rafters and fixtures such as doors and windows – timber was the most widely used load-bearing material. Carpentry practices varied around the country, as can be seen in the different ways in which walls and roofs were constructed. In southern and eastern England box frames were widely used to bear the weight of the roof. Although examples can be found of paired curved posts or 'crucks' doing the job, this system was much more common in the North and West. Smallholders, labourers and cottagers could not afford the services of a craftsman and had to build their homes themselves with whatever materials were readily to hand – mud, wood and thatch.

The homes of a large proportion of the population were not comfortable places in which to live. Their interiors were dark and gloomy; windows were unglazed and therefore shuttered to keep out the draught, while smoke from the open hearth filled the rooms. Damp rose up from the earthen floors or through ill-fitting shutters and holes in the roof. They were also cramped and crowded; not only did people have to carry out the daily routine of living in a confined space but they were also hindered by the clutter of household and farm goods all around them. Above all, there was little privacy, except perhaps for the head of the household.

Apart from the evidence of the houses themselves, weighted towards the homes of the more prosperous villagers, there are the documentary records to consider. They largely comprise manorial and estate material. Surveys of different sorts – extents, IPMs and the Hundred Rolls – give some information, though normally of a general nature. The premises are described in terms of messuages, tenements and cottages, perhaps indicating the type and size of houses but hardly providing a full account. The documents may mention the location of the properties, possibly revealing evidence of expansion on to the wastes as the population grew in the period before the early fourteenth century. Occasionally, details are given of the manor house. Other surveys refer to mills, an important piece of information, especially if the mode of power is noted. Water-mills were introduced into England in the late twelfth century and from these sources it is possible to calculate how quickly they spread around the country.

Manorial accounts are much more specific, although they do not usually describe the housing stock as such. This has to be deduced from the entries, many of which record the costs of erecting and repairing buildings on the estate. One may have to look through the whole document for relevant information but this is not always necessary; in many cases the accountant collected all building expenses together and wrote them down on the document under a separate subheading. Major items of expenditure might include the wages of the craftsmen and other persons employed, and the cost of the materials. These were often noted in minute detail.

The evidence makes it possible to assess construction costs, especially if the dimensions of the building are given, and also learn of the materials used. At Kibworth Harcourt (Leicestershire) building accounts reveal that the houses had cruck frames standing on stone footings. The mud walls were strengthened with small timbers, wherever necessary, and plastered over. Houses of three bays were common, and the largest one had eight bays.[10]

Other information can be found in the manor court rolls. As essential resources such as timber and stone were traditionally manorial monopolies; tenants who wanted to build, extend or repair their homes, had to come to court for permission to obtain the materials. For the sake of economy, and as a labour saving measure, materials were reused whenever possible and timber and stone from one house regularly ended up in the walls or roof of another. This process often required a licence, too. In the period after the plague of the mid-fourteenth century there was considerable activity of this sort as tenants pulled down derelict houses for materials to improve their own. Manorial lords were generally in favour of the practice but they sought to punish those who allowed their properties to fall into disrepair. Manor court rolls are full of presentments for the offence.[11]

In the records of the court baron there may be references to tenants having to build houses of a certain size as a condition of being granted a holding. In Worcestershire in the late fourteenth and fifteenth centuries the homes of peasants acquiring property on the various estates most commonly had three bays, followed at a distance by those with two and four bays.[12] Deeds and leases may contain similar information. According to the terms of a lease granted to a tenant at Wigston Magna (Leicestershire) in 1405, the lessee had 'to make or cause to be made a house upon the said tenement of three paires of "forkes" [crucks] within the term of three years under penalty of twenty shillings.'[13] A Chertsey Abbey deed of 1484–5, granting a messuage and land to John Bartholomew of Englefield (Surrey), describes the house as possessing a hall, chambers, a kitchen and two barns.[14]

'The Great Rebuilding'

In the period from the mid-sixteenth century improvements in the standard of housing occurred which some have claimed as revolutionary. Even contemporaries noticed the changes: writing in his *Survey of Cornwall* (published 1602) of the homes of the county's husbandmen, Richard Carew observed that traditionally they had comprised 'walles of earth, low thatched roofes, few partitions, no planchings or glasse windowes, and scarcely any chimnies, other than a hole in the wall to let out the smoke . . . but now most of these fashions are universally banished, and the Cornish husbandman conformethe himselfe with a better supplied civilitie to the Easterne patterne.'[15]

Prof. W. G. Hoskins was among the first modern scholars to comment upon this phenomenon.[16] Since his pioneering study local research in many parts of the country has confirmed his account, although refining the timing and pace of the movement by region. Increased profits from agriculture paid for the improvements and thus the initiators were the farmers who had considerable surpluses to sell in the market.

With extra money in their pockets, many of them decided to improve the quality of their lives by converting their cramped single-storeyed houses into more spacious homes. First floors were put in, perhaps in a piecemeal fashion, so that the open hall might remain after the rest of the house had been boarded over. Additional accommodation was provided in the form of one or more cross-wings. With more rooms, the hall gradually lost its prominent position as the various functions which had been carried out there were hived off to more specialized rooms. The service area was enlarged, notably by making the kitchen an integral part of the house. If one had previously existed outside the house, it was used as a storage shed. In the homes of craftsmen one of the rooms often served as a workshop. More space for sleeping was created by constructing bed chambers upstairs, though the parlour long remained the best bedroom in the homes of many farmers. Houses became lighter and more airy not only because of the insertion of chimney stacks but also because of the greater use of glass as the period progressed. The use of brick either as infill, as a façade or as a cladding material similarly improved the standard of comfort by making the houses warmer and less draughty.

Such developments can be examined in some detail because of the information contained in probate inventories. Many inventories list the contents of the house room by room, making it possible to work out the function of each. Naturally, the size of a house and the improvements that were made varied according to the wealth and status of the occupant. From the inventories it is easiest to investigate the homes of the prosperous villagers; they were more likely to have had their goods appraised than were the small farmers, craftsmen and labourers. In this respect inventories cannot be used to provide a comprehensive survey of the housing stock of a community. Moreover, post-Restoration inventories tend to be less informative than those made earlier. Rooms might still be given but often the goods are not separately listed. Many do not mention individual rooms and even those that do have omissions.

Of the other sources, manorial and estate records such as accounts, leases, rentals and manor court rolls can still be looked at. Indeed, early modern surveys may furnish more evidence than medieval ones. Some give a general description of each building, others note the size, normally in bays, of the house and outbuildings. They may even list rooms. Parliamentary surveys of the mid-seventeenth century often did: in a survey of Lord Craven's Shropshire estate in 1652–3 this information was regularly included.[17]

Glebe terriers provide similar details of the homes of the clergy. In some dioceses it was the custom to record the parsonage and outbuildings in terms of bays of building. In others, descriptions were more precise. According to Prof. Hoskins, the documents often go 'more fully into the materials of which the house is built, and the way in which it is laid out, than any probate inventory would do.'[18] Also useful, though not as common, are the faculty papers, deposited in the diocesan archive. If, in the eighteenth century, an incumbent wanted to make alterations to the parsonage, he had to obtain a

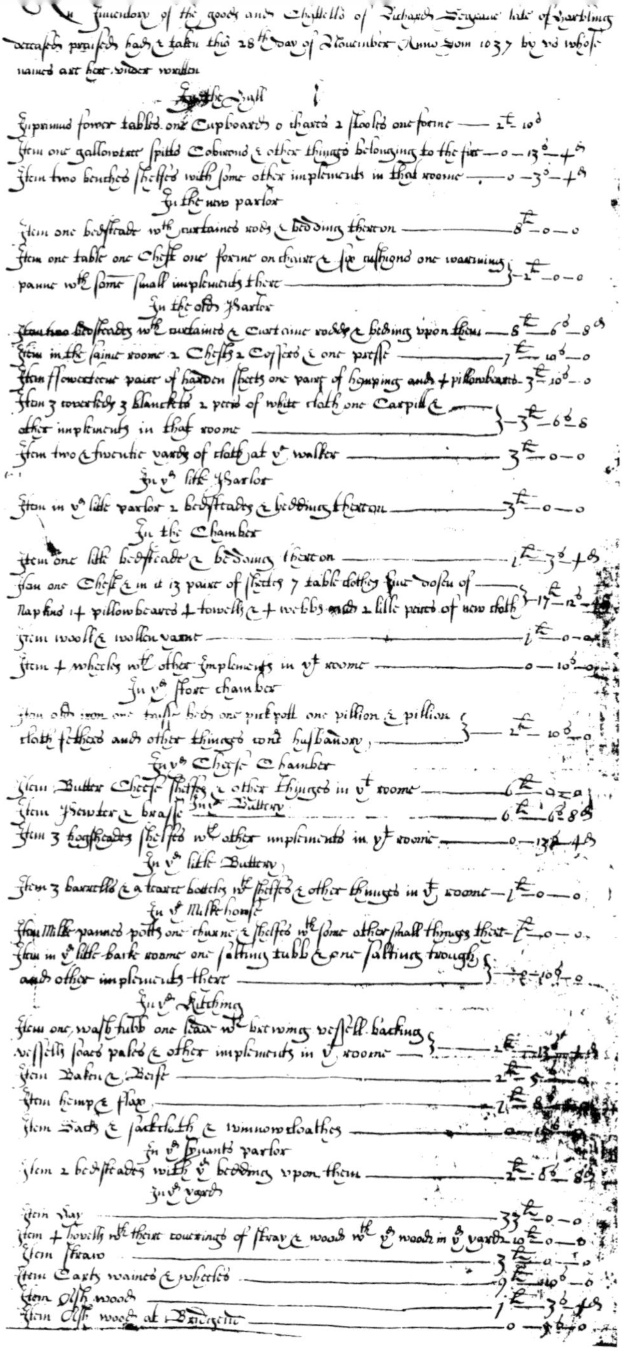

An Inventory of the goods and Chattells of Richard Segrave late of Horbling deceased praised had & taken this 28th day of November Anno Dom 1637 by us whose names are here under written

In the Hall

Imprimus fower tables one Cupboard 6 chairs 2 stooles one forme — 2li 10s

Item one gallowtree spitts cobirons & other things belonging to the fire — 0 – 13s – 4d

Item two benches shelfes with some other implements in that roome — 0 – 3s – 4d

In the new parlor

Item one bedsteade with curtaines rods & bedding thereon — 8li – 0 – 0

Item one table one Chest one forme one chaire & six cushions one warming panne with some small implements there — 2li – 0 – 0

In the old Parlor

Item two bedsteads with curtaines & curtaine rodds & bedding upon them — 8li – 6s – 8d

Item in the same roome 2 Chests 2 Coffers & one presse — 1li – 10s – 0

Item fowerteene paire of harden sheets one paire of hempen and 4 pillowbeares — 3li – 10s – 0

Item 3 coverlids 3 blanckets 2 peece of white cloth one Carpitt & other implements in that roome — 3li – 6s – 8d

Item two & twentie yards of cloth at ye walker — 3li – 0 – 0

In ye little Parlor

Item in ye little parlor 2 bedsteads & bedding thereon — 3li – 0 – 0

In the Chamber

Item one little bedsteade & bedding thereon — 1li – 3s – 4d

Item one Chest & in it 13 paire of sheets 7 table clothes five dosen of napkins 14 pillowbeares 4 towells & 4 webbs and 2 little peece of new cloth — 17li – 12s – [illegible]

Item woolle & wollen yarne — 1li – 0 – [illegible]

Item 4 wheeles with other implements in yt roome — 0 – 10s – 0

In ye fore chamber

Item old iron one truss bedd one pickfork one pillion & pillion cloth fethers and other things with husbandry — 2li – 10s – 0

In ye Cheese Chamber

Item Butter Cheese shelfes & other things in yt roome — 6li – 0 – 0

Item Pewter & brasse — 6li – 6s – 8d

In ye Buttery

Item 3 hogsheads shelfes with other implements in yt roome — 0 – 13s – 4d

In ye little Buttery

Item 3 barrells & a leather bottle with shelfes & other things in yt roome — 1li – 0 – 0

In ye Milkehouse

Item Milke pannes potts one churne & shelfes with some other small things there — 1li – 0 – 0

Item in ye little back roome one salting tubb & one salting trough and other implements there — [illegible] – 10s – 0

In ye Kitching

Item one wash tubb one lead with brewing vessell backing vessells soes pales & other implements in ye roome — 2li – 13s – 4d

Item Bacon & Beife — 2li – [illegible]

Item hempe & flax — [illegible]

Item Sacks & sackcloth & winnowcloathes — [illegible]

In ye servants parlor

Item 2 bedsteads with ye bedding upon them — 2li – 6s – 8d

In ye yard

Item Hay — 33li – 0 – 0

Item 4 hovells with their coverings of straw & wood with ye wood in ye yarde — 10li – 0 – 0

Item Straw — 3li – 0 – 0

Item Cart waines & wheeles — 9li – 10s – 0

Item Ash wood — 1li – 3s – 4d

Item Ash wood at Bridgend(?) — 0 – [illegible]

42 The probate inventory of Richard Segrave, a farmer from Horbling (Lincolnshire), 28 November 1637. The appraisers carefully noted each room in his house and the contents in them.

faculty (licence) to do so.[19] Not only do these documents indicate the nature of the proposed changes but as they were often accompanied by a plan they show them in a visual way too.

The proliferation in the number of maps in the early modern period, as well as improvements in their quality, adds an extra dimension to the study of buildings. Many estate maps give bird's-eye views of houses and buildings erected on land belonging to the owner and might show whole villages if the estate encompassed most of the manor, township or parish. Thus, the whole of the village of Little Wenlock (Shropshire) is included on a map of 1727, drawn up for the Forester family.[20] The houses are shown in some detail and include such features as cross-wings, gables, windows, doors and chimneys. Apart from the fact that this particular surveyor carried out a number of commissions for the local gentry, the care with which he made the map and the details of the houses illustrated give one confidence in the way he depicted them. This is not always the case and anyone, when studying a map, should take care before accepting the accuracy of the buildings drawn on them. One way to gauge this is to compare existing houses with sketches of them on the map.

Paintings and drawings provide another source of visual evidence, but although houses may be better drawn and painted in full colour, they still could be inaccurately portrayed. Vernacular buildings did not form the main subject matter of many paintings of this period, though they can often be found in them, completing the scene. Inevitably, the artist paid greater attention to the central themes – perhaps a portrait, a landscape or a country seat – and painted in the background details in a generalized way.

Estate and farm accounts record the cost of improvement, while diaries and commonplace books might add personal comments on the process. In the household book which Robert Furse, a Devonshire yeoman, wrote in 1593, he describes the alterations he had made to his home since succeeding to his estate in 1572. This work, he tells us, involved adding a porch and entry to the house, a ceiling to the hall, and glazing the windows. He probably built the granite newel stair on the back wall as well.[21] Information also appears in the correspondence. Land agents reported on the state of the houses on the estate, and on the repairs that needed to be done or which were being carried out. They discussed possible improvements with their masters and kept them informed on the progress of any project. Negotiations with craftsmen and labourers concerning wages and conditions were noted and comments made on the standard of their work.

Some indication of the size of houses can be obtained from the hearth tax returns, as individuals paid on the number of fireplaces they had in their homes. Obviously a connection existed between the two but the relationship was not a precise one, as shown in the research undertaken by Margaret Spufford in which she linked Cambridgeshire hearth tax entries with individual probate inventories.[22]

The houses of the people who benefited from the economic changes of the sixteenth and seventeenth centuries are the most striking. Not only are they well documented but many of them still stand in the village streets today. They were outnumbered, however, by the homes of the poorer sections of society, dwellings which have largely disappeared and only exist in documents or under the soil. Contemporaries wrote about these buildings, often in shocked terms which reflect their social background. Celia Fiennes, in her travels in the 1690s, saw many examples of bad housing, especially in the North, the least prosperous part of the country. Between Penrith and Carlisle she observed 'little hutts and hovels the poor live in like barns some have them daub'd with mud-wall others drye walls.'[23]

Thousands of cottages built by squatters on waste land are referred to in the manor court rolls, sometimes indicating the size of the building. These cottages are also depicted on contemporary maps, such as the one made of Lineal Common (Shropshire) in *c.* 1600.[24] These cottages were one or two bays long with timber-framed walls and a chimney. By combining the two sources we discover that a cottage and garden labelled Copnall's Croft on a map of part of the Wealdmoors in the 1630s had been built by Robert Copnall forty years earlier. In 1594 he had been fined at the manor court for a cottage 'newly erected'.[25]

If most of this building activity had been prompted by individual initiative, formal provision was regularly made for the homeless too – perhaps for an aged or infirm parishioner. The record of such proceedings might overlap a number of sources, notably parish accounts, vestry minutes, manor court rolls and quarter sessions' papers. Discussion of individual cases might take place at a meeting of the vestry and if an agreement could be reached, a patch of ground would be sought. Often, the lord of the manor allowed a piece of the waste to be used. Sometimes, the matter had to be dealt with by the magistrates and they might order land to be set aside and a cottage built. If the building was put up at the parish's charge, details of the expenditure appear in the accounts of the overseers of the poor.[26] More commonly, they list costs incurred in maintaining existing cottages.

The hearth tax returns reveal, not surprisingly, that a large proportion of those exempted on grounds of poverty were living in the smallest houses, those with one hearth. As noted above, probate inventories cannot be used to provide an accurate picture of the standard of housing of the labourers because those whose goods were appraised were among the wealthiest of their class. Indeed, they often appear to be indistinguishable from small-scale husbandmen. Occasionally, pauper inventories survive among the records of the overseers of the poor, since the goods of paupers belonged to the parish after their death.[27]

Housing developments since the mid-eighteenth century

Changes continued to take place after the mid-eighteenth century. By 1700 the design of farmhouses was being influenced by classical motifs, as Renaissance ideas percolated down through the social strata.[28] During the course of the eighteenth century the process accelerated as houses were built or modified to conform to contemporary canons of polite taste. In this respect, the homes of many prosperous farmers were passing beyond the bounds of the vernacular tradition.

This development was nation-wide but is perhaps most noticeable in open field communities where upon enclosure new farmsteads were built in the middle of the consolidated fields. A guiding principle was that of symmetry; typically farmhouses were built of two full storeys, comprising a doorway flanked by two windows on either side and five windows on the first floor.[29] Because of the arrangement of the hall and parlour on the ground floor extra space had to be found. This was provided for at the rear of the house either as a parallel range or as a cross-wing. The influence of the Renaissance can also be seen in the detailed features of the house, in the use of new styles such as sash windows and in the decoration around doors and windows.

At a lower level, many labourers continued to live in substandard housing, crammed into converted farmhouses, or in homes which they had built themselves or which had been thrown together by speculators seeking to maximize their returns for the lowest possible outlay.[30] With the decline of living-in, farmers and landowners had to give greater consideration to the provision of houses for their work-force. To a certain extent a distinction can be made between open and closed communities, in which the sprawling and ill-planned buildings of the former villages contrast with the neat, well-ordered and unified appearance of the latter. Nonetheless, there was a connection between the two. The pretty estate villages, with their decorative and highly stylized homes, could be kept that way because they were small and manageable. Often only the permanent workers were housed there. Other labourers had to find alternative accommodation and inevitably they moved into nearby open villages, adding to the housing problem there.

During this period the stock of farm buildings underwent considerable improvement. Earlier farmsteads had contained outbuildings, essential to the work of the farm, but as Roy Brigden observes in his book, *Victorian Farms*, 'farms were commonly made up of an amalgam of buildings that had accumulated over the centuries to no logical plan, were unsuited to present conditions and were, in any case, falling into disrepair.'[31] Later farm buildings, in contrast, especially those erected during the nineteenth century, were planned and constructed in a more scientific way. A good deal of reorganization and rebuilding was undertaken, the aim of which was to improve efficiency and increase output.[32] Greater consideration was also given to power sources, whether by the installation of wheel-houses for horse gins, the cutting of a leet to drive a water-wheel or the housing of a steam engine.

Large landowners, with their greater resources, took the lead in such matters and therefore estate records provide some of the best sources of evidence of developments, as well as information on traditional themes (size of houses, room functions, construction materials and so on). Building projects were discussed in estate correspondence and, if implemented, progress was reported in further letters. More than before, improvement schemes were likely to be accompanied by diagrams, showing floor plans and elevations. Account books reveal the costs involved and the timing and pace of the building work. The audit books of the Coke family of Holkham (Norfolk), for instance, contain details of changes that were made on the estate. From them two distinct phases can be discerned: in the first, covering the period up to 1850, emphasis was placed on building new houses and premises (or remodelling existing ones), whereas in the second, spanning the years 1868–83, it switched to the improvement of farm buildings.[33]

Improvements on the Holkham estate cost thousands of pounds and it is therefore no surprise to note the growing interest shown by farmers and landowners in insuring their property. More fire insurance policies were taken out which, because they describe the premises (and the goods and machinery) being insured, can be used to examine the state of farm buildings in the countryside. Details of the rooms were not normally recorded, though if goods or machinery were included in the policy, the places where they were being kept were mentioned. The size of the house and any ancillary buildings can be estimated from the references to the number of bays they contained, a piece of information that is often included in the description. The sum of money for which the property was insured may also indicate size. The materials used in the construction of the house and outbuildings were highly relevant to the insurer and this information was usually noted down.

Sales catalogues deal with the disposal of houses and land on large estates but they have wider application as even small freehold properties were involved. They often fully describe the house, listing its rooms and associated outbuildings and giving an indication of the construction materials used. Smaller properties, however, might be recorded in less precise terms. Even more detailed are the notices drawn up to accompany disposal sales of household goods. In some ways they are very similar to probate inventories. No valuations are given, but the auctioneer moved around the house, room by room, recording the items and giving them a lot number. As many of the sales were advertised in the local newspaper, some information might be found there too. Today we would still look in newspapers for details of houses but for the original documentation, we would examine the papers in estate agents' offices.

Sales catalogues normally include a large-scale map of the properties being sold and can be used to work out the dimensions of the buildings. Deeds drawn up in the last hundred years or so are also more likely to contain a plan of the premises than earlier ones. The ground-floor plan of individual

Particulars,

AND

CONDITIONS OF SALE,

OF THE

VALUABLE MANOR

OF

Great Bookham,

NEAR LEATHERHEAD, SURRY;

WITH

COURTS, LEET AND BARON, RIGHTS, AND ROYALTIES, &c. &c.

TOGETHER WITH THE

LORD'S RIGHT OF THE SOIL,

AND OF

GROWING TIMBER THEREON,

ON

BOOKHAM AND RANMORE COMMONS,

OF GREAT EXTENT,

THE ONE COVERED WITH FINE OAK, THE OTHER WITH BEECH AND OTHER TIMBER,

ALSO

SOLE FARM, FREEHOLD,

THE LAND TAX (EXCEPT ON ABOUT THIRTY-NINE ACRES) REDEEMED,

WITH A SUBSTANTIAL

Brick-Built Farm House,

CAPITAL BARNS, AND OTHER BUILDINGS;

AND

384 ACRES

OF

ARABLE, MEADOW, AND PASTURE LAND,

CONTIGUOUS TO

The Village of Bookham, and joining to Fetcham, Bookham Grove, Eastwick Park, and other distinguished Properties, in a country scarcely to be surpassed for Scenery, respectability of Inhabitants, and facilities for Field Sport.

The same will be Sold by Auction,

By Mr. CHRISTIE,

AT THE AUCTION MART,

IN BARTHOLOMEW LANE,

On WEDNESDAY, JULY the 2d, 1823,

AT ONE O'CLOCK PRECISELY,

IN EIGHTEEN LOTS.

Particulars may be had at the office of Mr. LOVERIDGE, Solicitor, Charlotte Street, Bloomsbury; of JOHN SMALLPIECE, Esq. Steward of the Manor, Guildford, Surry; at the AUCTION MART, and at the office of Mr. CHRISTIE, Pall Mall, where a Map may be seen;—and of Mr. THOMAS LA COSTE BANKER, at Chertsey, who has for several years been Land Steward of the Estate, and is intimately acquainted with all the details of the Property.

43 Sale particulars of Sole Farm, Great Bookham (Surrey), 2 July 1823.

properties can be seen by looking at other large-scale maps, notably the tithe and 25-inch Ordnance Survey maps. On the latter, features such as an added wing at the side of a house can be spotted. Sales catalogues may include photographs of some of the properties involved, adding to the pictorial record of the recent past. Photographs, as a source, offer striking evidence of building changes over the last century. Apart from furnishing information on houses long since pulled down, they might also portray existing buildings before late twentieth-century modernization.

Tax records can also be examined in a general way to evaluate the standard of housing in a particular locality. Descriptions in the land tax returns or in the parish rate assessments indicate the type of housing to be found there. The size of the assessments can also be analysed, though if land is attached to a property, it is a less effective guide. Additions to and subdivisons from individual assessments are illuminating, perhaps indicating an extension to the house or its conversion into tenements. More detailed information can be obtained from the records of the reformed land tax of 1910. Field books, in particular, often contain a considerable amount of material. For instance, 2 Myrtle Cottages, Leatherhead Road, Chessington (Surrey) comprised a 'semi detached brick and slated cottage containing Sitting Rm. Kitchen & Scullery 3 Bedrooms (3rd. leads from 2nd.) outside closet & shed. Rent 7/-, cold water, 20′ Frontage.'[34]

For the homes of the labourers a further source becomes available in the nineteenth century. As part of the government's enquiries into the condition of the rural work-force, evidence was heard concerning the cottages in which they lived.[35] Conditions varied enormously. Thus the Royal Commission on Housing in 1885 could report that in Cheshire Lord Tollemache had recently built 300 excellent cottages, while in Wiltshire bedrooms were found which were not high enough to stand up in and where the rotting thatch dropped filth on to the sleepers' heads. The reports of local medical officers also showed that a considerable amount of insanitary and substandard housing remained. At a national level Chadwick's reports revealed the same picture: many labourers lived in squalid homes, one- or two-roomed hovels built of mud and thatch, and damp because of a lack of flooring. Washing, cooking and drinking facilities were equally primitive. This state of affairs persisted to the end of the nineteenth century and beyond, a fact confirmed by reports, literary evidence and the testimony of old people.

Summary

A study of the history of rural buildings, using the documents referred to in this chapter, reveals that the homes of people of different social classes moved beyond the scope of vernacular architecture at varying times. In the Middle Ages even some of the larger houses possessed vernacular qualities, though these had virtually disappeared by the end of the period. During the course of the sixteenth and seventeenth centuries they were followed into the sphere of polite architecture by the bulk of the homes of the gentry. By 1700, too, the houses of prosperous farmers were beginning to cross the threshold. On the other hand, the dwellings of many labourers did not enter the vernacular zone until the eighteenth century or even later.

Today, houses are normally no longer constructed according to the vernacular tradition. Even the modest homes of the mass of the population conform to national styles and are built of materials often brought in from a distance. Improvements in transportation had the effect of breaking down the old reliance on local resources, while the development of mechanization brought with it mass production. There has been a price to pay for this progress, however, for these changes have had an adverse effect on the landscape. Buildings constructed out of alien materials are obtrusive and jarring to the eye, whereas those dug or quarried locally blend in naturally with their surroundings. The clock cannot be turned back to reduce the visual impact, but care should be taken whenever buildings are designed and erected. Architects should be aware of environmental factors and bear them in mind at the planning stage, in terms of scale and design, as well as in the materials used.

Notes

1 The governance of rural England

1. E. Miller & J. Hatcher, *Medieval England: Rural Society and Economic Change 1086–1348* (Longman, London, 1978), pp. 19–22
2. P. D. A. Harvey, 'Manorial Records', *Archives and the User*, 5 (British Records Assoc., London, 1984), pp. 45–9, 60
3. *Ibid.*, pp. 29–38; Miller & Hatcher, pp. 191–5
4. Harvey, pp. 17–22
5. *Ibid.*, pp. 2–3
6. *Ibid.*, pp. 10–11
7. C. S. Orwin & E. H. Whetham, *History of British Agriculture 1846–1914* (David & Charles, Newton Abbot, 1971), pp. 182, 186–7
8. W. E. Tate, *The Parish Chest: a Study of Parochial Administration in England* (Cambridge University Press, Cambridge, 1969), p. 84
9. J. H. Bettey, *Church and Parish: a Guide for Local Historians* (Batsford, London, 1987), p. 54
10. Tate, pp. 44–5
11. *Ibid.*, p. 177
12. *Ibid.*, pp. 242–50
13. A. L. Beier, *The Problem of the Poor in Tudor and Early Stuart England* (Methuen, London, 1983), pp. 23–5
14. Tate, pp. 14, 18–20
15. *Ibid.*, p. 8; Orwin & Whetham, pp. 294, 331
16. Tate, pp. 188ff.
17. This paragraph is based on information kindly supplied by Dr. D. B. Robinson, the Surrey County Archivist
18. P. Clark & P. Slack, *English Towns in Transition 1500–1700* (Oxford University Press, Oxford, 1976), pp. 126–7; P. J. Corfield, *The Impact of English Towns 1700–1800* (Oxford University Press, Oxford, 1982), pp. 157–8
19. C. G. A. Clay, 'Landlords and Estate Management in England', in J. Thirsk, ed. *The Agrarian History of England and Wales, V, 1640–1750*, ii, p. 245; J. V. Beckett, *The Aristocracy in England 1660–1914* (Basil Blackwell, Oxford, 1986), p. 151
20. J. B. Harley, 'Maps for the Local Historian; a Guide to the British Sources, 2, Estate Maps', in *The Amateur Historian*, 7, vii (1967) p. 226–7

21. C. G. A. Clay, *Landlords*, p. 198; C. G. A. Clay, 'Lifeleasehold in the Western Counties of England 1650–1750', *Agric. Hist. Rev.*, 29, ii, 1981, pp. 9–12
22. A. A. Dibben, 'Title Deeds 13th. – 19th. Centuries', *Helps for Students of History*, H72 (Historical Association, London, 1971), pp. 9–12
23. J. R. Wordie, *Estate Management in 18th Century England* (Royal Historical Society, 1982), p. 40
24. This section is based on Bettey, pp. 42–7, 77–81; D. M. Owen, 'Short Guides to Records, 8, Episcopal Visitation Books', *History*, 49 (1964), pp. 185–8
25. J. Thirsk, 'Sources of Information on Population 1500–1760', in J. Thirsk, *The Rural Economy of England* (Hambledon Press, London, 1984), pp. 21–2, 25–6
26. D. M. Barrett, 'Short Guides to Records, 13, Glebe Terriers', *History*, 51 (1966), p. 36
27. Bettey, pp. 48, 81–4; F. G. Emmison, *Archives and Local History* (Phillimore, Chichester, 1978), pp. 39–40
28. P. Riden, *Local History: a Handbook for Beginners* (Batsford, London, 1983), p. 62
29. B. Trinder & J. Cox, *Yeomen and Colliers in Telford* (Phillimore, Chichester, 1980), p. 5
30. J. S. Moore, 'Probate Inventories: Problems and Prospects', in P. Riden, ed., *Probate Records and the Local Community* (Alan Sutton, Gloucester, 1985), pp. 18–19
31. P. Riden, *Record Sources for Local History* (Batsford, London, 1987), pp. 179–80
32. E. J. Evans, *The Contentious Tithe: the Tithe Problem and English Agriculture 1750–1850* (RKP, London, 1976), pp. 16–17
33. R. J. P. Kain & H. C. Prince, *The Tithe Surveys of England and Wales* (Cambridge University Press, Cambridge, 1985), pp. 7–9
34. *Ibid.*, p. 6; Evans, pp. 17, 42–6
35. Kain & Prince, pp. 3, 5, 32–3, 66–7, 86
36. N. Landau, *The Justices of the Peace 1679–1760* (University of California Press, Berkeley, 1984), pp. 6, 8–9, 27–9
37. J. S. Morrill, *The Revolt of the Provinces* (George Allen & Unwin, London, 1976), pp. 66–70
38. Riden, *Record Sources*, p. 87
39. Emmison, p. 24
40. Riden, *Record Sources*, pp. 89–90
41. *Ibid.*, p. 87
42. *Ibid.*, pp. 26–7
43. S. B. Chrimes, *An Introduction to the Administrative History of Medieval England* (Basil Blackwell, Oxford, 1959), pp. 113, 136–140, 199–200, 206, 213–16
44. Riden, *Record Sources*, pp. 52–4
45. *Ibid.*, pp. 55–6
46. G. R. Elton, *England under the Tudors* (Methuen, London, 1955), pp. 83, 176, 419–20
47. Riden, *Record Sources*, pp. 162–3
48. *Ibid.*, pp. 119–22
49. *Ibid.*, pp. 118–19
50. *Ibid.*, pp. 122–3
51. Chrimes, pp. 29–32

52. Riden, *Record Sources*, pp. 29–30
53. R. Welldon Finn, *Domesday Book: a Guide* (Phillimore, Chichester, 1973), pp. 17–24
54. J. B. Harley, 'The Hundred Rolls of 1279', *The Amateur Historian*, 5, i (1961), pp. 9–15
55. A. R. H. Baker, 'Evidence in the "Nonarum Inquisitiones" of Contracting Arable Lands in England during the Early Fourteenth Century' in A. R. H. Baker, J. D. Hamshere & J. Langton, eds., *Geographical Interpretations of Historical Sources* (David & Charles, Newton Abbot, 1970), pp. 85–6
56. M. W. Beresford, 'The Lay Subsidies, part I – 1290–1334', *The Amateur Historian*, 3, viii (1958), pp. 101–5
57. D. Pennington, 'The War and the People', in J. Morrill, ed., *Reactions to the English Civil War 1642–1649* (Macmillan, London, 1982), pp. 127–30
58. Baker, p. 85
59. W. G. Hoskins, *The Age of Plunder*, (Macmillan, London, 1976), pp. 123–4
60. M. Turner & D. Mills, *Land and Property: the English Land Tax 1692–1832* (Alan Sutton, Gloucester, 1986), pp. 1–6
61. B. Short & M. Reed, 'An Edwardian Land Survey: the Finance Act 1910', *Journal of Society of Archivists*, 8, ii, 1986, pp. 95-103
62. M. W. Beresford, 'The Poll Taxes of 1377, 1379 and 1381', *The Amateur Historian*, 3, vii, 1958, pp. 271–8
63. C. Russell, *The Origins of the English Civil War* (Macmillan, London, 1973), pp. 83–9; Riden, *Record Sources*, p. 61
64. Riden, *Record Sources*, p. 63
65. R. Howell, 'Short Guides to Records, 7, Hearth Tax Returns', *History*, 49 (1964), pp. 62–5
66. Riden, *Record Sources*, p. 30
67. W. C. Richardson, 'Records of the Court of Augmentations', *Journal of Society of Archivists*, 1, 1955–9, pp. 159–68
68. C. A. F. Meekings, ed., 'The 1235 Surrey Eyre', I, *Surrey Record Society*, 31, 1979, pp. 4–6
69. J. S. Cockburn, *A History of English Assizes 1558–1714* (Cambridge University Press, Cambridge, 1972), pp. 16–19; Elton, pp. 176–8
70. Cockburn, *Assizes*, pp. 130–1; M. Blatcher, *The Court of King's Bench 1450–1550* (University of London Press, London, 1978), p. 2
71. Riden, *Record Sources*, pp. 28–9; Elton, pp. 412–17; Evans, pp. 44–5

2 Village society

1. Miller & Hatcher, *Medieval England: Rural Society and Economic Change 1086–1348* (Longman, London, 1978) p. 22
2. W. G. Hoskins, *The Midland Peasant* (Macmillan, London, 1965), pp. 8–9
3. R. Lennard, *Rural England 1086–1135* (Clarendon Press, Oxford, 1959), p. 341; Miller & Hatcher, p. 24
4. Lennard, pp. 349–53
5. Miller & Hatcher, p. 24
6. *Ibid.*, pp. 123, 145–6

7. *Ibid.*, pp. 143–4
8. J. Z. Titow, *English Rural Society 1200–1350* (George Allen & Unwin, London, 1969), pp. 153–60
9. For example M. K. McIntosh, 'Land, Tenure and Population in the Royal Manor of Havering, Essex, 1251–1352/3', *Economic History Review*, 33, i (1980), pp. 17–31
10. Miller & Hatcher, p. 145
11. For example, C. Dyer, *Lords and Peasants in a Changing Society* (Cambridge University Press, Cambridge, 1980), pp. 350–1
12. C. Howell, *Land, Family & Inheritance in Transition* (Cambridge University Press, Cambridge, 1983), pp. 42–3
13. J. L. Bolton, *The Medieval Economy 1150–1500* (Dent, London, 1980), pp. 214–15
14. Dyer, *Lords and Peasants*, pp. 236–43
15. Bolton, pp. 218–19
16. Dyer, *Lords and Peasants*, p. 246
17. J. M. Bennett, *Women in the Medieval English Countryside: Gender & Household in Brigstock before the Plague* (Oxford University Press, Oxford 1987), pp. 22–4
18. Bolton, p. 239
19. Dyer, *Lords and Peasants*, p. 350
20. Hoskins, *Age of Plunder*, pp. 19–21
21. E. Kerridge, 'The Movement of Rent, 1540–1640' in E. M. Carus-Wilson, ed., *Essays in Economic History*, II (Edward Arnold, London, 1962), pp. 208–26
22. E. Hopkins, 'The Re-leasing of the Ellesmere Estates, 1637–42', *Agricultural History Review*, 10, i (1962), pp. 14–28. Also see E. Hopkins, 'The Bridgewater Estates in North Shropshire in the First Half of the Seventeenth Century', unpub. London Univ. M.A. dissertation, 1956, pp. 71–2, 87
23. Hereford & Worcester Record Office (Worcester), Probate Will of Thomas Nayshe of Rushock, 1620/137; Merchant Taylors' Records, IX, 113–15
24. K. Wrightson & D. Levine, *Poverty and Piety in an English Village: Terling 1525–1700*, (Academic Press, New York, 1979), p. 104
25. *Ibid.*, p. 103
26. M. Spufford, *Contrasting Communities* (Cambridge University Press, Cambridge, 1974), pp. 76–85
27. *Ibid.*, pp. 66–70
28. V. Skipp, *Crisis and Development*, (Cambridge University Press, Cambridge, 1978), p. 80
29. F. G. Emmison, *Archives and Local History* (Phillimore, Chichester, 1974), p. 58
30. J. V. Beckett, *The Aristocracy in England 1660–1914* (Basil Blackwell, Oxford, 1986), pp. 198–9
31. Clay, 'Lifeleasehold', p. 87
32. Shropshire Record Office, Attingham Park Colln., 112/2698
33. *Ibid.*, 112/2388
34. R. Gough, *Antiquityes and Memoyres of the Parish of Myddle* (Salop County Council, Shrewsbury, 1987), pp. 66–70
35. M. Turner, *English Parliamentary Enclosure* (Dawson, Folkestone, 1980), pp. 163–70

36. M. Turner, 'The Land Tax, Land and Property: Old Debates and New Horizons', in M. Turner & D. Mills, eds. *Land and Property: The English Land Tax 1692–1832* (Alan Sutton, Gloucester, 1986), pp. 1–6. Also read D. Grigg, 'A Source on Landownership: the Land Tax Returns', *The Amateur Historian*, 6, v (1964), pp. 152–6
37. S. Banks, 'Parish Ownership and the Land Tax Assessments in West Norfolk; a Comparison with the Tithe Surveys', in Turner and Mills, *Land and Property*, p. 48
38. M. Turner, *op. cit.*, p. 16
39. Turner, *English Parliamentary Enclosure*, p. 162
40. F. M. L. Thompson, *English Landed Society in the Nineteenth Century* (RKP, London, 1971), p. 27
41. BPP 1874 LXXII, *Returns of Owners of Land 1872–3*
42. Beckett, *The Aristocracy*, p. 85
43. Rep. of Royal Comm. on Poor Law, H.C. 44 (1834) xxvii-xxxviii

3 Population trends

1. D. B. Grigg, *Population Growth and Agrarian Change: an Historical Perspective* (Cambridge University Press, Cambridge, 1980), pp. 283–5
2. Miller & Hatcher, *Medieval England: Rural Society and Economic Change 1086–1348* (Longman, London, 1978), p. 29
3. *Ibid.*, pp. 160–1, 243–6, 250–1
4. *Ibid.*, pp. 143–5
5. Dyer, *Lords and Peasants*, p. 90
6. Miller & Hatcher, p. 31
7. Dyer, *Lords and Peasants*, p. 237
8. W. G. Hoskins, 'The Population of an English Village 1086–1801: A Study of Wigston Magna', in W. G. Hoskins, *Provincial England* (Macmillan, London, 1963), pp. 182–3
9. M. W. Beresford, 'The Poll Taxes of 1377, 1379 and 1381' *The Amateur Historian*, 3, vii (1958), pp. 271–8
10. Howell, *Kibworth Harcourt*, p. 210
11. B. A. Hanawalt, *The Ties that Bound* (Oxford University Press, Oxford, 1986), p. 197
12. Miller & Hatcher, pp. 43–4
13. D. Hey, *Family History and Local History in England* (Longman, London, 1987), pp. 29–34
14. Howell, *Kibworth Harcourt*, p. 47
15. Dyer, *Lords and Peasants*, p. 366–8
16. J. Thirsk, 'Sources of Information on Population', p. 19
17. Hoskins, 'Population of an English Village', p. 185
18. British Museum, Harleian, 594, 595, 618
19. E. A. Wrigley & R. S. Schofield, *The Population History of England 1541–1871* (Cambridge University Press, Cambridge, 1989 edn.) p. 35
20. C. T. Smith, 'Population', *Victoria County History of Leicestershire*, III (London, 1955), pp. 166–74

21. Thirsk, 'Population', pp. 20–2
22. *Ibid.*, p. 20–1
23. W. G. Hoskins, *The Age of Plunder* (Longman, London, 1976), pp. 14–18
24. C. J. Harrison, 'Elizabethan Village Surveys: a Comment', *Agricultural History Review* 27, ii (1979), p. 86
25. M. Drake, ed., *Population Studies from Parish Registers* (Local Population Studies, Matlock, 1982), pp. v–xxxiv
26. D. M. Palliser, 'Dearth and Disease in Staffordshire 1540–1670', in C. W. Chalklin & M. A. Havinden, eds., *Rural Change and Urban Growth 1500–1800* (Longman, London, 1974), p. 57
27. D. M. Palliser, *The Age of Elizabeth* (Longman, London, 1983), p. 55
28. P. Laslett, *Family Life and Illicit Love in Earlier Generations* (Cambridge University Press, Cambridge, 1977), pp. 65–6
29. P. Clark, 'Migration in England during the late Seventeenth and early Eighteenth Centuries', in P. Clark and D. Souden, eds., *Migration and Society in Early Modern England* (Hutchinson, London, 1987), p. 218
30. *Ibid.*, p. 223
31. P. Edwards, 'The Development of Dairy Farming on the North Shropshire Plain in the Seventeenth Century', *Midland History*, 4 (1978), p. 177
32. Grigg, *Population Growth*, p. 168; N. Tranter, *Population since the Industrial Revolution* (Croom Helm, London, 1973), p. 97
33. Grigg, *Population Growth*, p. 168
34. *Ibid.*
35. W. G. Hoskins, *The Midland Peasant* (Macmillan, London, 1965), pp. 212, 217, 227–8, 261–2, 273
36. M. W. Flinn, *British Population Growth 1700–1850* (Macmillan, London, 1970), pp. 12–13
37. Guildford Muniment Room, PSH/Bk. G/8/2
38. J. A. Cole & M. Armstrong, *Tracing Your Family Tree* (Equation, Bath, 1988), p. 64
39. Hey, *Family History*, p. 212
40. Shropshire Record Office, 499/1

4 Earning a living

1. P. Edwards, *Farming: Sources for Local Historians* (Batsford, London, 1991), chapter 7
2. L. F. Salzman, ed., 'Ministers' Accounts of the Manor of Petworth 1347–1353', *Sussex Record Society*, 55 (1955), pp. 1–11
3. Titow, *English Rural Society 1200–1350* (George Allen & Unwin, London, 1969) pp. 138–44
4. Petworth Accounts, p. 10
5. Hanawalt, *The Ties that Bound* (Oxford University Press, Oxford, 1986), pp. 157–61
6. For the early modern period see A. Kussmaul, *Servants in Husbandry in Early Modern England* (Cambridge University Press, Cambridge, 1981), pp. 3–4
7. Hanawalt, pp. 141–55

8. Petworth Accounts, p. 7
9. S. A. C. Penn, 'Female Wage-earners in Late Fourteenth-Century England', *Agricultural History Review*, 35, i (1987), p. 2
10. *Ibid.*, p. 3
11. *Ibid.*, p. 5
12. This section is based upon Bennett, *Brigstock*, pp. 120-9
13. This section is based upon J. Birrell, 'Peasant Craftsmen in the Medieval Forest', *Agricultural History Review*, 17 ii (1969), pp. 91–107
14. Edwards, *Farming*, pp. 139–40
15. This topic is discussed in J. Thirsk, *Economic Policy and Projects* (Oxford University Press, Oxford, 1978), pp. 1–23
16. For example C. B. Phillips, 'Town and Country: Economic Change in Kendal', in P. Clark, ed., *The Transformation of English Provincial Towns* (Hutchinson, London, 1984), pp. 99–132
17. Hoskins, *The Midland Peasant*, pp. 227–9
18. Lincolnshire Archive Office, SWINDERBY PAR 23/1
19. E. Melling, ed., *Kentish Sources III: Aspects of Agriculture and Industry* (Kent County Council, Kent, 1961), pp. 32–59
20. Shropshire Record Office, Forester Colln. 1224/Boxes 296-7; Charlton-Meyrick Colln. 625/Box 15
21. Oxford and Chester have good runs of early modern market toll books which list occupations
22. P. Edwards, *The Horse Trade of Tudor and Stuart England* (Cambridge University Press, Cambridge, 1988), p. 127
23. M. Spufford, 'The Limitations of the Probate Inventory', in J. Chartres & D. Hey, eds., *English Rural Society, 1500–1800: Essays in Honour of Joan Thirsk* (Cambridge University Press, Cambridge, 1990), pp. 142–6
24. Lichfield, J. R. O., Probate John Williamson of the parish of Whitchurch, 4 October 1694
25. Edwards, *Farming*, pp. 165–6
26. This section is based upon Hey, *Family History*, pp. 151–72
27. A. Rogers, *Approaches to Local History* (Longman, London, 1977, edn.), p. 89
28. S. MacDonald, 'The Diffusion of Knowledge among Northumberland Farmers, 1780–1815', *Agricultural History Review*, 27, i (1979), p. 36
29. Hey, *Family History*, p. 154
30. Edwards, *Farming*, pp. 146–7
31. *Ibid.*
32. T. V. Jackson, 'The Sun Fire Office and the Local Historian', *Local Historian*, 17, iii (1986), pp. 142–3
33. R. Hillier, 'Auction Catalogues and Notices: their Value for the Local Historian', *Local Historian*, 13, iii (1978), pp. 131–9
34. This section is based upon G. Shaw, 'The Content and Reliability of Nineteenth-century Trade Directories', *Local Historian*, 13, iv (1978), pp. 205–9
35. Rogers, p. 87
36. Hey, *Family History*, p. 152

5 The peasant world

1. K. Thomas, *Religion and the Decline of Magic* (Penguin, Harmondsworth, 1973), pp. 681–98
2. J. A. Sharpe, *Crime in Early Modern England 1550–1750* (Longman, London, 1984), p. 123
3. J. H. Bettey, *Church and Parish: a Guide for Local Historians* (Batsford, London, 1987), p. 68
4. D. Hey, 'The Pattern of Nonconformity in South Yorkshire 1660–1850', *Northern History*, 8 (1973), pp. 86–118
5. Bettey, pp. 49–50
6. *Ibid.*, pp. 84–5
7. Spufford, *Contrasting Communities* (Cambridge University Press, Cambridge), p. 246
8. Bettey, p. 73
9. J. Morrill, 'The Church in England 1642–9', in J. Morrill, ed., *Reactions to the English Civil War 1642–1649* (Macmillan, London, 1982), p. 89–114
10. D. M. Owen, Short Guides to Records, 8, 'Episcopal Visitation Books', *History*, 49 (1964), pp. 185–8
11. Spufford, *Contrasting Communities*, pp. 268–9
12. Sharpe, *Crime*, p. 27; Bettey, pp. 35, 48
13. J. C. Jeaffreson, ed. *Middlesex County Records*, old series, 1 (Greater London Council, London, 1972), *passim*
14. J. A. Sharpe, *Early Modern England: a Social History 1550–1760* (Edward Arnold, London, 1987), pp. 244–5
15. Hey, *Family History*, p. 131
16. Spufford, *Contrasting Communities*, p. 260
17. R. W. Ambler, 'A Lost Source? The 1829 Returns of Non-Anglican Places of Worship', *Local Historian* 17, viii (1987), pp. 483–9
18. *Ibid.*, pp. 486–7
19. Bettey, pp. 134–7
20. Gough, *Myddle*, *passim*
21. Bettey, p. 90
22. B. Reay, 'Popular Religion', in B. Reay, ed., *Popular Culture in Seventeenth-Century England* (Croom Helm, London, 1985), p. 96
23. Wrightson & Levine, pp. 119-20, 156–7
24. *Ibid.*, 156–7
25. S. A Peyton, 'The Churchwardens' Presentments in the Oxfordshire Peculiars of Dorchester, Thame and Banbury', *Oxfordshire Record Society* (1928), p. 68, quoted in Thomas, *Magic*, p. 190
26. Thomas,, *Magic*, p. 192
27. *Ibid.*, p. 191
28. R. W. Malcolmson, *Life and Labour in England 1700–1780* (Hutchinson, London, 1981), p. 86–7
29. Thomas, *Magic*, p. 212
30. A. D. J. Macfarlane, 'Witchcraft in Tudor and Stuart Essex', in J. S. Cockburn, ed., *Crime in England 1550–1800* (Methuen, London, 1977), pp. 73–4
31. *Ibid.*, pp. 72–3

32. *Ibid.*, pp. 76–7, 79
33. J. Lawson & H. Silver, *A Social History of Education in England* (Methuen, London, 1973), pp. 43–4, 46
34. *Ibid.* pp. 68–72
35. *Ibid.*, pp. 182–4
36. *Ibid.*
37. Gough, *Myddle*, p. 31
38. D. Cressy, *Literacy and the Social Order: Reading and Writing in Tudor and Stuart England* (Cambridge University Press, Cambridge, 1980), p. 2
39. D. Cressy, *Education in Tudor and Stuart England* (Edward Arnold, London, 1975), p. 28; Spufford, *Contrasting Communities*, p. 187
40. Lawson & Silver, pp. 100–2, 165
41. *Ibid.*, pp. 191–2
42. Cressy, *Education*, p. 37
43. Lawson & Silver, pp. 239–41
44. Surrey Record Office, 3628/1
45. Lawson & Silver, pp. 241–3
46. G. F Bartle, 'The Records of the British and Foreign School Society', *Local Historian*, 16, iv (1984), pp. 204–6
47. Lawson & Silver, p. 268
48. P. Horn *The Victorian Country Child* (Alan Sutton, Gloucester, 1985), pp. 47ff.
49. Rogers, p. 205
50. Lawson & Silver, pp. 316–18
51. P. Horn, *Labouring Life in the Victorian Countryside* (Alan Sutton, Gloucester, 1987), p. 39
52. F. Thompson, *Lark Rise to Candleford* (Oxford University Press, Oxford, 1948), p. 171
53. Archives of Bookham Middle School, Surrey, log books *passim*
54. Lawson & Silver, p. 324
55. M. Spufford, *Small Books and Pleasant Histories* (Methuen, London, 1981), *passim*
56. Cressy, *Literacy*, pp. 54–61
57. *Ibid.*, p. 106–7
58. R. A. Houston, 'The Development of Literacy: Northern England, 1640–1750', *Economic History Review* 2nd. series, 35, ii (1982), pp. 199–216
59. Cressy, *Literacy*, pp. 67–78
60. R. S. Schofield, 'Dimensions of Illiteracy in England 1750–1850', in H. J. Graff, ed., *Literacy and Social Development in the West* (Cambridge University Press, Cambridge, 1981), pp. 206–9
61. Bettey, p. 63
62. *Ibid.*, pp. 56–7
63. H. S. Bennett, *Life on the English Manor* (Cambridge University Press, Cambridge, 1956), p. 264
64. *Ibid.*
65. R. W. Malcolmson, *Popular Recreations in English Society 1700–1850* (Cambridge University Press, Cambridge, 1979), p. 10
66. Hanawalt, p. 318, footnote 10
67. Malcolmson, *Popular Recreations*, pp. 6, 9

68. *Ibid.*, p. 11
69. Gough, *Myddle*, p. 63
70. Malcolmson, *Popular Recreations*, pp. 17–18
71. *Ibid.*, pp. 56–8
72. Gough, *Myddle*, p. 54
73. W. A. Leighton, 'Early Chronicles of Shrewsbury 1372–1606', *Trans. Shrops. Arch. Soc.*, 3 (1980), p. 318
74. Gough, *Myddle*, pp. 58, 78
75. P. Clark, *The English Alehouse: A Social History 1200–1830* (Longman, London, 1983), p. 115
76. *Ibid.*, p. 169
77. *Ibid.*, p. 154
78. Jeaffreson, Middlesex County Records, I, p. 97
79 A. J. Willis, *Winchester Consistory Court Depositions 1561–1602* (A. J. Willis, Hambledon, 1960), p. 34
80. Malcolmson, *Popular Recreations*, pp. 89ff.
81. *Ibid.*, p. 147
82. *Ibid.*, p. 149
83. Horn, *Victorian Country Child*, p. 180
84. B. Bushaway, *By Rite: Custom, Ceremony and Community in England 1700–1880* (Junction Books, London, 1982), p. 146
85. Malcolmson, *Popular Recreations* p. 146
86. Horn, *Victorian Country Child*, pp. 183–4
87. Bushaway, p. 261
88. R. W. Malcolmson, 'Leisure', in G. E. Mingay, ed., *The Victorian Countryside*, II (RKP, London, 1981), p. 612
89. Bennett, *Brigstock*, p. 24
90. R. W. Malcolmson, *Life and Labour in England 1700–1780* (Hutchinson, London, 1981), p. 105
91. Bennett, *Brigstock*, pp. 22, 104, 213–15
92. R. P. Hastings, 'Private Law-enforcement Associations', *Local Historian*, 14, iv (1980), pp. 226–32
93. G. C. Homans, *English Villagers of the Thirteenth Century* (Harper & Row, New York, 1970 edn.), p. 326
94. C. Herrup, *The Common Peace; Participation and the Criminal Law in Seventeenth-Century England* (Cambridge University Press, Cambridge, 1987), pp. 25–6
95. G. R. Elton, *England under the Tudors* (Methuen, London, 1955), pp. 412–17
96. Tate, p. 178
97. J. J. Tobias, *Crime and Police in England 1700–1900* (Gill & Macmillan, Dublin, 1979), pp. 96–101
98. Surrey Record Office, CC98/4/1 Examination and Appointment Book 1851–66
99. J. S. Cockburn, ed., *Crime in England 1550–1800* (Methuen, London, 1977), p. 114
100. Harvey, Manorial Records, pp. 46–7
101. H. S. Bennett, *The English Manor*, p. 199
102. Tobias, p. 137
103. Landau, p. 209ff.

104. Horn, *Labouring Life*, p. 222
105. C. A. F. Meekings, ed., 'The 1235 Surrey Eyre', *Surrey Record Society*, 31 (1979), pp. 5–6
106. Cockburn, *Crime*, p. 28
107. E. J. Hobsbawm & G. Rudé, *Captain Swing* (Lawrence & Wishall, London, 1969)
108. Bushaway, pp. 25–7
109. Surrey Record Office, CC98/1/2 Chief Constable's Report to the J.P.s, Easter Sessions 1853
110. J. A. Sharpe, *Crime in Seventeenth-century England: a County Study* (Cambridge University Press, Cambridge, 1983), pp. 9–11

6 Family and neighbourhood

1. Bennett, *Brigstock*, p. 24
2. Howell, *Kibworth Harcourt*, p. 210
3. A. V. Peatling, ed., Surrey Wills, *Surrey Record Society*, V (1921), p. 33
4. Bennett, *Brigstock*, pp. 80–2
5. Z. Ravi, *Life, Marriage and Death in a Medieval Parish: Economy, Society and Demography in Halesowen 1270–1400* (Cambridge University Press, Cambridge, 1980), pp. 60–4
6. R. A. Houlbrooke, *The English Family 1450–1750* (Longman, London, 1984), p. 63
7. *Ibid.*, p. 64
8. Hanawalt, p. 96
9. *Ibid.*, p. 201
10. *Ibid.*, pp. 67ff.
11. E. Toms, ed., Chertsey Abbey Court Rolls Abstract, *Surrey Record Society*, 21 (1954), p. 105
12. Miller & Hatcher, p. 141
13. Hanawalt, pp. 77–8
14. *Ibid.*, p. 71
15. Bennett, *Brigstock*, p. 144
16. M. W. Flinn, *British Population Growth 1700–1850* (Macmillan, London, 1970), p. 30
17. Sharpe, *Early Modern England*, p. 40
18. *Ibid.*, p. 41
19. Rev. T. Priestley, ed., The Register of Albrighton near Wolverhampton, *Shropshire Parish Register Society* (1899), p. 53
20. Sharpe, *Early Modern England*, p. 41
21. Grigg, *Population Growth*, pp. 166–8
22. M. Blaug, 'The Myth of the Old Poor Law and the Making of the New', *Journal of Economic History*, 23 (1963), pp. 151–84
23. Guildford Muniment Room, PSH/Bk. G/1/1
24. Warwickshire Record Office, Dr 198/1(a)
25. J. A. Cole & M. Armstrong, *Tracing your Family Tree* (Equation, Wellingborough, 1988), p. 60

26. J. G. W. Lewarne, Fetcham Parish Registers, *Procs., of Leatherhead & District Local History Society*, I, viii (1954), p. 7
27. Hey, *Family History*, p. 51
28. Wrightson & Levine, p. 77
29. Miss Auden, ed., The Register of Donington, *Shropshire Parish Register Society* (1900), pp. 32–46
30. Cole & Armstrong, p. 64
31. D. V. Glass, 'Two Papers on Gregory King', in D. V. Glass & D. E. C. Eversley, eds., *Population in History: Essays in Historical Demography* (Edward Arnold, London, 1965), pp. 169–73
32. Tate, p. 50
33. Dyer, *Lords and Peasants*, p. 270
34. Hanawalt, pp. 91–2
35. *Ibid.*, p. 91
36. *Ibid.*, p. 92
37. *Ibid.*, p. 90
38. Dyer, *Lords and Peasants*, p. 311
39. Hanawalt, pp. 229–35
40. Howell, *Kibworth Harcourt*, p. 158
41. Toms, Chertsey Abbey Court Rolls, Abstract, p. 136
42. P. Laslett, *The World We Have Lost – Further Explored* (Methuen, London, 1983), p. 92
43. A. Macfarlane, 'The Myth of the Peasantry', in R. M. Smith, ed., *Land, Kinship and Life-cycle* (Cambridge University Press, Cambridge, 1984), p. 344
44. R. T. Spence, 'The Graham Clans and Lands on the Eve of the Jacobean Pacification', *Trans. Cumb. & Westmor. Antiq. & Arch. Soc.*, N.S., 80 (1980), p. 80
45. K. J. Allison, 'An Elizabethan "Census" of Ealing', *Ealing Local History Society*, members papers, no. 2 (1962), *passim*
46. Laslett, *The World We Have Lost*, p. 96
47. Rogers, p. 41
48. Laslett, *The World We Have Lost*, p. 101
49. G. Nair, *Highley: the Development of a Community 1550–1880* (Basil Blackwell, Oxford, 1988), pp. 111–19
50. Lichfield J. R. O., Will of John Fletcher of Albrighton, 26 May 1618
51. Miller & Hatcher, pp. 24–5
52. Houlbrooke, pp. 150–1
53. Miller & Hatcher, p. 146
54. Dyer, *Lords and Peasants*, p. 110
55. Bennett, *Brigstock*, pp. 62–3
56. Z. Razi, 'Family, Land and the Village Community in Later Medieval England', *Past & Present*, 93 (1981), pp. 3–36
57. R. H. Hilton, *The English Peasantry in the Later Middle Ages* (Clarendon Press, Oxford, 1975), pp. 31–5
58. Hanawalt, p. 167
59. Peatling, Surrey Wills, p. 90
60. Ealing Census, *passim*

61. A. Kussmaul, *Servants in Husbandry in Early Modern England* (Cambridge University Press, Cambridge, 1981), pp. 121ff.
62. W. M. Williams, *The Sociology of an English Village: Gosforth* (RKP, London, 1956), pp. 38–40
63. Surrey Record Office, Great Bookham Census 1881
64. Hanawalt, pp. 79–80
65. *Ibid.*, pp. 80–1
66. Razi, Halesowen, pp. 147–9; Razi, 'Family Land and the Village Community', pp. 22–7
67. Gough, *Myddle*, *passim*
68. Hanawalt, p. 167
69. Lambeth Palace Library, Will of Nicholas Waxham of Putney (Roehampton)
70. Wrightson & Levine, pp. 99–100
71. *Ibid.*, p. 100
72. P. Edwards, *The Horse Trade of Tudor and Stuart England* (Cambridge University Press, Cambridge, 1988), p. 85
73. A. M. Everitt, 'The Marketing of Agricultural Produce', in J. Thirsk, ed., *The Agrarian History of England and Wales, IV, 1500–1640* (Cambridge University Press, Cambridge, 1967), p. 557
74. Edwards, *Horse Trade*, pp. 81–6
75. Shropshire Record Office, Shrewsbury Quarter Sessions' Papers, Shrewsbury Corp. Records, Bundle 2214
76. P. J. Bowden, *The Wool Trade in Tudor and Stuart England* (Frank Cass, London, 1971), pp. 101–6
77. Bennett, *Brigstock*, pp. 24, 28, 30, 37, 76
78. *Ibid.*, pp. 24, 181

7 Rural housing

1. Surrey Record Office, Great Bookham Tithe Map 1839
2. Emmison, *Archives and Local History*, p. 55
3. Guildford Muniment Room, PSH/Bk. G/8/6
4. Short & Reed, *An Edwardian Land Source*, pp. 95–103
5. Riden, *Local History*, p. 59
6. Surrey Record Office, Land Tax Returns, Great Bookham
7. Public Record Office, E179/188/481
8. M. W. Barley, *The English Farmhouse and Cottage* (RKP, London, 1961), pp. 19–20
9. The section on medieval developments is based on *ibid.*, pp. 3–37
10. Howell, *Kibworth Harcourt*, p. 57
11. *Ibid.*, pp. 55–6
12. R. H. Hilton, *A Medieval Society: the West Midlands at the End of the Thirteenth Century* (Cambridge University Press, Cambridge, 1983), pp. 95–6
13. Hoskins, *The Midland Peasant*, p. 284
14. Chertsey Abbey Cartularies, II, i, *Surrey Record Society*, 12 (1958), p. 34
15. F. E. Halliday, *Carew's Survey of Cornwall* (Angus M. Kelley, New York, 1969), p. 124

16. W. G. Hoskins, 'The Rebuilding of Rural England, 1570–1640', in W. G. Hoskins, *Provincial England* (Macmillan, London, 1963), pp. 131–48
17. Bodleian Library, Oxford, Parliamentary Surveys of Lord Craven's Estate, nos. 16–17, 19–21, 23
18. W. G. Hoskins, *Local History in England* (Longman, London, 1959), p. 132
19. S. Davies, 'The Documentary Sources of Vernacular Architecture', *Local Historian*, 12, v (1977), pp. 236–7
20. Shropshire Record Office, Forester Colln., 1224/1/59, Map of Little Wenlock 1727
21. Quoted in Hoskins, 'Rebuilding of Rural England', p. 133
22. M. Spufford, 'The Significance of the Cambridgeshire Hearth Tax, *Cambs. Antiq. Soc. Procs.*, 55 (1962), pp. 53–64
23. C. Morris, ed., *The Journeys of Celia Fiennes* (The Cresset Press, London, 1947), p. 202
24. Shropshire Record Office, Bridgewater Colln., 212/Box 466/2, Map of Lineal Common *c.* 1610. Shropshire Record Office, Sutherland Colln. 38/5; Staffordshire Record Office, Sutherland Colln., D593/J/20A/1
25. Shrops. R. O., Sutherland Colln., 38/5; Staffs. R. O., Sutherland Colln., D593/J/20A/1
26. Barley, pp. 245–6
27. For example F. G. Emmison, 'Relief of the Poor at Eaton Socon, Bedfordshire, 1706–1834', Beds. Hist. Rec. Soc., 15 (1993), pp. 33–4
28. Barley, p. 243
29. *Ibid.*, pp. 253–4
30. A. Armstrong, *Farmworkers: a Social and Economic History 1770–1980* (Batsford, London, 1988), pp. 57–8
31. R. Brigden, *Victorian Farms* (The Crowood Press, Ramsbury, 1986), p. 23
32. *Ibid.*, pp. 28–36
33. S. W. Martins, 'The Farm Buildings of the Agricultural Revolution', *Local Historian*, 12, viii (1977), p. 414
34. Short & Reed, An Edwardian Land Survey, p. 99
35. E. Gauldie, 'Country Homes', Mingay, The Victorian Countryside, II, p. 533

Further reading

1 The governance of rural England

BETTEY, J. H., *Church and Parish: A Guide for Local Historians* (Batsford, London, 1987)

CLANCHY, M., *From Memory to Written Record: England 1066–1307* (Edward Arnold, London, 1979)

EMMISON, F. G. & GRAY, I. *County Records* (Historical Association, London, 1961)

EMMISON, F. G., *Archives and Local History* (Phillimore, Chichester, 1974)

HARVEY, P. D. A., 'Manorial Records', *Archives and the User*, 5 (British Records Assoc., London, 1984)

PORTER, S., *Exploring Urban History: Sources for Local Historians* (Batsford, London, 1990)

RIDEN, P., *Record Sources for Local Historians* (Batsford, London, 1987)

SIMPSON, A., *The Wealth of the Gentry 1540–1660* (University of Chicago Press, Chicago, 1961)

TATE, W. E., *The Parish Chest: a Study of Parochial Administration* Cambridge University Press, 1969)

WEST, J., *Village Records* (Macmillan, London, 1962)

2 Village society

CLAY, C. G. A., *Economic Expansion and Social Change: England 1500–1700, I, People, Land and Towns* (Cambridge University Press, 1984)

EDWARDS, P. R., *Farming: Sources for Local Historians* (Batsford, London, 1991)

HORN, P., *The Rural World 1780–1850: Social Change in the English Countryside* (Hutchinson, London, 1980)

MILLER, E. & HATCHER, J., *Medieval England: Rural Society and Economic Change 1086–1348* (Longman, London, 1978)

MILLS, D. R., *Lord and Peasant in Nineteenth Century Britain* (Croom Helm, London, 1980)

SLACK, P., *Poverty and Policy in Tudor and Stuart England* (Longman, London, 1988

3 Population trends

CHARLTON, C., 'Historical Demography: Games to Play with Parish Registers, in A. Rogers, ed. *Group Projects in Local History* (Dawson, Folkestone, 1977)

DARBY, H. C., *Domesday Geography of England* (Cambridge University Press, 1952 onwards)

DRAKE, M., ed., *Population Studies from Parish Registers* (Local Population Studies, Matlock, 1982)

DYER, C., *Lords and Peasants in a Changing Society: the Estates of the Bishopric of Worcester 680–1540* (Cambridge University Press, 1980)

GRIGG, D. B., *Population Growth and Agrarian Change: an Historical Perspective* (Cambridge University Press, 1980)

HOSKINS, W. G., 'The Population of an English Village 1086–1801: a Study of Wigston Magna', in W. G. Hoskins, *Provincial England* (Macmillan, London, 1963)

THIRSK, J., 'Sources of Information on Population 1500–1760', in J. Thirsk, *The Rural Economy of England* (Hambledon Press, London, 1984)

WRIGLEY, E. A., *Population and History* (McGraw-Hill, New York, 1969)

WRIGLEY, E. A., & SCHOFIELD, R. S., *The Population History of England 1541–1871* (Cambridge University Press, 1989)

4 Earning a living

ARMSTRONG, A., *Farmworkers: a Social and Economic History 1770–1980* (Batsford, London, 1988)

BOLTON, J. L., *The Medieval Economy 1150–1500* (Dent, London, 1980)

CLAY, C. G. A., *Economic Expansion and Social Change: England 1500–1700, II, Industry, Trade and Government* (Cambridge University Press, 1984)

EDWARDS, P. R., *Farming: Sources for Local Historians* (Batsford, London, 1991)

GLENNIE, P., 'Distinguishing Men's Trades: Occupational Sources and Debates for Pre-Census England', *Historical Geography Research Series* no. 25 (1990)

HORN, P., *Labouring Life in the Victorian Countryside* (Alan Sutton, Gloucester, 1987)

KUSSMAUL, A., *Servants in Husbandry in Early Modern England* (Cambridge University Press, Cambridge, 1981)

MALCOLMSON, R. W., *Life and Labour in England 1700–1780* (Hutchinson, London, 1981)

5 The peasant world

BETTEY, J. H., *Church and Parish: a Guide for Local Historians* (Batsford, London, 1987)

BUSHAWAY, B., *By Rite: Custom, Ceremony and Community in England 1700–1880* (Junction Books, London, 1982)

CLARK, P., *The English Alehouse: a Social History 1200–1830* (Longman, London, 1983)

HAWKINS, D. T., *Criminal Ancestors: a Guide to Historic Criminal Records in England and Wales* (Alan Sutton, Stroud, 1992)

HORN, P., *The Rural World 1780–1850* (Hutchinson, London, 1980)

LASLETT, P., *The World We Have Lost – Further Explored* (Methuen, London, 1983)

MALCOLMSON, R. W., *Popular Recreations in English Society 1700–1850* (Cambridge University Press, 1979)

MINGAY, G. E., ed., *The Vanishing Countryman* (Routledge, London, 1989)
SHARPE, J. A., *Crime in Early Modern England 1550–1750* (Longman, London, 1984)
SHARPE, J. A., *Early Modern England: a Social History 1550–1760* (Edward Arnold, London, 1987)
STEPHENS, W. B., & UNWIN, R. W., *Materials for the Local and Regional Study of Schooling 1700–1900* (British Records Association, London, 1987)
THOMAS, K., *Religion and the Decline of Magic* (Penguin, Harmondsworth, 1973)
TOBIAS, J. J., *Crime and the Police in England 1700–1900* (Gill & Macmillan, Dublin, 1979

6 Family and neighbourhood

BENNETT, J. M., *Women in the Medieval English Countryside* (Oxford University Press,
1987)
HANAWALT, B. A., *The Ties that Bound: Peasant Families in Medieval England* (Longman, London, 1984)
HEY, D., *Family History and Local History in England* (Longman, London, 1987)
HORN, P., *The Victorian Country Child* (Alan Sutton, Stroud, 1985)
HOULBROOKE, R. A., *The English Family 1450–1700* (Longman, London, 1984)
LASLETT, P., *Family Life and Illicit Love in Earlier Generations* (Cambridge University Press, 1977)
STOE, L., *The Family, Sex and Marriage in England 1500–1800* (Weidenfeld & Nicolson, London, 1977)

7 Rural housing

BARLEY, M. W., *The English Farmhouse and Cottage* (RKP, London, 1961)
BRIGDEN, R., *Victorian Farms* (The Crowood Press, Ramsbury, 1986)
BRUNSKILL, R. W., *Illustrated Handbook of Vernacular Architecture* (Faber & Faber, London, 1971)
HARVEY, J. H., 'Sources for the History of Houses', *Archives and the User*, no. 3 (British Records Assoc., London, 1974)
HOSKINS, W. G., 'The Rebuilding of Rural England 1570–1640', in W. G. Hoskins, *Provincial England* (Macmillan, London, 1963)
MACHIN, R. A., 'The Study of Traditional Buildings' in A. Rogers, ed. *Group Projects in Local History* (Dawson, Folkestone, 1977)
SPUFFORD, M. 'The Significance of the Cambridgeshire Hearth Tax', *Cambs. Antiq. Soc. Procs.*, 55 (1962)

Index